DANCE THEATRE OF HARLEM

A HISTORY · A MOVEMENT · A CELEBRATION

DANCE THEATRE OF HARLEM

A HISTORY · A MOVEMENT · A CELEBRATION

JUDY TYRUS

PAUL NOVOSEL

www.kensingtonbooks.com

The authors have made diligent efforts to include internet addresses that are accurate at the time of publication; however, neither the author nor the publisher is responsible for inaccurate or incomplete addresses, or for changes occurring after this book was printed and published. Moreover, the publisher and the author have no control over any such third-party internet sites or the content contained thereon, and are not responsible for any such content.

DAFINA BOOKS are published by

Kensington Publishing Corp.
119 West 40th Street
New York, NY 10018

All Kensington titles, imprints, and distributed lines are available at special quantity discounts for bulk purchases for sales promotions, premiums, fund-raising, educational, or institutional use.

Special book excerpts or customized printings can also be created to fit specific needs.
For details, write or phone the office of the Kensington sales manager: Kensington Publishing Corp.,
119 West 40th Street, New York, NY 10018, attn: Sales Department; phone 1-800-221-2647.

The Dafina logo is a trademark of Kensington Publishing Corp.
ISBN-13: 978-1-4967-3360-3
ISBN-10: 1-4967-3360-6

First Dafina hardcover printing: November 2021

10 9 8 7 6 5 4 3 2 1

Printed in the United States of America

for

Satoko and Jack Tyrus

Helen and Michael J. Novosel

The state that the world is in today, and all the preaching going on, makes movement take on a different value. The aesthetics of dance—the beauty of it, the line of it, the physicality of it—that's communication . . . that's freedom.

—*Arthur Mitchell*

TABLE OF CONTENTS

Introduction: viii

INTRODUCTION

This book is the first history of Dance Theatre of Harlem (DTH). It tells of one of the greatest classical ballet companies in the world. It tells of some of the greatest ballet dancers in the world. It tells how they danced the greatest ballets in the world. It tells how they proved against all odds that classical ballet can, and should, flourish beyond skin tone. This is the story of Dance Theatre of Harlem, a community-based ballet company, primarily African American, from its meager beginnings to its glory days; in crisis, in revival. Here is the sweeping chronicle from inception in a Harlem garage in 1969 to the Company and School's triumphant 50th anniversary in 2019. DTH continued its existence online during the COVID pandemic, and through the civil rights movement known as Black Lives Matter.

This book covers DTH's evolution, season by season, during two great periods of change in America's history: the 1960s social revolution that brought diversity to the fore, and the advent of the technologies that ushered in the digital age. The rapid changes were breathtaking. In a mere 50 years, DTH made its indelible mark on American cultural history and on the world of ballet, dancing through barriers of traditionalism, bias, and prejudice.

The DTH narrative begins just four years after the 1965 Jim Crow laws of the American South were overruled. It is focused, though not solely, on dancers with African heritage. We authored this book for the DTH fan, the dancer, the academic, those who love ballet, and those who simply want to know the miraculous story. It is indeed a story of survival.

As archivists organizing items to be preserved at DTH, we discussed the need for a single printed work that covered the Company's history. The archive held valuable primary sources and an extensive photo collection. We realized that a rendering of a DTH history would be a *Gesamtkunstwerk*, a work that is made from many art forms. Research toward that goal included examining ballet histories, films, videos, photography, dance criticism, dance pedagogy, and choreography. The extensive quotes by Arthur Mitchell have been sourced from writings, interviews, dissertations, lectures, and dancers. Though our work has been in-depth, not all research has been exhausted. For instance, Karel Shook, cofounder of DTH, wrote numerous articles on the art of dance that have not been examined, leaving a gold mine for future scholars.

Dance Theatre of Harlem: A History, A Movement, A Celebration (DTHHMC) comes with a host of online ancillary readings at www.DTHbook.org. Readers and researchers can access additional resources that include an updated list of DTH ballets, a list of Company members, materials on multiculturality, glossaries, and research materials.

This book is written chronologically for historical and reference purposes. However, within each chapter material may appear to be presented nonsequentially due to the subject matter and the duration of various activities. Dance critics and reviewers of record have been quoted extensively. Press sources are cited in the text with byline, headline, and date of publication. Dates have been added to the photo captions unless the date was not identified on the print, nor if the photo was taken some time after the premiere.

Although a portion of our research comes from DTH archival materials that have been processed (where each item is assessed, environmentally preserved, logged, labeled, inventoried, placed, digitized, managed, and protected), a large portion of the archive has been left unprocessed at the time of publication.

This book uses selective sociological vocabulary. Describing people as "Black" or "White," except when within a direct quote, has been avoided. We believe that to divide the entire human race into two colors continues segregation, stereotyping, othering, intolerance, and feeds an us-versus-them mentality. Another vocabulary choice was to excise the word "race" and its cousins "racist" and "racism," a classification (social construct) left over from the eighteenth century, in favor of the more humanist but equally charged term "cultural bias," denoting that "culture" includes all nationalities and ethnicities. We have made our best effort to respect each individual's heritage, ethnic makeup, nationality, culture, or other identity, a vocabulary that levels the playing field toward acceptance of the diversity of all people. This mirrors DTH's pursuit of cultural equality. The struggle endured by ballet dancers because of skin tone is a story of the pursuit of civil rights in the United States. Our aspiration, in telling this great story, is to shift the mindset away from skin tone and generalizing to valuing and respecting each person's, and each dancer's, own heritage, culture, and talent.

In 1999, Dance Theatre of Harlem was named one of America's Irreplaceable Dance Treasures by the Dance Heritage Coalition. These treasures are defined as entities that have made an impact on the art form and achieved artistic excellence, enriched the nation's cultural heritage, and enhanced the lives of future generations, and are worthy of international recognition. We hope the following pages will illuminate this honor, and serve critical discourse and scholarship in the future, becoming the first source for understanding Dance Theatre of Harlem—in historical context, through its artistic continuum, and as the bold American experiment in cultural diversity that it is.

—Judy Tyrus and Paul Novosel, December 1, 2019

PART ONE

CHAPTER 1

ARTHUR MITCHELL

What we started out to do, to prove, was that black children,
given the same opportunity as white children,
could be great dancers.

—*Arthur Mitchell in* The Lexington Herald-Leader

Arthur Mitchell told dancers to allow the light to hit their cheekbones. (Photo: Martha Swope, ©NYPL)

THE TRIP TO BRAZIL

On Thursday, April 4, 1968, civil rights activist Dr. Martin Luther King Jr. was assassinated on the balcony of the Lorraine Motel in Memphis, Tennessee. A few days after, Arthur Mitchell was boarding a flight at JFK Airport. He was traveling to South America to initiate a national ballet company for Brazil. While on board this flight, as this story has been told time and time again, one astonishing revelation jolted his entire being. This epiphany, this idea, would eventually be made real and change forever the lives of thousands of people in the world of classical ballet.

Mitchell's life was built on fortuitous and exceptional events. He became an international ballet star who from an impoverished childhood in Harlem went on to become the first permanent African American principal male dancer in George Balanchine's esteemed New York City Ballet. (The honor of the first African American male dancer of New York City Ballet goes to the Dunham-trained Arthur Bell, in 1950.) Mitchell's talent, hard work, determination, and discipline challenged the commonly held perception that African Americans could not dance classical ballet. His love of the arts moved him to build a world where classical dancers would know that the only difference between them was their ability to perform, regardless of their culture, class, creed, or skin tone. He built a space where people could train to become the best human dance beings possible. He built a place where learning the discipline of classical ballet was a means to high artistic expression.

He said, "It takes a long time for us to find what we are capable of and what our means of expression are. I think that I was a born dancer. I mean I was born to dance—I first think physically and then I think intellectually. I respond to any kind of movement automatically, and I think that is my natural means of expression. I think dance is the mother of all art forms. Even before a child is born, when it is still in the womb, it kicks—and kicking is movement, singing and music come afterward." Arthur Mitchell Jr. was born on March 27, 1934, headfirst and feet kicking.

FAMILY AND EARLY YEARS

Willie Mae Mitchell (née Hearns) and Arthur Mitchell Sr., native to Savannah, Georgia, married there, and then relocated to Pennsylvania. After three years they moved again to Harlem, 112th Street between 7th Avenue and Lenox Avenue. At the time of his birth, Arthur had an older sister, Frances Marie, 14 years his senior, and soon after four more siblings: Charles William, Laura Mae, Herbert Gerald, and Shirley Elizabeth.

Arthur Mitchell Sr. worked as a riveter at the Brooklyn Navy Yard. Self-taught in other trades, he also worked as a carpenter, plumber, automotive mechanic, and building superintendent. The family was quite poor, and for practical purposes moved several times. The young boys of the family, Charles and Arthur, spent their time assisting their father with his work. Mitchell would remember, "My father was the superintendent of the apartment buildings. When the dumbwaiters were broken, we collected the garbage from door to door in huge burlap bags. There were two buildings comprised of six floors and four apartments on each floor. By the time we reached the basement, not only were the bags quite heavy, but we were also dirty and smelly ourselves. So, the rest of the time I took baths."

Raising children who were very close in age was not easy, but fortunately, all of the siblings enjoyed each other's company. Mitchell recalled, "There were so many of us, we always shared everything." Daily life was filled with work and chores, but on Sundays, all was put aside.

Church was a central part of life, a meeting place in the neighborhood, especially for Willie Mae Mitchell and her friends. She took her children to Convent Avenue Baptist Church where Arthur Mitchell Jr. sang in the choir. This was likely Arthur Mitchell's first exposure to music and live performance. He would later admit, "Dad wouldn't go to church because he believed that all preachers were crooks, and he didn't believe in the goodness that they talked about when he had such a hard life."

In 1937, the family moved to West 114th Street and later to West 139th Street. When Mitchell was four, his mother took him to the playground across the street from their apartment. Showing independence and curiosity, he chose to follow the kindergartners from the playground into class. (Arthur Mitchell would later admit that he had *nerve*.) The school officials soon contacted his mother and allowed him to attend the school unofficially, because of his age. When he turned five, he was officially enrolled as a kindergartner. Willie Mae would reveal that the school authorities approved of her son attending kindergarten at such a young age because he was "always so clean and so nicely dressed." Mitchell carried the attribute of dressing well throughout his life.

His activities at school included playing rhythm-band instruments. He played maracas and performed for all the parents on Fridays. "My mother tells me that when I was a child I loved to dance and that, when guests would come to the house, I would hide behind the door until everyone was seated; she says that I would then emerge and start performing—totally untrained—with lots of guts as usual."

As the eldest son, Mitchell took responsibility and contributed to family earnings. At the age of seven, he shined shoes and sold newspapers. His father was incarcerated when Mitchell was 12. "I was always a very old child. And I guess that's what set me up for being able to administer. There was a street-wise I acquired because I've always supported my family and taken care of them."

Harlem, the culturally diverse entertainment capital of the world, was a productive atmosphere for bootleggers, prostitutes, and the numbers racket. To protect the family, the Mitchells moved to safer havens on West 151st Street, and subsequently to West 143rd Street, where the youngsters spent most of their childhood. At a young age, Mitchell found steady work at a butcher shop around the corner from their apartment and used his earnings to support and care for the family. Mitchell would later recall that the butcher paid him in meat.

As all young people try on personalities like new clothes, it was no different for Mitchell during his middle school years. He was a member of a local street gang called the Rebels and then later, the Hill Top Lovers. He occasionally played basketball in a nearby park. "I remember my red satin jacket with 'Artie' written over the left pocket." He attended Public School #143, and in 1944 joined the Police Athletic League Glee Club, gaining performing experience at nine years old. A few years later, in 1949, his sister Frances Marie passed away from diabetes.

A teacher at Mitchell's school noticed him hamming it up at a social event, dancing the Lindy Hop and The Jitterbug. Recognizing his raw talent, the teacher suggested that he attend a new public high school being formed specifically for talented teens and urged Mitchell to enter. Conceived by educational thinker and creative whirlwind Franklin Keller, the school was located on West 46th Street in the Times Square Theater District (now the Jacqueline Kennedy Onassis School for International Careers). Simply named the Performing Arts School, it merged later

DRESS CODE FOR DANCERS

MITCHELL WAS ALWAYS CONSCIOUS OF FIRST IMPRESSIONS AND DEMAND-
ing respect through dress. When the Company began to tour, he categorically insisted that
Company dancers follow a strict dress code. There were levels of dress by which the Company
had to abide: casual, planned casual, cocktail, semiformal, or black tie. This dress code appeared
on the Company's touring schedule to assure that everyone, not only dancers but Company staff
as well, traveled with appropriate clothing.

LEFT: Dressed in black tie. *Top row left to right*: Joselli Audain, Robert Garland, Arthur Mitchell, and Christina Johnson.
Bottom row left to right: Melanie Person, Charmaine Hunter, Cicely Tyson, and Yvonne Hall (Photo: Courtesy of the
Dance Theatre of Harlem Archive)

RIGHT: The Company dressed in planned casual, Jamaica, 1970. (Photo: Roy O'Brien, Courtesy of the Dance Theatre
of Harlem Archive)

with the Upper Manhattan High School of Music & Art and eventually became the High School of the Performing Arts (HSPA) in 1961. By 1984, it had been renamed Fiorello H. LaGuardia High School of Music & Art and Performing Arts and had moved to a new building located at what is now Lincoln Center.

The stars aligned for Mitchell. While attending Public Junior High School #43, Mitchell auditioned for the School of Performing Arts in the fall of 1949 with help from African American vaudevillian Tom Nip. Tom taught him a routine to "Steppin' Out with My Baby," by Irving Berlin. Mitchell also choreographed a solo he called "Wail" to music by Béla Bartók. Fortuitously, the audition panel included John Martin, critic for *The New York Times*, Martha Graham, modern dance luminary, and Lincoln Kirstein, impresario and founder of New York City Ballet. Mitchell recalled, "The other auditionees who had been studying either ballet or modern dance were performing with classical ballet, there I was—with this rented top hat, white tie and tails, but when my number was called, I came out and sold. I have always felt, however, that they accepted me because they needed male dancers."

Arthur Mitchell's class, Manhattanville Junior High School, 1949. Mitchell is top row, third from left. (Photo: Courtesy of the Dance Theatre of Harlem Archive)

He became one of the first graduates from a high school dedicated solely to the arts. Dancing for hours during the school day must have been heavenly for many students. For more than 60 years, Keller's performing arts school succeeded beyond expectations, giving the world many star performers including Liza Minnelli, Eliot Feld, Daniel Day-Lewis, Ben Vereen, and indubitably, Arthur Mitchell. One of Mitchell's classmates, Hattie Wiener, recalled that he could be seen in the HSPA lunch hall practicing the mambo with Suzanne Pleshette. She also recalled how good-looking he was, and how the HSPA faculty was entirely supportive of the students and made them feel like stars. She also stated that the faculty, many of whom considered themselves "leftists," provided a support system for all of the young artists, including their gay students.

For Mitchell, high school was a turning point that lay the foundation for his strong will, determination, and fighting spirit. He was talented and good-looking, but not a natural ballet dancer. Despite having long legs, his body lacked flexibility and his feet had little natural arch. One of his teachers suggested that he give up dance altogether, but another, Nanette Charisse (the sister of famous dancer Cyd Charisse), encouraged him to study ballet. "I made up my mind that I would not only become a dancer, but that I would try to be one of the best dancers in the school." He realized that gaining dance experience was all-important, so he danced as much as possible.

He took the first steps toward a dance career by becoming a member of the Repertory Dance Company at HSPA and choreographing "Primitive Study," presented by the Altoona Undergraduate Center in Altoona, Pennsylvania. His concentration of study was modern dance, and he performed with great dancers and choreographers, namely Donald McKayle, John Butler, Louis Johnson, Sophie Maslow, and Anna Sokolow. Some of these incredible artists would eventually teach, choreograph, and set signature works for DTH.

When Mitchell was 17, the Greater New York Committee for State of Israel Bonds invited him to dance for the Chanukah Festival of Light. Mitchell: "It was fun . . . can't you just see me in 1952—as black as I am—selling bonds for Israel?"

BROADWAY DEBUT

While still in high school, Arthur Mitchell made his Broadway debut as a dancer in the 1952 revival of Virgil Thomson and Gertrude Stein's opera *Four Saints in Three Acts*. It had choreography by William Dollar, choral direction by William Jonson, and artistic and musical direction by the composer. With a multicultural cast, the original 1934 production featured the choir of Eva Jessye, the first African American female choral conductor to receive international distinction. Ethel Linder Reiner, producer of Leonard Bernstein's *Candide* and N. Richard Nash's *The Rainmaker*, among other shows, discovered Mitchell, who was tagging along with a friend and not actually intending to audition. She was said to have exclaimed at the audition table, "My God, you'll make a perfect angel!" God listened, and Mitchell was cast as one of the six angels. Leontyne Price portrayed Saint Cecilia, the patron saint of music, and later became a "patron saint" for DTH.

Another revival of *Four Saints*, produced in Paris, represented the United States in the International Festival of the Arts. It was well received, and shows were added. Debuting on Broadway and traveling abroad were highly memorable experiences for Arthur Mitchell, but the most memorable were during breaks when there were opportunities to sing informally. The impromptu jam sessions were "absolutely incredible—music that you could not have paid enough to hear." Rawn Spearman, Billy Daniel, Olga James, Martha Flowers, and Leontyne Price were among the singers. Louis Johnson, Robert Curtis, Carolyn Jorrin, Billie Allen, and Helen Taitt were the other dancers. Mitchell returned from Paris to graduate, gaining a certificate in modern dance, and becoming the first male dancer at HSPA to receive the first award for greatest improvement.

Mitchell's dream was to attend a university, and Bennington College offered him the opportunity with a scholarship. At the same time, Lincoln Kirstein at the School of American Ballet (and a Performing Arts High School board member) likewise offered Mitchell a scholarship. The choice was difficult. He was aware that an African American had never become a permanent member of New York City Ballet. Inequity and segregation existed in the dance world, and Mitchell knew he was skating on intolerant ice. In one instance, at an audition, he and a fellow performer noticed that a special code was being used on audition cards, the letters *W* and *N*, designations for "white" and "negro." At other auditions, because of his skin tone, "No" was the blunt judgment. He would ruminate: "Well, Arthur, you have got to beat them at their own game. If you can take what *you have* as a black dancer—a sense of rhythm, a style, and a way of moving—and couple that with the discipline and the training of classical ballet—you will be in a totally different class from anybody. There will be no white dancer and there will be no colored dancer like you." He eventually chose to attend the School of American Ballet.

Katherine Dunham

KATHERINE DUNHAM WAS CALLED "MATRIARCH AND QUEEN MOTHER OF
black dance" by Joyce Aschenbrenner in her book *Katherine Dunham: Dancing a Life*, and
"dancer Katherine the Great" by the *Washington Post*. Dunham cut an unprecedented swath of

African American dance history in the twentieth
century as a solo dancer. She choreographed ballets, Hollywood movies, television, and Broadway
shows. She was a movie star (*Stormy Weather*),
Broadway star (*Cabin in the Sky*), wife, mother,
award-winning author, educator, lecturer, art-
ist-in-residence, anthropologist, and company
founder. Of Dunham Arthur Mitchell would
write, "As a researcher, Dunham went to the vir-
gin sources to gather material, which with astonishing genius she translated into theatre pieces
that communicated expressively without distort-
ing or vulgarizing the original." From forming her
own dance company, Ballet Négre, to choreographing a new production of *Aida* for the Metropolitan Opera, to touring nationally and internationally with her company, she was yet another
planetary sphere in whose orbit Arthur Mitchell and Karel Shook would rendezvous.

Though Katherine Dunham's style was eclectic, she knew that ballet was the base discipline
for all other forms of presentational ethnic dance. She had studied ballet with Ludmilla Sper-
anzeva, Vera Mirova, Mark Turbyfill, and Ruth Page. Her students included a plethora of performers and dancers who went on to become substantial names in American entertainment—
Shirley MacLaine, Gregory Peck, Warren Beatty, Eartha Kitt, Sidney Poitier, Alvin Ailey, and,
as fate would have it, Arthur Mitchell.

Katherine Dunham in costume for the dance revue *Bamboche*, 1962 (Photo: Granger)

EARLY CAREER
AND DANCE STUDIES

In 1952, Karel Shook was teaching at the Katherine Dunham School of Dance and heard about Mitchell. He requested that Mitchell come to see him and told him that he had all the possibilities of becoming a first-class dancer if he would *work*. That vote of confidence coupled with the word *work* was like a magic potion for Mitchell: "If *work* was all that was required—well that was easy." Shook gave him a Dunham scholarship, and from that time, befriended, mentored, and eventually collaborated with him to establish Dance Theatre of Harlem. Trust developed very early in their relationship.

At the Dunham School, Mitchell received a dance education that asked questions about cultural diversity, sociology, anthropology, and philosophy. This liberal arts aesthetic exposed him to interrelated disciplines that eventually shaped DTH as a school of the allied arts, not just a dance school. This holistic approach to ballet gave him the idea to learn about cultures, to research, and to seek ways to make choreography more relevant to the dancers and audience. He learned how ballet is an art of arts. Thirty years later, his company's ballets *Giselle* and *Firebird* would become the quintessential examples of cultural adaptation. James Haskins, in *Black Dance in America*, quotes Dunham: "You must know the entire complex, the musical instruments, the rhythms, the songs and what they are and how they are used, the language, and the interrelationships among all the elements in this immense cycle that goes with a single dance."

At 18, Mitchell's focus on dance switched into high gear with classes at the School of American Ballet and private lessons with Karel Shook at Dunham. Having to support his family, he worked part-time. This cut into his training and lessons. Shook offered him a teaching position in the school, where future luminaries of dance Geoffrey Holder, Alvin Ailey, and Mary Hinkson were training in ballet. This atmosphere was part of Mitchell's gateway to greatness.

Determined, dedicated, and passionate, Mitchell had a regimen and stuck to it. His longtime friend and Martha Graham star dancer Mary Hinkson said of him, "You talk about discipline—I mean he was possessed with this whole thing. He would awaken at 8:00 to do his pre-barre exercises so that his body would be ready for his first class of the day." Shook said that Mitchell "could work for hours and hours every day and he accepted gracefully every correction that was ever given to him."

Mitchell devoured what School of American Ballet's curriculum had to offer. He went to every audition posted. He studied there with the Ballets Russes dancer Madame Felia Doubrovska, whom he revered. He worked with Natanya Neumann and Shirley Broughton, appearing in Broughton's *Introduction and Quartet*. Most importantly Mitchell captured the attention of Lincoln Kirstein and George Balanchine.

In 1953 he reconnected with Louis Johnson, whom he danced with in *Four Saints*, and choreographed a new work, *Lament*, that premiered at New York City Ballet Club's Third Annual Choreographers Night. During the summer, Mitchell joined Donald McKayle and Company, which debuted at the Jacob's Pillow Dance Festival. The Company performed at venues that included the 92nd Street Y and the Brooklyn Academy of Music. Mitchell danced some of McKayle's most famous works, including *Games*, *The Street*, and *Nocturne*. It is important to mention that Louis Johnson introduced Mitchell to Doris Jones and Claire Haywood who established the Washington, DC–based Jones-Haywood Dance School. It offered classes to multicultural students. Johnson and Mitchell who both had performed at the school's annual performance were thereafter invited to teach. Mitchell sustained a long association with the school.

In 1954, William Dollar, who had choreographed the Broadway revival of *Four Saints in Three Acts*, gave Mitchell his first opportunity to dance classical ballet in public with Ballet Theatre Workshop. Ordinarily these performances involved students associated with Ballet Theatre School (BTS), but Mitchell had no connection. It was a turning point for Mitchell—that Dollar saw talent and went out of his way to explore it. Experimental in nature, these workshops gave students the opportunity to dance within a purely classical framework. Mitchell danced in Dollar's *Concerto* and *Out of Eden*.

It was not uncommon for students to pick up outside engagements. In *Arabian Nights (A Musical Extravaganza)*, produced in 1954 by Guy Lombardo at the Jones Beach Marine Theater, Mitchell was the only African American in the cast of over 100 performers. The performance starred Wagnerian tenor Lauritz Melchior. Lombardo was a big swing band conductor known as "Mr. New Year's Eve," remembered best for playing "Auld Lang Syne" from the Waldorf Astoria Hotel at the drop of the ball in Times Square. Lombardo's many extravaganzas featured a number of up-and-coming showbiz personalities such as Gene Nelson, Arthur Treacher, and Dom DeLouise. Arthur Mitchell considered his appearance in the extravaganza to be "a feather in my cap."

In the early 1950s, American writer Truman Capote traveled to Haiti, and taken by its charm, used the local culture in one of his works. Frequenting the bordellos was his inspiration for a short story that he adapted into book and lyrics for *House of Flowers*, a Broadway musical with score and additional lyrics by Harold Arlen. It was produced by Saint Subber and ran for three years. Mitchell, then age 19, played a townsperson in the chorus. Opening in December 1954, *House of Flowers* starred Pearl Bailey with a cast including Rawn Spearman, Delores Harper, Juanita Hall, Alvin Ailey, Carmen de Lavallade, Diahann Carroll, Frederick O'Neal, Josephine Premice, and Geoffrey Holder (who would later create *Dougla* and other ballets for DTH). The score for *House of Flowers* is best remembered for the use of steel drums in the orchestration. Three steel drummers from Geoffrey Holder's Dance Company were specially brought in from Trinidad.

Theatre folk, like no other, have an uncanny way of bonding and forging friendships when doing a show. Top talent surrounded Mitchell and he built a Rolodex to be envied. Nevertheless, it is the totality of experience that molds and forms an artist. A revealing stint, often eclipsed by his work with New York City Ballet, is Mitchell's work with John Butler.

JOHN BUTLER

John Butler performed in Robbins's *On the Town* and in Martha Graham's *Appalachian Spring*. He most notably created the role of Curly in the historic dream ballet of *Oklahoma!* As a choreographer, he created a number of ballets that entered the world repertoire, including *Carmina Burana* and the Billie Holiday tribute *Portrait of Billie*. In the early 1950s, he became the permanent choreographer for *The Kate Smith Show* on television. With the money he made, he formed and toured his own group, aptly named the John Butler Dance Company.

In 1955, Butler offered Arthur Mitchell work, and even though Mitchell had his heart set on becoming a member of New York City Ballet, he accepted. Geoffrey Holder and his wife, Carmen de Lavallade, also danced in Butler's company. That the position was in an integrated company was most interesting for Mitchell. Though this was a time of resistance to African American performers, the seeds of acceptance had begun to grow. If *fine art* requires nothing besides talent, time, and refinement, then anyone on Mother Earth is a candidate. This was the consciousness that embedded itself in the national thinking during those decades of unquestionable change. Arthur Mitchell lived in this consciousness.

John Butler fused modern dance with classical ballet.

The decades of change beginning with the "Age of Anxiety" through the late 1970s were an epoch of fusion in the arts. Bernstein mixed jazz figures with classical. Picasso developed abstraction from ancient Cycladic art. Arthur Mitchell and Karel Shook supported the blending of classical ballet with soul, jazz, and contemporary music, creating a niche in the dance world. Later, DTH choreographer Robert Garland would go on to describe his own style as *neoclassic urban contemporary*.

Mitchell danced in Butler works *Three Promenades with the Lord, Malocchio—The Evil Eye*, and *Clowns and Angels*. In 1955, the company was renamed the John Butler American Dance Theatre. It embarked on a European tour, appearing in the Festival Internazionale Del Balletto at the Piccolo Theatre in Geneva, Switzerland. Though the tour was artistically successful, the travel was demanding and arduous. It gave Mitchell a vantage point of life as an artist on tour, which trained him for his future work. He would hand on the fruits of this life to his dance progeny. Unfortunately, as happens so often in the arts, money ran out, and Butler realized that he could no longer wear hats of both administrator and artist. The company lasted for one season. But from the start, both Mitchell and Butler were launched into stunning careers.

NEW YORK CITY BALLET

At the end of the Butler tour, on August 24, 1955, Mitchell received a telegram from Lincoln Kirstein, then managing director of the New York City Ballet, offering him the opportunity to dance as a permanent member of the corps de ballet. The contract paid $90 a week. Accepting fulfilled Mitchell's dream and changed the course of his life.

Mitchell never wanted to draw attention to the fact that he was African American. "Jackie Robinson was making headlines in baseball, and I said that I didn't want any publicity about being a Negro barrier breaker. At my first performance, no one knew I was coming out. Jacques d'Amboise was shooting *Seven Brides for Seven Brothers* in L.A. and I debuted in his *Western Symphony* role partnering Tanny [Tanaquil Le Clercq, Balanchine's wife] when I stepped onto the stage. Some guy right behind the conductor, cried out, 'Oh my God! They got a . . . [In telling the story, Mitchell laughs while censoring the word.]' And the place went crazy. The audience was catcalling, 'Give him a chance!'"

Western Symphony served as Arthur Mitchell's debut on September 7, 1955. Choreographed by George Balanchine, it stitched together American melodies orchestrated and arranged by the renowned Hershy Kay. Originally done in practice clothes, and later dressed by Karinska in Old

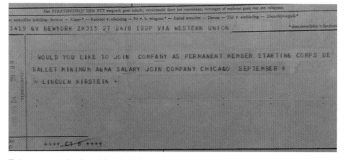

Telegram to Arthur Mitchell from Lincoln Kirstein (Courtesy of the Dance Theatre of Harlem Archive)

West costume, the luminary cast included Diana Adams, Herbert Bliss, Janet Reed, Nicholas Magallanes, Patricia Wilde, André Eglevsky, Tanaquil Le Clercq, and Jacques d'Amboise.

When Mitchell first began at the School of American Ballet, George Balanchine became aware of his potential as a classical dancer. Mitchell was very handsome, with a chiseled face and long legs. As a father figure and mentor, Balanchine explained to him the importance of making choices: "You made the choice to become a dancer, now stick to it. Learn everything there is to learn."

And learn he did. From the workings of the back office to the footlights, he absorbed the professional world of dance: stage design, music production, costuming, and historic choreography, all those things that make theatre magic.

In the rehearsal studio, the power of observation reigns supreme. Dance is visual. If the human body contains about 700 muscles, in a piece with 25 dancers, 17,500 muscles must line up in space, with precision, every split second—the position of each toe, leg, finger, hand, and head. Fighting for perfection means constant repetition of thousands of positions, steps, and combinations. Observation—for the ballet master in front of the mirror and the dancer in the mirror—is essential. Hundreds of corrections in class and in rehearsal, with George Balanchine and Jerome Robbins no less, would be deposited in Mitchell's toolbox. His keen sense of observation fueled his relentless push to keep dancers on the edge, aiming for perfection—you worked until you bled. These tools of the trade would be useful not only in becoming a world class dancer, but in someday becoming the leading ballet maker in Harlem.

At New York City Ballet, Mitchell also danced in the corps of Robbin's *Fanfare*, *The Pied Piper*, and *The Concert*, and in Balanchine's *Allegro Brillante*. Because he was a quick study, Mitchell could be relied upon to cover a part if needed. New York City Ballet did not limit the number of performances he could dance. This meant a steady flow of managing life in New York, life in ballet, and life on tour—11 European cities. He danced much of the repertoire; his career rapidly blossomed, and he became the only African American premier ballet dancer in North America. Although a barrier breaker, Mitchell was not the only one. Maria Tallchief, with Osage Nation heritage, was the first Native American principal dancer with NYCB. She and Arthur Mitchell would go on to dance at least two premieres, *Piège de Lumière* and *Panamerica*.

George Balanchine felt protective of Mitchell. Balanchine always said, "If Mitchell doesn't dance, New York City Ballet doesn't dance." The dancers supported him as well.

Though he had complete and unquestionable support from Balanchine, touring for this singular dancer had its challenges. "It was a very lonely tour, because it was very hard for me to relate to the people then . . . I have always been a very earthy, relaxed person and being the only black in the company, there was no one with whom I could communicate. . . . Everyone was very kind to me, but I felt like an outsider because I was not a ballet-oriented, ballet-minded person."

Performing with high-powered talents and egos can be difficult. Was Mitchell's sense of isolation from being a part of something new and inexpressible? Or were deep-seated cultural issues simmering just below the surface? Did Mitchell long for his own people? A more familiar culture? Some of these questions would be echoed later by DTH dancers who guested with nonintegrated companies.

TOP: Arthur Mitchell and Tanaquil Le Clercq in Balanchine's *Western Symphony* (Photo: Courtesy of the Dance Theatre of Harlem Archive).
BOTTOM: New York City Ballet in Baku, Azerbaijan, 1962. Arthur Mitchell, in a striped shirt, is kneeling in the second row. (Photo: Marlene Mesavage DeSavino, Courtesy of the Dance Theatre of Harlem Archive)

The Black and White of *Agon*

In 1928, George Balanchine began a trilogy of ballets that began with *Apollo*, continued in 1948 with *Orpheus*, and completed with *Agon* in 1957. *Apollo* was Balanchine's first collaboration with Igor Stravinsky, and the ballet was presented by Diaghilev's Ballets Russes. It has been said that the trilogy is what made New York City Ballet and Balanchine's work historic.

All three ballets used music by Stravinsky. The first two were mythical, but the last, *Agon*, was different. A seventeenth-century dance manual was used as the ballet's inspiration, and it was the first ballet in which Stravinsky used twelve-tone music and irregular meters. Balanchine stripped away many narratives from his early ballets—it was a modernist approach, and *Agon* was the epitome.

Provocative with splits, the use of pelvis tilts, and stark athleticism, *Agon* was performed with minimalist black leotards and had no set, just tights and lights. It came to be known as a *leotard ballet*, or a *black and white* ballet.

Balanchine eliminated the sets and costumes of *Concerto Barocco* and *The Four Temperaments* in 1951, both to be performed in practice clothes. In a *New York Times* article (11/25/2007), Alastair Macaulay proclaimed that "modernism had never gone so far before."

Agon was indeed Balanchine's first modern ballet, and ballet's salute to the modernist age. As one of the 12 dancers in the cast, Arthur Mitchell partnered with Diana Adams in the pas de deux, acting as a sculptor molding a statue. As Adams posed and contorted, Mitchell held, supported, carried, lifted, sustained, stabilized, and even whispered to his partner, "Relax!" To *The New York Times*' Jack Anderson (1/13/1993), Mitchell later said of the duet and its unusual pivots and balances, "Diana's nervous intensity made the whole pas de deux work because it's not so much the difficulty of the steps or how flexible you are, it's the precariousness." Mitchell would later present Balanchine's *Agon* in the DTH repertoire.

Not only was *Agon* a singular sensation, but it was also a turning point for Stravinsky as a composer. It was a transitional piece from diatonic to the twelve-tone composing technique that gave the music an edgy and acerbic panache. Balanchine: "As always in his ballet

Diana Adams and Arthur Mitchell in Balanchine's *Agon*, 1957 (Photo: Martha Swope, ©NYPL)

scores, the dance element of most force was the pulse—Stravinsky's strict beat is authority over time, and I have always felt that a choreographer should place unlimited confidence in this control." Mitchell would say to his dancers, "Find the pulse, people!"

In an essay penned by Mitchell, he states that *Agon* is "the definitive ballet of the neoclassical style." He recalls that the creation process of the ballet was fascinating. "Stravinsky was in Los Angeles working on the music. Each time he finished a page of music, he would mail the one page to Mr. Balanchine. Therefore, we could only go so far with the ballet [choreography] until we received another page of music by mail from Mr. Stravinsky."

Mitchell was keen to notice how Balanchine could bring daily life into choreography. He said Balanchine was a "master at using natural movement from the street. I remember one morning, he arrived for rehearsal and his knee was bothering him; he was limping. So, he added the limp to the choreography. The *toe, flat, toe, flat* step that the boys do came out of that day."

Adding to *Agon*'s preeminence, Balanchine chose to throw caution to the wind and use multicultural casting, pairing Diana Adams with Mitchell. "Do you know what it took for Balanchine to put me, a black man, on stage with a white woman?" said Mitchell. "This was 1957, before civil rights. He showed me how to take her [holding her delicately by the wrist]. He said, 'put your hand on top.' The skin colors were part of the choreography. He saw what was going to happen in the world and put it on stage."

The thinking that ballet needed multiculturality was not based solely on an idea that was born in the 1960s. As early as the 1930s, Balanchine had a creative impulse, or perhaps a mental image, of skin tone playing out in casting and onstage. In 1933 Lincoln Kirstein wrote a 16-page letter to A. Everett Austin Jr., director of the Wadsworth Atheneum, revealing an "unrealized dream" that Balanchine harbored. This was in the early days when Kirstein and Balanchine were formulating their ideas to create a new original ballet company. Balanchine described his hope to stage a ballet including "four white girls and four white boys, about 16 years old, and eight of the same, negros." It would be easy to surmise that this could have been a gesture of tolerance, but one thing is for certain: Balanchine and Kirstein lamented the fact that not enough was done to include all cultures in ballet.

Anna Kisselgoff, in the April 5, 1987, edition of *The New York Times*, wrote a masterful study on Balanchine's contribution to modern ballet. She distilled and theorized how the advantages of Balanchine's deconstructivist ballets benefited DTH. Balanchine stripped away the scene, the plot, the character names; "we see only the dancer dancing. . . . This aesthetic, which redefined classicism, made it possible for dancers of any culture finally to be judged exclusively as classical dancers. No one can say that DTH's women look out of place in Balanchine's *Allegro Brillante*. They are required to dance, not to persuade us they are Rhenish maidens—and as led by Virginia Johnson and Donald Williams, *Allegro Brillante* remains DTH's model of Balanchine style." Kisselgoff declares, "Balanchine . . . provided an escape hatch for those who think like Mr. Mitchell—and for himself."

Deconstructivist ballet has the useful side effect of diminishing production budgets. Performing ballets with only lights and tights is more affordable; however, this was never a grave concern for George Balanchine nor Arthur Mitchell. Balanchine's rationale was to expose the lines of the body, exhibit technique, and eliminate distraction.

OTHER EARLY ROLES

Gian Carlo Menotti's *The Unicorn, The Gorgon and the Manticore*, a madrigal ballet, premiered on October 19, 1956. Choreographed by John Butler, Mitchell danced the role of the unicorn, and *Life Magazine* hailed it as the best new ballet of the season; a fable about swanky, haughty high hats who are saying through dance, "We detest all, except, what by fashion is blest." Three mythical creatures, who fall from being in style as walking pets, represent the three stages of man (and Menotti's career).

The year 1958 brought Arthur Mitchell tours of Japan, the Philippines, and Australia. He performed *Stars and Stripes*, *Bourrée Fantasque*, and *The Four Temperaments*. The press in Sydney, Australia, gushed, "One has waited for the

opportunity to grant the dancer Arthur Mitchell his due praise. In this ballet [*The Four Temperaments*], he revealed himself as a dancer from the tips of his hands to the tips of his feet. He is never static. He dances as no one else with a native aptitude for rhythm and with always a beautiful classical expression."

Concerning his role of Phlegmatic in *The Four Temperaments*, Mitchell said: "I like dancing Phlegmatic—not only for the technique of it, but for the dramatic quality which the dancer can portray through movement. I like working from the standpoint of a theme or an idea. Even when I am working on abstract pieces, I try to give myself an emotional story line or something from which to draw the abstract movements." In the studio, and when choreographing, he insisted that his dancers always needed to have a reason to move, an inner meaning, subtext, a story line, or a character of sorts. If there was a character, he demanded dancers to delve deeper and find motivation for every movement.

For the Fourth International Congress of Iranian Art and Archaeology of 1960, Balanchine choreographed *The Figure in the Carpet*, a large dance work with extravagant scenery and costumes. It was an eighteenth-century court divertissement. Envisaging a tribute to the congress, Lincoln Kirstein and Mitchell imagined a fully dressed ballet that would portray the creation of the Persian carpet in dance terms. Mitchell would portray an African prince, the Ooni of Ife, with his consort. Concerning the production, Jacqueline Quinn Moore Latham, who documented much of Arthur Mitchell's early years, states: "Balanchine asked Mitchell to find a black girl with whom he could dance a pas de deux as the representatives from Africa. He called Mary Hinkson (a Martha Graham dancer who

George Balanchine and Arthur Mitchell rehearsing the role of Phlegmatic from *The Four Temperaments* (Photo: Martha Swope, ©NYPL)

would later teach at DTH). She auditioned and received the role to enthusiastic reviews. Walter Terry, dance critic of the *New York Herald Tribune*, called their performance 'exceptionally lively and majestic.' Mitchell considered this 'marvelous little divertissement' the lowering of another barrier, because Mary Hinkson was the first black girl ever to dance with the New York City Ballet."

Hinkson was also the first African American woman to dance in the Martha Graham Dance Company. Although resistant to being seen through a cultural lens, she knew that she would be. In 1966, she told *Dance Magazine*, "We will have to speak of the 'Negro dancer' until people are finally considered only on the grounds of their talent and merit."

In 1958 classical composer Gian Carlo Menotti founded a music and arts festival staged in Spoleto, Italy. Highlighting the performing and visual arts of Europe and the Americas, it was named the Festival of Two Worlds, with Spoleto and its sister city, Charleston, South Carolina, hosting. Invited to the third festival in 1960, Mitchell danced with Akiko Kanda in three dances that he choreographed. For the fourth festival in 1961, he appeared with Kanda again, dancing the three dances from the previous festival plus *Dance of The Seven Veils* in the Luchino Visconti production of Richard Strauss's *Salome*. Menotti penned a play for Mitchell entitled *Il Pegno*, for which Mitchell learned his Italian lines phonetically. The Spoleto Festival and DTH from then on would have a rich congruent history. It was another place on the globe where multicultural ballet was welcomed, celebrating high-level artifice and raising the bar for acceptance of cultural diversity.

NYCB, in 1960, premiered *Panamerica*, subtitled "An evening-long collection of eight short pieces." This music-and-dance tour through countries of Central and South America used indigenous classical pieces by composers from Heitor Villa-Lobos to Alberto Ginastera. Mitchell danced in *Mexico*, the fourth movement, choreographed by Balanchine with music by Carlos Chávez. Other choreographers of the evening included Gloria Contreras and Jacques d'Amboise.

What is interesting here in the repertoire is Balanchine's decision to use nationality, not only for entertainment purposes, but to explore the subtleties and nuances of cultural diversity. Here is witness to the learning power of dance. It is exactly this that Mitchell took to heart, but the outcome was quite different than what one might have expected. In the beginning years of DTH, Mitchell was determined to dispel the myth that African Americans could not dance classical ballet, and soon after the birth of the Company, he did. He himself was using

Mary Hinkson and Arthur Mitchell in New York City Ballet's *The Figure in the Carpet*, 1960 (Photo: Martha Swope, ©NYPL)

color as the armament to buck the European system, by having an "all Black" company. However, he soon realized that art superseded everything. He witnessed that not only "Black," but *multicultural* dancers from all over the world sought out DTH, further proving that skin tone was in no way a hindrance to achieving artistic excellence. It was only in interviews that Mitchell spoke of cultural equality, and rarely in the studio.

In 1960 *Modern Jazz: Variants* premiered at City Center with Arthur Mitchell, Diana Adams, Melissa Hayden, and John Jones. Choreographed by Balanchine, it had a commissioned score by Gunther Schuller, who had once played French horn in the American Ballet Theatre (ABT) Orchestra. Schuller coined the term *third stream* to describe the fusion of classical and jazz as a music genre—he simmered in the hotbed of musical innovation of 1950s and '60s New York City. Aaron Copland invited him to Tanglewood, he taught at the Manhattan School of Music, recorded with Miles Davis, and played with the Metropolitan Symphony Orchestra. He composed over 180 works. By melding the influences of Bernstein, Stravinsky, and Copland, Schuller produced hybrid pieces of music art. Balanchine thrived on innovation and the avant garde, but it had to have universal appeal and commerciality. Mitchell found himself in the heartbeat of this New York "new."

As Balanchine held Russian dancers in high esteem, Mitchell did as well. He highly admired the work of Georgian dancer Vakhtang Chabukiani, who in the twentieth century gave prominence and prestige to the male dancer's explosive balletic solo that dazzles the audience. On a trip to Russia, Chabukiani asked if Mitchell would cover a performance of *Othello*. Mitchell also danced the role in Munich. Concerning the role Mitchell stated "Most people show [Othello] shuffling. No. That's not him at all. He has fire and energy, a maleness that supersedes what the everyday is about. It excited me to do that role because I thought that I tried to bring a little bit of dimension to it. I must say it was very successful because Clive Barnes [*New York Times* dance critic] saw a performance and he said it was one of the best Othello's he had ever seen on stage, speaking or dancing."

Other than dance luminaries, Mitchell held admiration and respect for prominent personalities in arts and letters: "Lincoln Kirstein because of his tenacity in terms of fundraising and as an administrator and a wherewithal to get what he wants done. As a dancer, I would say Erik Bruhn had a tremendous impact on me. Paul Robeson, because his sound was so wonderful and so full—there was a wonderful strength in him. I always loved to sing . . . I wish I could be a singer, too . . . Langston Hughes was another man that I found fabulous. He is a writer. He had wonderful wit. He was a gentleman. He was incredible. Then there was someone in history who really influenced my life an awful lot—Henri Christophe, the president of the first republic in the western hemisphere, Haiti—from being a slave to that!"

ROLES AND TRANSITIONS

Shakespeare's *A Midsummer Night's Dream* became source material for another choreographic fete by Balanchine in 1962. New York City Ballet presented it at City Center to critical acclaim, with Mitchell dancing the role of Puck. It was set to Mendelssohn's score of incidental music by the same name, plus a plethora of Mendelssohn's other classical works including a symphony, an intermezzo, a nocturne, and some overtures. It was Balanchine's first completely original full-length ballet. It opened NYCB's first season at the New York State Theater in April 1964. Balanchine made use of Mitchell's comic gifts as well as his speed and agility in the role of Puck. To the costume, Mitchell added an important touch: he used Albolene Moisturizing Cleanser (the substance dancers use to remove makeup) to outline the muscles on his arms, legs

Arthur Mitchell in George Balanchine's *A Midsummer Night's Dream* (Photo: Martha Swope, ©NYPL)

and torso, sprinkling a mixture of red, gold, and silver glitter on top. The ballet was made into a made-for-television movie directed by Dan Eriksen and supposedly supervised by Balanchine. Clive Barnes in *The New York Times* (4/18/1967) wrote that Arthur Mitchell was a "smilingly human Puck." However, Barnes was disenchanted with the overall transmutation of live dance to television. No doubt the drab colors, skimpy television scenery, and early TV camera technology created a flat, ineffective presentation. There were no Flycam™ aerial shots, high-def color, nor any of the on-location technology that in the twenty-first century produces stunningly beautiful digital productions of dance and opera, sometimes shot with 10 cameras or more.

Mitchell, at this time, experienced performing in a brand-new state-of-the-art facility that would house one of the most noted ballet companies in the world. Construction of the New York State Theater was completed in 1964, and in 2008 it was renamed the David H. Koch Theater.

George Balanchine choreographed the pas de deux in *Pithoprakta*, the second dance of *Metastaseis and Pithoprakta* for Mitchell and Farrell in 1968. The score for these two orchestral works by Iannis Xenakis (*Metastaseis* composed 1953–54; *Pithoprakta* composed 1955–56), where the title translates loosely as "actions through probability," is rendered by using numbers and values from scientific laws and physics schemes. Like atonal, twelve-tone serial music, these techniques of composition produce stochastic music that sounds spiky, noisy, clashy, and dissonant—"modern classical" music. In the 1960s the pejorative phrases to express this twentieth-century music would be *far out* or *out there*. *Time* magazine wrote: "It was a long way from *Swan*

Lake, and it drew a few boos on opening night at Lincoln Center last week, but George Balanchine's new ballet is added proof of the inventiveness of the nation's number one choreographer.'"

That same year, Suzanne Farrell and Mitchell performed a Balanchine ballet that was a bit more earthy, *Slaughter on Tenth Avenue,* with tonal music by Broadway's Richard Rodgers, orchestrated by the unparalleled Hershy Kay. The ballet was originally created for the 1936 Broadway musical *On Your Toes,* and it was the first full ballet used in a musical to advance the plot. Mitchell danced the role of the Hoofer.

The year 1968 was a good one for Mitchell. Not only was he involved with the Broadway musical *Sweet Potato,* but he also appeared on television: *The Jackie Gleason Show, The Tex and Jinx Show, Look Up and Live, Camera Three, Omnibus, The Tonight Show Starring Johnny Carson, Tonight with Belafonte, USA: Dance,* and *Something Different.*

Mitchell had peaked in a stunning career with NYCB. Dancing major Balanchine roles on television, in concert, and on Broadway made him a celestial superstar of dance. Unfortunately, his father would never see his triumphs. Arthur Mitchell Sr. died on July 1, 1965. Mitchell recalled his last visit with his father in an interview held January 13, 1971: "My father who was always a fighter said to me, 'I'm tired, I'm really just tired.'"

TOP LEFT: George Balanchine rehearsing *Slaughter on Tenth Avenue* with Arthur Mitchell and Suzanne Farrell, 1968 (Photo: Martha Swope, ©NYPL)

BOTTOM LEFT: Candice Bergen and Arthur Mitchell's promotional photo for the movie *The Day the Fish Came Out,* 1967 (Photo: Michael Cacoyannis)

RIGHT: The Broadway marquis for *Sweet Potato,* 1968 (Photo: Courtesy of the Dorothy Louden Foundation)

REQUIEM AND RISING

In 1968, Mitchell had just lived through Dr. Martin Luther King Jr.'s assassination. He was paired once again with Suzanne Farrell to dance *Requiem Canticles* (1968), in honor of King. The ballet used Stravinsky's music by the same name, scored for orchestra and singers with Latin texts taken from the Catholic requiem liturgy. It was performed only once, on May 2, 1968. Of it, Stravinsky said, "I am honored that my music is to be played in memory of a man of God, a man of the poor, a man of peace." *Requiem Canticles* was used at Stravinsky's funeral, and according to his widow, "He and we knew he was writing it for himself." Conducted by Robert Irving, with Margaret Wilson, contralto, and John Ostendorf, bass, the costumes

and candelabra were by Rouben Ter-Arutunian and lighting by Ronald Bates. The dancers appeared in long white shrouds bearing three-branched candelabra. A woman searches among them and at the end a figure in purple representing Dr. King is raised up. It was a powerful performance for dancers and audience alike. The impact must have been even more powerful for Mitchell. It was empowering. *Requiem*. Death. The will to rise up.

Later, on that flight to Brazil, it hit him. He had his astonishing revelation—a revelation that would change ballet history in America—the insatiable need and strong feeling to *take action!* The need *to do something!* As a firm believer in astrology, he knew his stars in the heavens were

aligning. He said, "Here I am going hundreds of miles away to give of my talents to persons in another country; I should be right here [Harlem] helping my own people."

With the country in the midst of rapid social and political revolution, Arthur Mitchell would begin a brave new chapter of his life—growing a dance company couched in the rationale of tolerance and benevolence. The first step? It all started with a call—to his teacher—Karel Shook. . . .

Arthur Mitchell and Suzanne Farrell in Balanchine's *Requiem Canticles*, 1968 (Photo: Martha Swope, ©NYPL)

CHAPTER 2

KAREL SHOOK

The art of making a dancer is one of the most painstaking occupations in the world.
It demands the precision of the architect, the patience of a lace-maker,
the courage and endurance of a mountain climber.

—*Karel Shook*, Elements of Classical Ballet Technique

Blood bone gut and heart,
nothing less or you'll never make it.

—*Karel Shook*

Karel Shook teaching class with stick in hand (Photo: Marbeth, Courtesy of the Dance Theatre of Harlem Archive)

As a principal founder of Dance Theatre of Harlem, Karel Shook was its keeper of aesthetic values and philosophies of teaching, as well as a prolific artist. He had a glorious career that surrounded him with the most illustrious names in dance. From his childhood to his work with DTH, he developed an uncanny sense of patience. In the studio, he taught with steadfastness, fortitude, and persistence. In life, he never wavered from what he wanted to do. His singular ability to focus and meticulously organize complemented Mitchell.

A CHILD THESPIAN

Karel Francis Shook was born on August 8, 1920, in Renton, Washington, to Ida Marie Tack, a Belgian, and Walter Burnell Shook, a machinist originally from Ohio. They met during World War I in Belgium, and during the Great Depression ran a 15-acre farm in rural Washington State. In his early schooling Karel was an A+ student, and being isolated in the rural northwest, he became an avid reader. In a 1973 *Dance Magazine* article written by Tobi Tobias, Shook recounted how, as a precocious child reading *Harper's Magazine*, which displayed pictures of entertainers and actresses, he asked his mother what actresses did. She told him they dressed up and played around on a stage. After an argument ensued between his mother and his grandmother, a hard-shell Baptist and a member of the Women's Christian Temperance Union who said that actresses were awful people, that was it—Shook knew what he wanted to be. He wanted to be just like Helen Hayes, an *actress*.

Though Shook's parents went to the theatre often, no one in his family was involved in thespian life. He had a mild appreciation for dance, doing jigs and folk dances of the time, but the theatre was his early ambition. Isolated farm life gave him a hunger for the big city. At the farm, Shook would dress up and put on performances. Although he felt very lucky to have wonderful teachers in his country school, he would often run away from home. Eventually, he ended up at the Seattle Repertory Theatre Company (SRC).

SRC (not to be confused with Seattle Repertory Theatre, begun in 1962) was founded by New Yorkers Florence and Burton James, and was housed in the Seattle Repertory Playhouse. This theatre still stands in the University District, renamed the Floyd and Delores Jones Playhouse. Though little is known about Karel Shook's early theatrical training, his experiences in the 1930s influenced his future career and his work at DTH.

In 1931, when Shook would have been ten years old, Florence and Burton James's successful theatre, having 20,000 subscribers, daringly produced *Uncle Tom's Cabin* with a multiracial cast to critical and popular acclaim. Subsequently they also produced *In Abraham's Bosom*, casting from Seattle's African American community, which led to the birth of the Negro Repertory Company. Sadly, even with these heroic accomplishments, the Jameses were brought up on charges in front of the Joseph McCarthy's House Un-American Activities Committee hearings of the 1940s. The conservative narrative of the time was ruthless toward those who favored inclusivity. Any activity outside the realm of a segregated Jim Crow America faced accusations of anti-American subversive behavior.

Also, at this time, the young Karel Shook got his first taste of the footlights, the affirmation of applause, the smell of the greasepaint, and the roar of the crowd. He must have felt the need to be a part of an artistic community, a very intimate experience, as anyone who has ever walked or danced the boards will attest. Perhaps this theatrical orbit influenced his perception and thinking of multiculturalism in the arts. A sensitive and artistic soul, Shook chose throughout his life to work with other cultures, seeing the beauty of diversity. In the book he authored, *Elements of Classical Ballet Technique as Practiced in the School of the Dance Theatre of Harlem*, Shook states, "Prejudices are sophisticatedly acquired tastes that destroy innocence, that state of purity in which man can be in accord with himself, his fellow men, and attuned to nature. . . . True dance, in any of its forms, is an expression of this innocence and it is through dance that man has the possibility to find himself again. Skin shades and ethnic backgrounds have little or nothing to do with it."

SHOOK'S EARLY STUDIES

At the age of 13, in 1934, Shook was awarded a scholarship to the Cornish School of Allied Arts (renamed Cornish College of the Arts in 1986) and became the special protégé of Nellie Cornish, its founder, who encouraged him to study ballet. There is no record of Shook's early teachers, but in 1973 Shook recounted his audition process to dance critic Tobi Tobias:

> When I was 13, I heard there was a scholarship audition for a summer course in theater at the Cornish School of Allied Arts in Seattle. I was determined to do this, so I scraped money together for carfare and got myself there in my little sweater and dungarees. When I came in, they said, 'what do you want?' And I said, 'I want to audition.' They said, 'You are too young, you can't audition.' So, they called out the director of the school, a little sort of dumpy woman in flowered voile, Nellie Cornish—a fabulous person—and she said, 'Oh my goodness, I don't know what to do with you; you're too young. Well wait here, boy, and we'll see.' I waited hours and hours and hours. When all the others had finished, she came out again and said, 'Oh God, that boy is still here.' Well then, she let me up there before the judges and I did the monologue from *Richard III* and there were great whisperings among them. Next came the poetry—I recited something from Lord Byron. Great whisperings again. Finally, for the singing—I announced that I had prepared a *pièce de résistance*, the scene of the death of Aase from *Peer Gynt*. Maria Ouspenskaya, the famous old Russian actress, who was on the panel, said, 'Oh, I do the mother with you!' No, I said, it's not necessary. I do both parts.

Nellie Cornish was a revolutionary in her time. A Seattle pianist, teacher, and writer, she began her learning establishment as an *allied arts school*—music as the main subject with other fine arts taught as well, including dancing, theatre, painting, design, and others.

The story of her pioneering success, beginning a school with six children in a small downtown office, and Mitchell and Shook beginning a dance school in a garage, have uncanny similarities. Both organizations went from meager beginnings to extraordinary success in a short time. It is also noteworthy that DTH would be formed as an allied arts school as well, teaching costuming, sewing, music, singing, stagecraft, and choreography. Both institutions had founders who thought outside the box and saw the larger picture—to make each student a well-rounded artist *and* a well-rounded individual. It was this kind of legacy that gave students, particularly African American students, an edge in a very difficult field in which to gain employment. Nellie Cornish eventually encouraged the young Shook to study dance. She told him that dance, modern and classical, would soon explode into an unimaginably huge art form. She knew wisely that it would provide a great opportunity for the svelte boy. During the embryonic years of DTH, Shook would say, "I'd like to see a rounded curriculum involving music, dance in many forms, drama—all the allied arts—historical and social study, to train the whole artist, who will approach dance as a form of human expression."

The list of luminaries that these organizations have produced is remarkable. Martha Graham taught at Cornish; Chet Huntley (of NBC's *The Huntley-Brinkley Report* news program) and Merce Cunningham were Cornish students. Similarly, DTH produced its own roster of eminent artists. The Cornish school, existing for over 100 years, and Dance Theatre of Harlem, existing for over 50, both leave a legacy as progressive pioneer schools in the American dance scene.

In 1937 the Ballet Russe de Monte Carlo, one of the first and largest ballet companies, performed in Seattle. At age 17 Shook auditioned and was hired—it was his ticket to New York. His first appearance with the company was in 1938 at the Metropolitan Opera House portraying the beggar in Paul Hindemith's 50-minute *Nobilissima Visione* (on the life of Francis of Assisi). The role was small but very important, and Shook's New York debut was tumultuous. Suffering from terrifying jitters, he mistakenly put on megastar Léonide Massine's costume. After the backstage dresser screamed frantically in cardiac arrest, and after the quickest costume change in dance history, the dresser pushed him onto the stage. Blinded by the lights, he finally located Massine onstage and was to kneel before him. He did, and Shook's wig fell off—onto Massine's feet. The next day, Shook was fearing the worst, but the ballet star said to him, "Oh, Karlousha very good, very good. But please in the future try to keep your clothes on."

At this point in his career, Shook had very little classical training. The ballets he was in were choreographed not in the classical sense but called mostly for character dancing. At the time, Balanchine was to choreograph *Serenade*, and could not find seven girl dancers who could dance on toe. This high bar signaled the need in Shook to have more schooling, so he went to Ballet Arts and studied with Edward Caton. Other teachers he held in high esteem were Alexandra Fedorova, Anatole Obukhov, Felia Doubrovska, and especially the engaging Pierre Vladimiroff, who, with an encyclopedic knowledge of dance, would

Karel Shook in costume and makeup (Photo: Courtesy of the Dance Theatre of Harlem Archive)

hold after-class conversations with his students for hours. Here, Shook was washed over with the rhetoric, stories, myths, and truths of the ballet world that, still today, transfer through oral tradition from teacher to student.

After rejoining Ballet Russe in 1941 and performing yet another season at the Metropolitan Opera in New York City, Shook began to develop an interest in choreography, staging, and teaching, but knew he needed to build a solid foundation by dancing *and* by doing. Seven years of hard work and travel followed, from 1941 to 1947. It was the old-style traveling show by train, making whistle stops across the country. Wisely, Shook realized being an international ballet star was not in the cards for him. Too many other interests would interfere with the kind of focus and singular attention needed for that level of accomplishment. For Shook, the *communication of dance* was more interesting. He became passionate about the pedagogy of dance, the mechanics, the art, its aesthetics, its social impact, its mysticism, and its cultural meanings—how dance intrinsically communicates. These leanings became the foundation of his philosophies of dance, eventually shaping DTH into a high aesthetic cultural institution.

In 1947, at the age of 27, Shook took a year's leave from dance. He threw open the window for some fresh air, focusing on languages, music, and writing. It was a time for reassessment of his interests and career.

His journey led him to explore a more mature aesthetic in his art. This paralleled the larger growth of dance arts in America. Ballet, primarily through the work of George Balanchine, began to dramatically refine its methods and aesthetics, its style and its look, its choreography, its scenery and costumes. In 1958 when creating his dream of an American ballet company, Lincoln Kirstein wrote, "I knew that what Balanchine made meant ballet to me, because ballet was about dancing to music, not about painting to pantomime." Shook saw the writing on the wall.

Shook spent 1949 with Balanchine's New York City Ballet. It was a notable year. Jerome Robbins joined that year as choreographer, Tanaquil Le Clercq and Nicholas Magallanes were guest dancers, Stravinsky's *Firebird* premiered as well as Emmanuel Chabrier's *Bourrée Fantasque*. Working with NYCB was a crowning point in Shook's career that he would draw on in his future as a master teacher. He had toured *Song of Norway* and *The Chocolate Soldier*, both choreographed by Balanchine.

Although Shook liked the atmosphere Balanchine created, he felt the dancing was unchallenging—"there was nothing for the men to get their teeth into." For better or worse, this brought him into the realm of Balanchine's methods and thinking. Ballet slowly became theory-driven. The aesthetic bar began to rise and Shook now had credentials.

BECOMING A TEACHER

Karel Shook's prolific writings on dance are rich sources of information. He would gradually develop his own philosophy and pedagogy. This knowledge would eventually become embedded in the soul of DTH. He believed that dancers should not live in a vacuum. They should have a life outside of dance. He encouraged them to break the seal, to explore other art forms, and to enjoy life. For the inquisitive or troubled student, his office door was open, and Shook was available and always approachable.

In 1950 Shook returned to Ballet Russe as a mime dancer, but with added responsibilities as teacher and assistant ballet master. He also began to choreograph. He was gaining hands-on experience in molding dancers. In the summer of 1952, he accepted the offer to take over the ballet department of the Katherine Dunham School of Dance. The position paid only $40 a week, but it would provide him the opportunity to develop his skills as a master teacher.

Working for Katherine Dunham would be yet another rich multiethnic learning experience for Karel Shook. Mary Hinkson, who taught Mitchell in high school and would later teach at DTH, brought Mitchell to study with Shook at the Dunham studio. Of Arthur Mitchell, Shook said, "He was simply a remarkable student. How does one say it? It is very easy to teach talented students—they teach themselves, so to speak. But Arthur was tremendously energetic—always laughing and always very happy." Shook was 13 years Mitchell's senior.

Dunham fused together the styles of Afrocentric movement from many cultures. This would foreshadow the fusions that would ultimately influence all dance in America, and season Alvin Ailey and Arthur Mitchell for their groundbreaking companies. Shook played an important role in this process. He, with Mitchell, explored the possibilities of dance styles with nothing excluded from the table. They both valued and knew the magic of collaboration. They were fearless in exploring new concepts and engaging other professionals to make it happen.

Shook's openness led him to try to understand all people. He treasured the ineffable human being. He loved learning and had boundless curiosity. He respected, gave dignity to, and totally accepted those of any culture. Shook would say, "I did not go to the Dunham School to teach black people. I went there to teach." Beyond this rhetorical statement lies a great virtue that Shook, Mitchell, and Balanchine possessed—the courage and will to *engage*, to go beyond *tolerance*. Dan Rather, news anchor and journalist, once said that tolerance means nothing without

Karel Shook at his typewriter, 1978 (Photo: Marbeth, Courtesy of the Dance Theatre of Harlem Archive)

engagement: "Tolerance alone is not sufficient; it allows us to accept others without engaging with them, to feel smug and self-satisfied without challenging the boundaries within which too many of us live. A society worthy of our ideals would be a much more inclusive one, a more integrated one." George Balanchine made a conscious choice to engage with Arthur Mitchell. Arthur Mitchell made a conscious choice to engage with Karel Shook. People of different cultures choose, or not, to engage with each other; that is, to step beyond the security of tolerance into full, active, and real participation with another. Befriending, talking, dancing. The reality is that society and the ballet companies that reflect that society are not fully integrated, and *engagement*, always the first step, has not always been fully practiced.

Shook was very happy at Dunham, but the experience was short-lived. After he taught there for just two years, in 1954, the Katherine Dunham School of Dance on West 43rd Street closed, just as the civil rights movement in New York City began to simmer.

Karel Shook teaching class, 1972 (Photo: Marbeth, Courtesy of the Dance Theatre of Harlem Archive)

HIS OWN SCHOOL

Not taking any career detour, Shook opened his own school, Studio of Dance Arts, at 705 Eighth Avenue at West 44th Street, just above Downey's Steakhouse. Students from the Dunham School followed him: Alvin Ailey, Donald McKayle, Billy Wilson, Carmen de Lavallade, and Geoffrey Holder. Arthur Mitchell and Alvin Ailey both

taught for Shook as well. Classes in ethnic dance were taught, as well as tap classes with Charles "Cholly" Atkins. With the increasing number of students, he soon outgrew the studio and found an abandoned post office on 69th Street. He corralled there a bevy of dancers, but due to

rising rents and all of the administrational and janitorial work that he had to do single-handedly, it became burdensome. As luck would have it, another opportunity opened, but one not without its challenges.

Most baby boomers will never forget *The Jackie Gleason Show*, a staple of evening entertainment for millions across America. The show featured the kaleidoscopic Busby Berkeley-style overhead-camera showbiz dance routines of the June Taylor Dancers circa 1957. The Taylor School of Dance wanted Karel Shook on their ballet faculty despite the possibility that African American dancers would follow him from the Dunham School. They did. Shook said, "It was instant integration and the school flourished." Shook initiated *engagement*. Even though Shook had professed not to do his art for "political, social, or personal feelings," his sheer presence, decisions, and personal interactions made a huge difference in many a dancer's life, consciously or not. In 1963, Mercedes Ellington, a triple-threat performer, granddaughter of jazz great Duke Ellington and daughter of Mercer Ellington, became the first African American to become a June Taylor Dancer.

Jackie Gleason on his show with integrated June Taylor Dancers
(Photo: CBS)

DUTCH NATIONAL BALLET

Sonia Gaskell, a Lithuanian Dutch dancer, was a member of Ballets Russes from 1927 to 1929. She founded the Netherlands Ballet Academy in the Hague just before 1961. The Amsterdams Ballet (*sic*) merged with the Nederlands Ballet and became the Dutch National Ballet in which Gaskell became artistic director, serving from 1961 to 1968. This volley for ballet presence created a healthy tension in the low country's ballet life. Thus, the "Dutch ballet wars" between those two groups ended. It was probably at her invitation in the fall of 1959 that Shook ventured to Amsterdam through their Ballet Russe connection. Gaskell asked him to be DNB's first teacher and ballet master. Shook found himself again in the position of forming, nurturing, and growing a dance entity in yet another culture.

His experience in the Netherlands would prove to be the most challenging in his career. He had hoped that this was to be an opportunity to mold dancers into his image of what a ballet dancer should be. In a sense, he was beginning with a fresh new canvas, taking the rich essence of dance, learned and lived, to be passed on to a new generation of young performers. And young they were. Very young. Inexperienced. All over the place. Some gifted. Some with ghastly training.

It was chaos. Shook thrived. It was a nearly impossible task. There was no school to serve as a feeding system for new recruits. The inside pressures were tremendous: grueling rehearsals, scheming and politicking among the dancers, betrayed allegiances, an immense repertoire, massive planning, training soloists, conducting rehearsals, and choreographing ballets—24 of them. The outside pressures were equally enormous: deceitful bureaucratic stratagems in hiring and firing, administrative pressures,

and an intensive touring schedule, all the while trying to keep standards as elevated as possible. When the company was out touring internationally, Shook would at times stay in Amsterdam, taking full creative charge of about 35 dancers who were engaged to do local performances. He said, "Everyone asked me how I did it. I just went in and did what needed to be done." He became quite the *régisseur*. He was 40 years old.

Despite working 16-hour days, in 1961 he managed successful seasons in Monte Carlo and in Barcelona with the Dutch National. His talent in choreography was used in *Alceste*, in *Da Capo*, and opera ballets for television. He had been commissioned to do four dance films in living color for Philips TV, the first ever television broadcasts in the Netherlands that contained commercials. They were done in good taste, but he was discomfited because the project did not interest him in the least. He flippantly had asked for a tremendous amount of money because he really didn't want the gig—and, as sometimes happens, he got both.

During this time, he had a chance to exercise his literary muscle, penning a successful series of articles for *Kunst van Nu (Contemporary Art)*. He organized an exhibit of company members' artwork for the foyer of the Opera Theatre during the 1966 Holland Festival. His own creations exhibited were wood carvings, ceramics, paintings, and drawings. He also worked in bronze and terra-cotta. A portfolio of his poems, *Beyond the Mist*, with lithographs by the celebrated painter Sam Middleton, was published in a limited edition by ARTA, the Hague, in 1968.

The culinary arts were another one of his talents and he would often tell dancers and staff of his latest creations. He was ahead of his time when he wrote *A Short*

Guide to Nutrition for Dancers. Never formally published, the guide was another of Shook's endeavors to form the whole dancer. Written at the beginning of the "foodie" craze of the 1980s, it calls on the dancer to sculpt a nutritional program that fits their natural rhythms and individual needs. "Know yourself and study yourself carefully," he orders. His theory was based on the adage "one man's meat is another man's poison." He posits that "Dancers, like jockeys, face a never-ending struggle to stay at minimum weight while maintaining an optimum of energy." At the time, he counseled dancers seeking advice in navigating the "diet jungle," where everything from the Atkin's high-fat plan to the starvation diet were the latest fads. Eating only popcorn or chocolate were some dancers' diets du jour. Shook and Mitchell banned juice and soda from the premises because of their sugar content.

This did not preclude him from subjectively naming nutritious foods and making some statements that were not exactly correct. Included were his exhortations that "doctors know nothing of nutrition . . . Zen fasting can kill a dancer . . . Strict vegetarianism can lead to colitis and cancer . . . Rubber practice clothes are lethal," and "Check out your sex life! And if necessary clean house! Frustrated women most generally overeat to compensate for frustration." And the cryptic "Where sex is concerned don't sell out cheap and don't underestimate yourself. This is a two-way deal that has to arrive at one point. If it doesn't, someone is going to have acid indigestion, with all its ramifications, and that someone will probably be you. If you have any hang-ups dare to be realistic, it may hurt for a while, but the pain will soon lessen, and you'll feel like a million dollars (as Doris Day would say)."

Though the idea of teaching nutrition may have been a knee-jerk reaction to the bulimia and anorexia epidemics hitting the newspaper headlines, Shook's *Short Guide* was a benevolent gesture to care for the well-rounded dancer, whom he encouraged to "Love life and all that goes with it! Get out and look at a tree or a plant, if you haven't done that yet. Observe those around you, the subway or bus is a good place to do this." His work in this area of health and nutrition foreshadowed the trend of ballet companies putting physical therapists and nutritionists on staff.

"On the First Death of Isadora Duncan" from *Beyond the Mist*, Shook's book of poetry (Photo: Courtesy of the Hague)

AMSTERDAM

Shook loved Amsterdam and believed that it was an artist's city. He agreed with the local saying that "Amsterdam is not a city—she is a lover!" His home there was idyllic, an authentic 1664 Dutch house on a Venice-like canal called Egelantiersgracht. The three-story home had a garden in which he loved to work and a second house in the back once used for servants.

While in Amsterdam, Shook also choreographed *The Tales of Hoffman, Rigoletto*, and *I Capuleti e i Montecchi*. He staged and choreographed *La Réjouissance d'Orphée et Eurydice*, a seventeenth-century court ballet that premiered in Sittard. By his own admission, "the costumes are ravishing—high plumes and big skirts in wonderful colors."

Most notably, he created the playful *Jazz Nocturne* for Sonja van Beers and Billy Wilson. Costumed by Ger Frenzen with music by Alex Philipsen, it combined jazz and classical dancing. (Billy Wilson, an African American dancer also invited to the company by Sonia Gaskell, starred in the Dutch National Ballet's *Othello*, created for him by Serge Lifar.)

Shook's time in the Netherlands was remarkable. Dutch National Ballet opened its arms to multicultural dancers in the early 1960s, and no doubt Shook and Gaskell were sensitive to the inclusiveness. Shook engaged with a cohort that was open to diversity and cross-culturality. Billy Wilson and Raven Wilkinson danced in the company at that time. In 2013 Michaela DePrince, ballet star of the film *First Position*, became a DTH Company member for a short while, then joined Dutch National Ballet in 2014.

Karel Shook's years in Amsterdam did not come without a caveat. As when in his earlier dancing career, he realized that he would not be a megastar dancer, it was in Amsterdam that he realized choreography was not his forte—but teaching was. Then Arthur Mitchell called. . . .

CHAPTER 3

BIRTH OF
A SCHOOL

I look forward to an America which will reward achievement in the arts as
they reward achievement in business or stagecraft. I look forward to an America
which will steadily raise the standards of expression and which will
steadily enlarge cultural opportunity for all our citizens. And I look forward to
an America which commands respect throughout the world not only
for its strengths but for its civilization as well.

—President Kennedy, as quoted in a Dance Theatre of Harlem program,
February 4, 1972, Music Hall, Cincinnati, Ohio

Arthur Mitchell teaching a ballet class, 1970. (Photo: Marbeth, Courtesy of the Dance Theatre of Harlem Archive)

THE AGE OF ANXIETY

Mitchell and Shook's creative act of birthing a school of classical dance, and soon thereafter a ballet company, would plant a seed on the streets of Harlem. That seed grew into a community of dance and would blossom into a global aesthetic entity. It became a force in the humanities, and a treasure of civilization. Dance Theatre of Harlem would go on to earn hundreds of awards worldwide and perform for the Queen of England. Arthur Mitchell would garner the United States National Medal of Arts and the Kennedy Center Honors. This company would amass a long list of firsts in the history of classical ballet and change forever the dance landscape in America's historical record. What followed was dissent from ballet tradition. What followed was proving Mitchell and Shook's doctrine, a tenet in four words: all can do ballet.

This turning point for classical ballet in the United States started as a simple idea. Mitchell wanted to *do something* for his people: get kids off the streets of Harlem and redirect their energy; give them the means to change the focus in their lives through dance. The challenge fueled Mitchell's bold spirit. Without compromise, he proved many wrong. "Yes, you can!" became Mitchell's mantra, a phrase used often in the dance studio to quell any self-doubt. He said, "The minute you tell me I can't, that's the moment I'm determined that I'm going to do it. I'm Aries. Nothing deters you."

Most historical epochs are known by one name—Medieval, Renaissance, Baroque. However, the names coined for the years in America from roughly 1950 to 1975 were many: the Beat Generation, the age of Women's Liberation, the Space Age, the Hippie Generation, the Drug Generation, the Age of Civil Rights, and collectively, the Age of Anxiety. Coined in a poem by W. H. Auden, this phrase captured the feeling of unrest during and after World War II in America:

> Redeem with a clear
> Configuration
> Of routes and goals
> The ages of anguish,
> All griefs endured
> At the feet of appalling
> Fortresses; may
> Your present motions
> Satisfy all
> Their antecedents.
>
> —W. H. Auden, *The Age of Anxiety*

Karel Shook and Arthur Mitchell on a typical day in the studio, 1968
(Photo: Marbeth, Courtesy of the Dance Theatre of Harlem Archive)

What followed, in the industrialized post-WWII years, was an unprecedented sea change in American behavior— socially, politically, sexually, and culturally. The pendulum would swing from the conservative to the radical, from the formal to the informal, from unanimity and conformity to countercultural revolutions and generation gaps. The status quo was cut with civil unrest and protest. The civil rights movement challenged bigotry and intolerance. Americans began for the first time to witness live televised images of the Vietnam War in their living rooms, courtesy of new satellites that circled the earth. Global communications and advanced technology turned viewers into eyewitnesses for the human race's first step on the moon. Local news carried live shots of civil riots in major cities.

Though the African American struggle for equality is generations old, and is still ongoing, the continuum of the civil rights movement brought fierce and tumultuous change. Two key events advanced the movement. Segregated schools were ruled unconstitutional in 1954 by the Supreme Court's ruling in *Brown v. Board of Education*, and, led by Dr. Martin Luther King Jr. and Rosa Parks, the Montgomery city buses were boycotted in 1955 to protest discrimination. Rights activists mobilized and Freedom Riders would bus into the segregated South. These events opened the door to social integration in all aspects of life.

Rock and roll, folk, funk, soul, and progressive jazz challenged smooth swing bands. Protest songs abounded, and the cry for freedom was heard in all parts of the artistic community. The young generation's mantra became "Turn on, tune in, drop out." Psychedelia reigned. It was the age of "Black Awareness." New York art galleries carried works by African American artists such as Jacob Lawrence and Romare Bearden. Arthur Ashe ruled as the US Open tennis champion, Shirley Chisholm became the first African American congressional representative, and Aretha Franklin ruled as the queen of soul music. It was in this high-speed critical epoch of change that Arthur Mitchell and Karel Shook lived. It was a charged time. It was the right time, and ballet would never be the same.

Close to home, with the Harlem riots of 1964 and 1969, and more globally in cultural segregation and human rights, political action and reaction stimulated two dance artists to create something in the social-artistic realm. It was an opportunity *to do something* that would make a difference, that would help, that would heal. Something that would ignite.

Arthur Mitchell onstage at the Cambridge University Summer Arts Institute (Photo: Sharon Perry)

THE 1960S DANCE SCENE
IN NEW YORK

In 1968, the dance scene in metropolitan New York was ripe to receive Mitchell and Shook's new endeavor. New styles were emerging, but its landscape was not so different from what one would find in the twenty-first century, notwithstanding the number of companies and the price of tickets. The Joffrey Ballet presented its 1968 fall season at New York City Center, a main dance venue that was celebrating its 25th anniversary. That season included its signature piece *Viva Vivaldi*, with a top ticket price of four dollars. The New York City Ballet presented at City Center as well, while New York City Community College on Jay Street in Brooklyn presented American Ballet Theatre in its Festival of the Arts with a company of ninety-five including orchestra, and a top ticket price of three dollars. The Harkness Ballet appeared for a run on Broadway at the Music Box. The assemblage simply known as *Dance Repertory 1969* presented the dance companies of Merce Cunningham, José Limón, Alvin Ailey, Twyla Tharp, Meredith Monk, Yvonne Rainer, and Don Redlich at the Billy Rose Theatre on West 41st Street, each allotted two or three evenings for their works.

Broadway played host to *Fiddler on the Roof, Cabaret*, and *Hair*. In 1969, the very year Dance Theatre of Harlem came into being, a multicultural version of *Hello, Dolly!* with Pearl Bailey as Dolly Levi opened on Broadway. It featured Cab Calloway, Mabel King, Clifton Davis, Ernestine Jackson, and Morgan Freeman, with Bailey winning a special Tony Award for her performance.

Filling the vacuum in the American dance world with a multicultural classical ballet company would not be something new. There were several attempts, which included Joseph Rickard's First Negro Classic Ballet, founded in 1948; Thelma Hill and Edward Fleming's New York Negro Ballet, in 1955, and Aubrey Hitchens's Negro Dance Theater, in the mid-1950s; there were others, but these were short-lived. What *was* new was the impetus that caused Mitchell and Shook to birth an African American ballet company, namely, the jolting shock of the assassination of Dr. Martin Luther King Jr. on April 4, 1968. The assassination of Robert F. Kennedy on June 6 of that same year became similar inspiration for Karel Shook.

Just after that fateful Thursday in April 1968, Arthur Mitchell had his pivotal revelation that led him to eventually forgo the Brazil project and instead return to Harlem to create a ballet school with a company that would become one of the finest in the world. And build he did. He built an internationally known premier classical ballet company that would perform in theatres and opera houses throughout six continents. Mitchell had an uncanny ability to work with young dancers, some as young as three, and motivate them to excellence. His attractive persona, infectious energy, and motivational skills became a magnet for young artists who reaped the benefits in their lives, in the studio, and ultimately onstage.

SHOOK'S "ABOUTNESS" OF DANCE

After the assassination of Senator Robert F. Kennedy, Karel Shook was known to say that his own work "had to have spiritual and emotional and social significance, as well as artistic." This notion for Shook, not as dramatic an epiphany as Mitchell's, cast him not only as an artistic collaborator, but as DTH's prolific sage and a staunch defender of the organization's doctrines of dance. He had a stellar career as a dancer, ballet master, and choreographer—author and poet as well. He had also been Arthur Mitchell's teacher.

In near-religious language, Shook articulated and synthesized DTH's aesthetics, methods, and goals. The writings that he left behind, after a much too short a time on this planet (and much too short of a time with DTH), elegantly tell what the institution should be. In one of his writings, "The Aboutness of Dance Theatre of Harlem," he states that it is: "About returning the arts to the people to whom they belong and in perceiving them as necessary to daily life as they always should have been. About the aristocracy of man—the marriage of the incontestable

Karel Shook and Arthur Mitchell during the studio renovation, 1971 (Photo: Marbeth, Courtesy of the Dance Theatre of Harlem Archive)

nobility of the watusi with the rarefied aristocracy of the court of Louis XIV. And it is about all that we will have to be if we hope to preserve our civilization."

Between both founders, this kind of rhetoric grew, not only justifying the existence of a multicultural ballet company and school, but also challenging the popular notion that people from cultures other than Euro-American were not suitable to dance classical ballet.

In 2012, nearly 50 years after DTH's inception, *The New York Times* dance reviewer Gia Kourlas wrote:

When the company went on hiatus in 2004 for financial reasons, it left a big hole in the American ballet scene. . . . After all this time a question remains: Is a predominantly black ballet company even necessary? Just a glance at the makeup of the two main troupes at Lincoln Center provides a swift yes.

Born out of the Age of Anxiety, the creation of Dance Theatre of Harlem is an example of anxiety calmed—and transformed, and only the beginning . . .

Arthur Mitchell teaching a ballet class, 1970 (Photo: Marbeth, Courtesy of the Dance Theatre of Harlem Archive)

Karel Shook teaching children ballet (Photo: Marbeth, Courtesy of Dance Theatre of Harlem)

PART TWO

CHAPTER 4

BEGINNINGS

The Seasons 1968–1971

What we started out to do, to prove, was that black children, given the same opportunity as white children, could be great dancers. . . . We proved that in just a few years. Then we wanted to take that company of black dancers and showcase them in the city, the country, and the world, to show people what black artists could do. We did that.

—*Arthur Mitchell in the* Lexington Herald-Leader

The young company c. 1969 (Photo: Marbeth, Courtesy of the Dance Theatre of Harlem Archive)

CONTROLLED
AVALANCHE

The birthing of Dance Theatre of Harlem was more of a process than a singular event. Because Arthur Mitchell and Karel Shook were charismatic, talented, focused, energetic, and lucky, it was a successful endeavor. Even more, there was a vacuum and a *need* in the Harlem of the late 1960s.

With the '60s revolutions in pop culture, it was hip to be new, different, shocking, and, best of all, good-willed. With big ballet and opera companies swimming in post-war money, and with the novelty of television, ballet's image was projected to American viewers across the country. Viewers gasped at ballet dancers becoming human

tornadoes and gulped at women who could dance on just the point of their toes—didn't that hurt? The medium became the message, and the dream—as Dr. Martin Luther King, Jr. posited—was for *all*. Not only for the Euro-American son or daughter of the well-heeled patron of the arts, but for the Afro-American child of Harlem.

Many times, Arthur Mitchell reiterated his own dream: "The establishment of a permanent school of ballet in the Harlem community [that] would encourage less privileged youngsters in the art and discipline of the dance, as well as instill 'pride of ownership' throughout that community." As Edward Kleban later said in his *A Chorus Line* lyric:

The Company in Arthur Mitchell's *Rhythmetron* (Photo: Marbeth, Courtesy of the Dance Theatre of Harlem Archive)

"Everyone is beautiful at the ballet." The civil rights movement's notion of opportunity opened doors to thousands of children, to *be* somebody, to *be* beautiful—and with Arthur Mitchell as teacher—to *be* dancers, to *be* artists and ambassadors representing the United States of America. It was "hip" to be "cool" and cool to be inclusive. Acceptance of African Americans into Eurocentric circles proceeded tentatively and slowly, but it did proceed.

Arthur Mitchell grew from his experiences of travel and gigging around the world. He gained information and expertise from the major players in ballet who would influence his life decisions. His choice-making was tested in the westernmost city on the continent of Africa—Dakar, Senegal. In 1966, the city was presenting the First World Festival of Negro Arts. Mitchell was asked to be the US dance chairperson, cobbling together 31 dancers of the highest caliber that included Paula Kelly, Carmen de Lavallade, and Claude Thompson. After grueling preproduction and rehearsals, the funding fell out. Mitchell and his dancers were replaced by Alvin Ailey and company. This was convenient for the festival organizers. The Ailey company had just run out of money while on tour and were stranded overseas with nowhere to perform. Mitchell refused a last-minute offer to dance a duet with Carmen de Lavallade, Geoffrey Holder's wife. It was "all of us, or nothing." This would not be the first time Mitchell would make blunt, painful decisions. It would also not be the last time funding fell out.

Mitchell left for Rio de Janeiro, in March of 1966, to create the first national ballet company for Brazil. Two women accompanied him: Gloria Contreras as choreographer and Suzanne Ames as recorder. He called it "a fabulous little company," but it was short-lived, lasting only three months, cut short by a military coup. The Brazilian government was eventually replaced, and the new ballet project was rebooted a year later, in 1967. Mitchell began traveling again to Rio while still appearing with the New York City Ballet.

Though Mitchell had never considered himself a choreographer, it was in Brazil that he ventured into creating a new work with *Rhythmetron*. With 31 dancers and Brazilian themes, it quickly became a major part of his oeuvre. Composed in 1968 on commission for 38 percussion instruments by Marlos Nobre, *Rhythmetron* premiered on June 11, 1968, at the Teatro Novo. It had three parts: *A Preparação*, *A Escolhida*, and *O Ritual*. It was restaged and then performed in Philadelphia, Pennsylvania, at William Penn High School with a cast of 27 future DTH dancers. Later, in 1974, when it was performed at the ANTA Theatre, Clive Barnes of *The New York Times* called it "a good piece . . . brilliantly danced by the company."

During this time, Mitchell realized that using indigenous folklore as source material had value for theming dance projects. Mitchell surveyed Christianity, Buddhism, and Candomblé for inspiration. Capoeira, an Afro-Brazilian kickboxing dance-game, captured his attention.

Most importantly, Mitchell began to learn what it was like to be the driving force of a dance company. He had artistic freedom, talented dancers, space, monetary resources, and the credentials. Mitchell said, "After Dr. King was assassinated, and there were all the eulogies, I ask myself: Arthur Mitchell, what can you do? When you pay homage, you do the thing that you do best—if you make music, you beat your drum; if you are a singer, you sing; if you are a dancer, you dance. Once I made up my mind to pay homage through dance, all I needed were money, work, and love."

HARLEM SCHOOL
OF THE ARTS

In 1939 in New York's Town Hall, a concert venue in the Broadway theatre district, a young soprano sang to a sold-out house and took New York by storm. The great conductor Serge Koussevitzky proclaimed, "It is a miracle! It is a musical revelation! The world must hear her!" She was the singer Dorothy Maynor, an African American who paved the way for other artists like Leontyne Price, Jessye Norman, Kathleen Battle, and Marian Anderson, the first African American singer at the Metropolitan Opera (1955). Though Maynor had performed and recorded music from hundreds of operatic roles, she never appeared on the opera stage.

Maynor pursued Arthur Mitchell for two years to offer him the position of dance master for the new ballet division of her newly founded arts center, later to be called Harlem School of the Arts (HSA). Mitchell was a known quantity and Maynor understood that his association with the school would add prestige. At first, Mitchell resisted. When Nancy Lasalle, an HSA board member, also asked Arthur Mitchell to steer the dance program, he finally accepted. He raised $25,000 seed money at start-up, and on July 8, 1968, three months after Dr. Martin Luther King Jr.'s assassination, the HSA dance program opened.

Upon the launch, Arthur Mitchell called his teacher and mentor Karel Shook, who was still in Amsterdam, inviting him to be ballet master and associate artistic director for the new endeavor. After eight years with the Dutch National Ballet, on July 31, 1968, Shook left Holland.

Beginnings can be complicated. During the summer of 1968, Mitchell offered an eight-week workshop with 30 students in the gymnasium of the community center at St. James Presbyterian Church, at 141st Street and St. Nicholas Avenue. The day after Shook arrived in New York, Mitchell left for Vancouver, British Columbia, where he was to star with George Grizzard, Carole Shelley, and Dorothy Louden in the pre-Broadway run of Noël Coward's *Sweet Potato*. It played 32 performances and the critics were ruthless. The July 23, 1968, edition of the *Province* used the headline, "You Expect People to Pay to See That?" Critic James Barber said it "Has no more hope of reaching Broadway then has Uncle Fred, with a lampshade on his head, doing the Charleston." Well, it reached Broadway.

Karel Shook and Arthur Mitchell on a typical day in the studio, Harlem School of the Arts, 1968 (Photo: Marbeth, Courtesy of the Dance Theatre of Harlem Archive)

Dorothy Maynor

THERE WERE FEW OPPORTUNITIES IN OPERA FOR AFRICAN AMERICANS during the 1930s and 1940s, when Maynor's voice was in its prime. She, like Arthur Mitchell and Karel Shook, made historic firsts. She was the first African American singer to appear in Constitution Hall with the National Symphony Orchestra, and the first African American

member on the Metropolitan Opera Board of Directors. She also recorded extensively for RCA Records under the baton of Arturo Toscanini and toured the world concertizing with major symphony orchestras.

In April of 1947, with the encouragement of her husband, Reverend Shelby Rooks, pastor of St. James Presbyterian Church, Maynor began an arts program for the youth of Harlem. It was incorporated as the St. James Community Center. In 1963, upon her retirement, it became known as Harlem School of the Arts (HSA). It used church facilities located at West 141st Street and St. Nicholas Avenue, in West Harlem. Classes were offered in music, ballet, modern dance, drama, and art to Harlem children for as little as 50 cents a lesson, which included musical instrument rental, and for piano students, an on-site practice room. Maynor taught voice and served as executive director until 1979. She had come to raise more than $2 million to eventually build a new facility for her school that had grown to more than 1,000 students.

Dorothy Maynor (Photo: Carl Van Vechten)

With book, music, and lyrics by the legendary Noel Coward, *Sweet Potato* played at the Ethel Barrymore Theatre from September through November of 1968 with 19 previews and 44 performances. While it received mixed reviews, *New York Times* critic Clive Barnes called Mitchell "one of the world's finest dancers." Barnes would go on to keep Mitchell and DTH on his radar because Mitchell was working at the top of his field on Broadway and in ballet. Prophetically, in the program bio, Mitchell wrote that he "has found time to serve as dance director at Dorothy Maynor's Harlem School of the Arts where he teaches ballet to youngsters in the community, many of whom he hopes will form the nucleus of a professional Negro Ballet company."

While Mitchell was away working on *Sweet Potato*, Shook took the reins of the HSA dance department and four-member company. This cadre of dancers would eventually become the first DTH Company. The professional dancers were Lydia Abarca, Gerald Banks, Walter Raines, and Llanchie Stevenson (now Aminah L. Ahmad); soon thereafter, Sheila Rohan, Patricia Ricketts, Virginia Johnson, Arturo Vivaldo, and Derek Williams. Johnson would go on to become DTH's *prima ballerina assoluta* and eventually its second artistic director. A young group of apprentices also joined around this time, including Valerie Bower, Susan Lovelle, Yvonne Hall, Cassandra Phifer-Moore, and Jewel Melchior.

Shook was in a good place, doing work that had social and spiritual significance—not to be confused with a religious theology associated with the church space he was working, but as a spiritual humanist. By seeing his work manifested in the less fortunate, he was actually ministering to himself. The human spirit is nourished when it nourishes others. In a sense, it was noblesse oblige; or in today's vernacular, "making a difference." In his own pseudosecular Christian language, "Our manifesto was being made flesh and blood."

Mitchell was awarded a matching Ford Foundation grant for $151,000 and moved the HSA dance department to a street-level garage adjacent to St. James Presbyterian Church. The funds were exhausted after the studio, designed by George Balanchine, was completed, but Shook maintained that everyone could work safely on the expensive wood-sprung dance floor, unlike cement floors that can cause shin splints. (This care for the dancer's safety carried on through the years. DTH would even tour with their own sprung floor stage deck.)

More and more dancers arrived daily. Shook loved to tell how on hot summer days the bay doors would be left open, and a crowd of onlookers would gather, causing more and more children to join the program. Mitchell would tell the male bystanders that there was no need to wear tights, cutoff dungarees were fine. In a short time, there would be 400 students with 16 professionals teaching.

LECTURE DEMONSTRATIONS

This fledgling dance institution began to find ways to reach out to the community. Open rehearsals were offered to audiences so that the community could see ballet in action. Performances were presented at various venues throughout the city.

Lecture demonstrations became routine and grew increasingly popular. The art of ballet and the making of an artist were illustrated so that everyone could understand and enjoy. These were also performed at impoverished schools where students couldn't imagine that such dancers even existed in classical ballet. Theatres filled with children were left with a powerful message: that given an opportunity, and through hard work, anyone can achieve great and beautiful things.

The first lecture demonstration was given on August 6, 1968, in Rensselaerville, New York, with Lydia Abarca, Gerald Banks, Walter Raines, and Llanchie Stevenson.

Arthur Mitchell leading a lecture demonstration wearing tights (Photo: Marbeth, Courtesy of the Dance Theatre of Harlem Archive)

Many more were presented in colleges, and at elementary and high schools to introduce students to the art of ballet and the investment of time it takes to become a classical dancer. These were rehearsed and highly polished presentations that Mitchell narrated, with dancers starting at the barre, showing center work, pointe, partnering, lifting, turning, and then finishing with a solo, a pas de deux or pas de trois, and a full-company dance.

Mitchell solicited audience participation by inviting audience members onstage to show that the latest social dances, at their core, contained ballet steps. Just as in the late 1950s Leonard Bernstein made music lovers through his *Omnibus* and *Young People's Concerts* on TV, Arthur Mitchell was making ballet lovers. He connected the classical ballet steps from Louis XIV's court with the dance craze of the moment. He was riveting. Shook would delight in seeing the dancers enter, perfect posture, elongated necks, beautiful perfect arms, gorgeous legs, and defined musculature. In his own words: "The dancers arrived onstage beautifully groomed and looking like dark gods and goddesses. Arthur used them all, even the youngest. The demonstration part of the program went like a dream. Arthur was his usual breathtaking self, and the kids danced like dark angels. The audience was enthralled, and when it was finished, applauded wildly." These demonstrations were an opportunity for Shook and Mitchell to see their dancers onstage—to test them and provide an opportunity for the dancers to "get out there and do it." Virginia Johnson recalls: "[Mitchell] conducted the first lecture demonstration in tights and the kids laughed so hard when he came onstage that the next performance he had on slacks. I have not seen him in tights for a lecture demonstration since."

Daily classes and rehearsals filled Mitchell's schedule. He also found time for outside bookings. In 1969 Mitchell procured the opportunity to stage his ballet *Ode to Otis* on a bill with the André Eglevsky Ballet Company. Staged at Half Hollow Hills High School in Huntington, Long Island, it included dancers Lydia Abarca, Walter Raines, Derek Williams, Gerald Banks, and Arturo Vivaldo, and drummer Verrill Adams. Gelsey Kirkland and Robert Weiss shared the bill with Balanchine's *Tarantella*. *Ode to Otis* was also performed in 1969 by the same cast for an Afro-American cultural exhibit sponsored by the New York Foundling Hospital, with the dance company billed as the Harlem School of the Arts Dance Company. Choreographed as a tribute to Otis Redding, an R&B singer who perished in a plane crash, according to a program note, the work was "abstract, at times savage, [and] is danced to shrill and eerie Coleridge-Taylor Perkinson's music. It deals with the frustrations and disappointments of this as they are striving, relaxing and striving again."

News of Mitchell's work spread throughout the city and the number of students grew, including expenses, and

Lecture demonstrations continued throughout the following decades, 1976. (Photo: Courtesy of the Dance Theatre of Harlem Archive)

with that, tension. Tensions between Mitchell and Maynor manifested over monetary issues, vision, and sharing power. In William Roger's book on Dorothy Maynor, *Dorothy Maynor and the Harlem School of the Arts: The Diva and the Dream*, he quotes a teacher as saying: "When you have two prima donnas working together, there is bound to be conflict." This may have been the cause of animosity between Arthur Mitchell and Dorothy Maynor, a divo of dance versus the diva of song, but most likely other events added to the irritations. Artistic egos the size of Saturn fueled the clashes, but the day-to-day tensions of running an educational business did as well. Balanchine had warned Mitchell: "Once you begin this, Arthur, you will never sleep again. You begin as an artist with just the idea of a school and a company in mind—but then you will meet dozens of other ramifications of which you never dreamed, there will be no more rest." To properly attend to his voracious creative impulse, and the work it brought forth, Mitchell had to make sacrifices. He had to forgo enticements, such as Hollywood, marriage, and other forces that beckoned. He would need to devote himself to the work.

Dorothy Maynor continued navigating the turbulent '60s by booking herself throughout the country, making speeches on the plight of urban arts. Wanda Toscanini Horowitz (chairperson of HSA's Women's Committee, conductor Arturo Toscanini's daughter, and the wife of pianist Vladimir Horowitz) had procured real estate for a new building. She complained that the HSA board was recalcitrant, and the Women's Committee lacked information as to how the school was being run, necessary for fundraising. Horowitz resigned and Maynor was shocked. At the time, Mitchell had the support of Lincoln Kirstein and George Balanchine. With Mitchell's hubris in ascension, he proclaimed that he was ready to build a "Harlem Lincoln Center." Lean and handsome, cocky and stubborn, with a million-dollar smile, Mitchell had obtained a high level of success with the school. He was ready to move on.

A BOARD OF DIRECTORS

On February 11, 1969, without Maynor knowing, and with the assistance of Mitchell's friend Charles De Rose, a financial planning consultant, Mitchell formed a culturally diverse nonprofit corporation with himself as president, George Balanchine first vice president, actress Cicely Tyson second vice president, actor Brock Peters third vice president, City Center board member Nancy Lasalle secretary, and Charles De Rose treasurer. Nonprofit status with tax exemption was granted on October 15, 1969.

with the discipline and professionalism of our approach." And to the dance community at large: "We had begun to show up the seams of the entire establishment of the dance world, and we were accomplishing, in a frightfully short period of time, what they knew they should have done years ago."

The lightning speed of the dance program's growth while Mitchell was at HSA yielded a good amount of creative output for Mitchell, Shook, and their retinue: *Ode to Otis*, with a score by Coleridge-Taylor Perkinson; the first movement of *Tones*, with original music by Tania León; and an adapted *Rhythmetron*, all of which would serve as the foundation of a solid repertoire that would continue to grow throughout the years.

In January of 1970, on the advice of Balanchine and Kirstein, Mitchell finally resigned from the HSA. He was replaced by Oleg Briansky and his wife, Mireille Briane, directors of the Saratoga Ballet Center at Skidmore College.

Regarding the situation at HSA, Shook believed that Maynor was not sympathetic with "what we were doing, or

LEFT: Karel Shook teaching class at Jacob's Pillow (Photo: Marbeth, Courtesy of the Dance Theatre of Harlem Archive)

RIGHT: *Left to right in foreground:* Arthur Mitchell and composer Coleridge-Taylor Perkinson, during the creation of *Ode to Otis*, 1969 (Photo: Marbeth, Courtesy of the Dance Theatre of Harlem Archive)

CHURCH OF THE MASTER

With no home, Mitchell and Shook accepted studio space generously offered by choreographer Glen Tetley, who had just folded his dance company due to financial problems. Tetley, a Cleveland-born Graham dancer/choreographer, appeared in and was dance captain for the original production of *Kiss Me, Kate* as well as choreographer for *Nureyev* on Broadway. His claim to fame as choreographer was fusing modern dance with ballet, and in 1969 he became codirector of the Netherlands Dance Theatre. After two months at the Tetley studio, according to Shook, "the incubation period was over, and we officially became 'DTH.'"

For anyone who desires to begin a dance entity, rehearsal and performance space is a primary concern. Dance needs space, and the right space comes with a huge cost. A dance studio and the money to support it are essential for making ballet. Insurance problems arose at the Tetley space, so DTH moved to another church basement, Church of the Master, across the street from Morningside Park at 122 Street and Morningside Ave.

Eventually Mitchell and Shook's School had grown to an enrollment of 600 and a Company of 24 members. It flourished and others were invited to teach, including Tanaquil Le Clercq, Cicely Tyson, James Truitte, Pearl Reynolds, and Mary Hinkson. Tania León was appointed music director and Daniel Barrajanos became the official drummer.

The observation deck at Church of the Master served as a sacrosanct space for VIPs. Mitchell's friends and prospective donors came to observe classes, rehearsals, and run-throughs. He loved to show off the Company where he himself could perform as a dancer, be "on," and play the role of the director. Working the room with a towel around his neck, Mitchell the showman, animated with

intensity, presented those in the gallery with a display of amazing talent. Popping up from his director's chair, he would partner dancers with a release of atomic energy, raising the heat in the room and exposing the hard work that goes into ballet. At times, for special invitees, he would actually rehearse a rehearsal and stage it!

Mitchell's presence in the studio was intimidating. He demanded he be called "Mr. Mitchell." When in the studio he held court. He would dissect a step to its raw

A Christmas portrait. *Left to right:* Tania León, Arthur Mitchell, Tanaquil Le Clercq, and DTH original board treasurer Charles De Rose (Photo: Marbeth, Courtesy of the Dance Theatre of Harlem Archive)

essentials, then have dancers do it over and over again to perfection. Mitchell used metaphors to help dancers understand corrections he gave in class and onstage. If he wanted the dancers to utilize their inner thighs to access more turnout, he would say, "bring the juicy part of the chicken leg." Or if he wanted dancers to be one with the music, he would say, "the music is the water and you are the swimmer, let it carry you." When his dancers were performing onstage, he would tell them to not press their lips together because it made the face lose its expression.

If one believes that the stars do align, then they did for Mitchell and Shook, in more ways than one. Mitchell was a believer in astrology, and upon meeting dancers for the first time would ask them their zodiac sign. Astrology was Mitchell's way of starting a personnel file, for better or for worse. It provided justification if a dancer was precise or detailed (Virgos) and gave him some idea of compatibility between dancers and himself. After identifying a personality via horoscope, Mitchell would ask to see the dancer's feet, to determine if they were "pretty." In ballet, this means that the foot has a high instep, and when it is pointed, it arches down toward the floor as much as possible. Even when feet were nearly perfect, Mitchell still insisted on stretching and strengthening.

Left to right: Luchino Visconti, Arthur Mitchell, and Cicely Tyson watching ballet from the observation gallery (Photo: Marbeth, Courtesy of the Dance Theatre of Harlem Archive)

ALVA GIMBEL AND
466 WEST 152ND STREET

Among the many who came to observe a rehearsal at Church of the Master was an "angel," Mrs. Alva B. Gimbel, of Gimbels store fame, who would become Dance Theatre of Harlem's first individual major benefactor. Taken with Mitchell and Shook's work, Gimbel told Mitchell that if he could find a permanent building, she would "present it." Mitchell was motivated.

The story of procurement is legendary: Mitchell gets into a cab, cab driver says a two-story garage is vacant, Mitchell asks, "Where?" cab driver says "152nd Street in Harlem," they drive there. Bingo. Transactions were made, papers signed, and Alva Gimbel presented Dance Theatre of Harlem with a home. It was like Christmas. At a cost of $365,000, the firm of Hardy, Holzman, and Pfeiffer renovated the space at 466 West 152nd Street. An additional $70,000 was raised by the dancers through extra performances.

The repertoire was expanded with works by Balanchine, Robbins, Holder, Louis Johnson, Lester Horton, John Taras, and Mitchell. The student enrollment in the school reached 1,000.

A 1969 brochure boasted stunning reviews: "A controlled Avalanche!"—Clive Barnes, *The New York Times*; "It's a Miracle!"—Walter Terry, *The Saturday Review*;

Arthur Mitchell with philanthropist Alva Gimbel of Gimbels department store fame (Photo: Marbeth, Courtesy of the Dance Theatre of Harlem Archive)

"Unique, impressive!"—Leonard Harris, CBS News; "Constantly Inventive"—Anna Kisselgoff, *The New York Times*. The Company roster included Gayle McKinney, John Jones, Roslyn Sampson, Gerald Banks, Patricia Ricketts, Clover Mathis, Llanchie Stevenson, James Thurston, Virginia Johnson, Derek Williams, Ronda Sampson, Samuel Smalls, Lydia Abarca, Walter Raines, and Sheila Rohan. The board of directors boasted Lincoln Kirstein, Arthur Mitchell, George Balanchine, Brock Peters, and Cicely Tyson.

The immediate public response to a multicultural ballet company called Dance Theatre of Harlem led to a myriad of isolated engagements including a benefit luncheon for Northside Center for Child Development at the New York Plaza Hotel and the Philadelphia Academy of Music. One of the first full-evening programs consisted of a lecture demonstration for act one, a performance of *Holberg Suite* for act two, and *Rhythmetron* for act three, performed at William Penn High School.

In August of 1970, DTH performed at Jacob's Pillow and was finally in their permanent home at 466 West 152nd Street, today known as the Everett Center for the Performing Arts. Open Houses, later called Sunday Matinées, quickly became a tradition. They were held monthly throughout the history of DTH to engage with the community. An open invitation was offered to all to see studio presentations of ballet, chamber music, dance companies, fashion shows, talks, and all types of performers. When the program was planned, a staff person or a celebrity would be chosen to host and emcee. These programs would be one to two hours in length, and some featured megastars. Some contained full ballets.

The first DTH Open House, c. 1971 with Susan Lovelle (Photo: Marbeth, Courtesy of the Dance Theatre of Harlem Archive)

MUSIC AND MUSICIANS

IN THE BASEMENT OF THE DTH STUDIOS, A LOCKED STORAGE ROOM HOLDS A WALL of bookshelves that house large, gray archival boxes. These contain the orchestrations of some the greatest music ever written for ballet. It is a priceless collection. Each box holds a conductor's full score and the individual parts for every instrument in a large symphonic orchestra. They include the conductor's pencil notes, cues, and tempos of each ballet as performed by the DTH Company. These scores were the road map for the hundreds of musicians that accompanied the dancers onstage: the conductors, instrumentalists, pianists, and singers, all of whom brought the glorious music of the world's greatest composers to life.

DTH has had a long tradition of giving live music a privileged place. Pianists and drummers were hired to provide live music for classes. The Company used live symphonic orchestral accompaniment with union musicians. Many celebrated musicians graced the conductor's podium, Charles Darden, Isaiah Jackson, Derrick Inouye, Jonathan McPhee, Boyd Staplin, Patrick Flynn, Milton Rosenstock, David La Marche, but the first was a woman.

Cuban-born Tania Justina León experienced what might be called a Cinderella story for any musician trying to make it in New York City. Originally hired as a pianist in 1969 by Arthur Mitchell, the 26-year-old was swept up into a world of music and dance royalty that was made up of the most illustrious names in show business. She became a prolific artistic force in the New York music scene as a composer, conductor, and educator, going on to win a Pulitzer Prize in music.

Many DTH musicians went on from being pianists to prominent musical careers. It was typical of Arthur Mitchell's way of throwing people into the deep water to make them swim on their own. If you had the drive, passion, and gumption, Mitchell would "give you a shot." Many created their own positions at DTH: a pianist could become a conductor or an archivist; a former Company dancer could become an exhibition curator or in-house photographer; a dancer could become ballet master or work in the school.

Karel Shook, Tania León, and Arthur Mitchell (Photo: Marbeth, Courtesy of the Dance Theatre of Harlem Archive)

The DTH Style

What would become DTH's modus operandi, and eventually its signature style, was the blending of classical ballet with Balanchine's neoclassical technique. Upon these two pillars, modern, jazz, and other styles were added. Balanchine admired ballet because of its full-bodied largesse as a dance form. It shared the same size theatre as opera, and his vision for it was as big. When working with Mitchell, the two would share and converse deeply. The classical and neoclassical styles are distinct from each other in numerous ways:

[Fig.4.1] Some differences between classical and neoclassical style

ANATOMY	CLASSICAL	BALANCHINE-STYLE NEOCLASSICAL
Arms and Hands	Rounded or extended, no wrists or dropped elbows, no tension	Could be hyperextended, flexed, elbows bent, wrists dropped; tension in hands might be visible
Feet	Pointed	Could be pointed or flexed
Legs	Placed and turned out	Could be turned in or hyperextended
	Weight on one leg or between both legs Placement on the leg	Weight off the leg Placement on and off the leg
	Static style	Freer style
Hips	Square and placed	Could be tilted, raised, or open
Full Body	All defined by the style	Sometimes everyday pedestrian movements were added to the choreography

Mitchell would then teach the classical and neoclassical techniques to his dancers so that they would have a foundation. This would enable them to do anything that came their direction, from choreographers like Alvin Ailey to Geoffrey Holder to Glen Tetley. Karel Shook reinforced the theory, teaching basic structure with repetition so that the student would understand how muscles worked. Once the foundation was laid and the techniques were mastered, Mitchell's dancers could execute steps at lightning speed in any style. The dancers used their classical technique in a way that was radically creative. It is interesting to note that Mitchell said, "It was called *Dance* Theatre of Harlem, not *Ballet* Theatre of Harlem, because it is theatrical dance grounded in classical ballet." This is what made DTH distinctive.

Louis Johnson's *Forces of Rhythm*, one of DTH's earliest signature pieces, is known for introducing the DTH style element called *tipping*. *Tipping* refers to the immediately recognizable sultry, poised power walk of DTH ballerinas.

GUGGENHEIM AND TOURING

In 1970, the Company's touring schedule expanded outside the US to Bermuda, the Bahamas, and Curaçao. The young Company performed Balanchine's *Concerto Barocco*, *Rhythmetron*, and *Tones* at Bermuda City Hall Theatre.

Curaçao saw a company of nine female dancers, eight male dancers, and 12 apprentices. Four ballets filled the program: *Rhythmetron*, *Holberg Suite*, *Ode to Otis*, and *Biosfera*. Clive Barnes in *The New York Times* (4/20/1974) called *Biosfera* "a science-fiction duet of alienation . . . an acrobatic pas de deux," with its "sinuous and adagio convolutions." Biosfera, two spheres, depicts the conflicts and fulfillments of two worlds—any two worlds, in fact, in an abstract sense of man and woman, right and wrong, celebrating duality. The music for *Biosfera* was originally a string quartet that was orchestrated by the composer, Marlos Nobre, for a larger ensemble.

Isolated engagements (including colleges and high schools) followed, and in January of 1971, the fledgling company performed their New York City debut at the Guggenheim Museum, Frank Lloyd Wright's 1950's hatbox-inspired masterpiece of architecture. A circular stage was constructed, and the audience observed from the spiraling ramps in its beehive atrium. Joseph H. Mazo of *Women's Wear Daily* (1/11/1971) wrote, "Technically, the

The Company in Balanchine's *Concerto Barocco*, c. 1970 (Photo: Martha Swope, ©NYPL)

dancers are marvels. The men perform lifts and leaps with such ridiculous ease that they may be cited for contempt of the Law of Gravity, while the women have the true toe-of-steel points that dig three inches into the stage floor."

Recognizing the high level of skill developed in DTH dancers, George Balanchine invited Mitchell and company to perform in New York City Ballet's gala benefit held in the spring of 1971. This was a one-off, and the only collaboration between Mitchell and Balanchine, called *Concerto for Jazz Band and Orchestra*, which included 21 dancers from NYCB and 23 dancers from DTH. Performed by Doc Severinsen and his orchestra from Johnny Carson's *The Tonight Show*, two of the three evenings were benefit performances with the proceeds going toward the renovation of the Company's new home. Clive Barnes of *The New York Times* (5/8/1971) thought the blend of symphonic and big band music was an attempt to "get with it" but ineffective, though well played. He went on to say, "It was great to see black dancers at the State Theatre; great and very unusual." Shook thought that the performance pigeonholed DTH as the "cliché idea of all black dancers—all they can do is jazz." He had also thought that

DTH should have been given the opportunity to dance a classical ballet.

Touring dates followed in Michigan, North Carolina, and Florida, including a Caribbean tour of Puerto Rico, St. Thomas, and St. Croix. *Agon* and *Forces of Rhythm* were added to the repertoire as well as *Fete Noire*. Of *Fete Noire*, Hubert Saal in *Newsweek* (4/29/1974) called it "a crisp showpiece in the classical tradition. . . . Mitchell calls it classical ballet with soul." In addition to Tchaikovsky, Louis Johnson's *Forces of Rhythm* was danced to a cornucopia of contemporary pop hits that included the Supremes' "Nathan Jones," Phil Spector's "Spanish Harlem," Rufus Thomas's "Breakdown," and the Hollies' "He Ain't Heavy, He's My Brother" sung by Donny Hathaway. This ballet was a masterwork because it combined ballet, ethnic, and modern dance using popular music. Clive Barnes was

LEFT: Arthur Mitchell and Karel Shook in a rare photograph during bows at the Guggenheim Museum, New York City debut, 1971 (Photo: Martha Swope, ©NYPL)

RIGHT: Mitchell and Balanchine in the studio (Photo: Martha Swope, ©NYPL)

known to say that this central aspect was "classicism with a difference—ballet noir rather than ballet blanc."

An early 1972 Company brochure included a press quote from *The New York Times* in which Barnes said, "Few, if any, companies have moved so far so fast, and this speed of progress is all the more remarkable when it is realized that many of the company's very young dancers have not been training for very long. Even so, in three years a valuable American dance company has been molded, and it was a pleasure to see it again."

LEFT: Louis Johnson and Sandi Phifer-Moore in a rehearsal of the "Shout" section of *Forces of Rhythm* (Photo: Marbeth, Courtesy of the Dance Theatre of Harlem Archive)

BELOW: New York City Ballet and DTH in Balanchine's *Concerto for Jazz Band and Orchestra,* Doc Severinsen is top left, 1971. (Photo: Martha Swope, ©NYPL)

OPPOSITE: Homer Bryant and Ronda Sampson (*in pink tights*) in a pose inspired by the ballet *Forces of Rhythm*; it would become the vision behind the logo designed by Artis Lane. (Photo: Courtesy of Homer Bryant, Program Courtesy of Playbill Magazine™)

The Seasons' Ballets

here is very little archival information about Mitchell's *One by One Equals Two* other than a *New York Times* review (12/6/1969) by Don McDonagh. McDonagh noted that "Derek Williams and Llanchie Stevenson displayed a brilliant attack in handling the intricacies of *One by One*. Miss Stevenson was the solitary girl reacting to the taut aggressiveness of Mister Williams, who pursued her with sharply correct accents."

Concerto Barocco, was the first Balanchine ballet performed by DTH in 1970. Originally choreographed for the students in Balanchine's school and premiering at Hunter College in 1940, it has come to be known as a piece that not only tests the artist's level of proficiency and achievement but is also pure music and pure dance. Costumed simply in white leotards and skirts, it was the entrée to Balanchine's neoclassical style. "If the score is truly a great one, suitable for dancing . . . [the ballet maker] will not have need of such devices and can present his impression of pure dance." William Mootz of the *Louisville Courier-Journal* (3/3/1973) wrote, "Of the works being danced here for the first time by the dance theater, Balanchine's *Concerto Barocco* possibly hurled the greatest challenge at the company. It was a challenge its dancers met with aplomb."

Mitchell's *Holberg Suite* premiered in 1970. A neoclassical ballet, it used as accompaniment *The Holberg Suite, Op. 40*, by Edvard Grieg. Clive Barnes in *The New York Times* (4/20/1974) spoke of Mitchell as a Russianist. "Like all of George Balanchine's favorite sons, Mr. Mitchell takes a Russian imperialist view to this kind of music, but he uses what he has learned with a most happy confidence and fluency . . . . it has its own choreographic grace."

Timperturbably Blue (1970) was a piece Arthur Mitchell choreographed for the National Association for the Advancement of Colored People's (NAACP) Benefit and Tribute to Duke Ellington. Held at the Felt Forum (the

Arthur Mitchell rehearsing the Company in his ballet *Tones* at the Guggenheim Museum (Photo: Marbeth, Courtesy of the Dance Theatre of Harlem Archive)

Theater at Madison Square Garden), it began at 8:00 p.m. and lasted until 1:45 a.m. The marathon of celebrities making an appearance included the Duke himself, Louis Armstrong, Peggy Lee, Roberta Flack, Eubie Blake, B.B. King, Ray Charles, and many other entertainers. The genius of the evening was the master of ceremonies Sammy Davis Jr., who heroically kept the audience spellbound for more than five hours.

Tones (1970) was choreographed by Arthur Mitchell to Tania León's original piano concerto. Of the work, Don McDonagh of *The New York Times* (4/27/74) said it was "excitingly danced. The six couples of the first movement careered through the decor of small hanging reflecting disks like vibrantly alert beings ready for any eventuality."

Jerome Robbins's *Afternoon of a Faun* entered the DTH repertoire in 1971. A later review by Anna Kisselgoff in *The New York Times* (5/3/1975) hailed it as "a stunning

TOP: Denise Nix and Eddie J. Shellman in Arthur Mitchell's *Holberg Suite*, c. 1979 (Photo: Marbeth, Courtesy of the Dance Theatre of Harlem Archive)

BOTTOM: Gayle McKinney and Roman Brooks in Lester Horton's *The Beloved* (Photo: Martha Swope, ©NYPL)

FOLLOWING SPREAD: The Company in Jamaica (Photo: Courtesy of the Dance Theatre Harlem Archive)

performance." She was astounded how dancer Ronald Perry kept a spellbinding stare into an imaginary mirror and Lydia Abarca's "radiant attitude." Mitchell brought in Cicely Tyson as an acting coach to give Abarca a lesson on internalizing emotions.

Fun and Games, by Arthur Mitchell with music by Piero Piccioni, was "a rather overheated ballet that contained more violence than invention." So said Clive Barnes in *The New York Times* (3/9/1971). Premiering shortly after the Company's New York City debut, "fun and games" here is characterized by a street gang's brutality.

James Truitte staged Lester Horton's *The Beloved*, a pas de deux for the young company. Clive Barnes of *The New York Times* (12/14/1971) said it "has been expertly revived by Mr. Truitte, who danced it first for Mr. Horton and later for the Ailey company. Mr. Horton's strong, almost static choreography remains as powerful as ever, and the work was most passionately danced by a terrified but calm Gayle McKinney and an impassively brutal Walter Raines."

CHAPTER 5

PINK TIGHTS
IN BLACK TEA

The Seasons 1972–1976

Art in this country cannot be so precious that it can only relate to a few.
Because good art relates to everybody . . . it's universal.

—*Arthur Mitchell, 1975*

Mel A. Tomlinson as the snake in Arthur Mitchell's *Manifestations* making his dramatic entrance by being flown in headfirst from the fly rails (Photo: Marbeth, Courtesy of the Dance Theatre of Harlem Archive)

THE TIMES

- 1972: Shirley Chisholm became the first African American congresswoman to announce her candidacy for the office of the president of the United States.

- The Equal Employment Opportunity Act, under President Lyndon Johnson, strengthened 1964 labor laws to prevent discrimination for reasons of race, religion, color, national origin, and gender.

- Watergate broke.

- 1974: The Negro Ensemble Company, the Hadley Players, and the Black Arts Repertory Theatre were fostered by the Council on Harlem Theatre.

- Hollywood stars Barbara McNair and Lucie Arnaz won $5,000 on the TV game show *$10,000.00 Pyramid*, which they donated to DTH.

- The Department of the Interior granted DTH a residency at the Ford's Theatre in Washington, DC.

BUILDING COMMUNITY

Harlem's gentrification cycle began roughly in 2001, when former President Bill Clinton made 55 West 125th Street his post-presidential office address. President Clinton once said, "Harlem always struck me as a place that was human and alive, where there was a rhythm to life and a song in the heart, where no matter how bad it was, people held up their heads and went on, and where, when things got good, people were grateful and cared about their neighbors." As the social revolutions affected all Americans, DTH continued to be unique, not only in the ballet world, but in Harlem as well.

In the early '70s, DTH instituted a large-scale community involvement program. Many of these activities echoed the model of African American protestant churches building community throughout the century: have *fellowship*, let people gather and talk. "Community is where community happens!" was the chant of the day. Mitchell and Shook knew that the churches and community centers of Harlem were immediate networks of people he could tap for assistance, support, and love. Arthur Mitchell employed his own family members for school support staff.

Neighboring organizations such as St. John's Baptist

Arthur Mitchell's sister, Shirley Mills (*standing*), teaching typing, 1976 (Photo: Marbeth, Courtesy of the Dance Theatre of Harlem Archive)

Church and the Wilson Major Morris Community Center were invited to participate in DTH's numerous events. The community center graciously allowed DTH to use their space for overflow dance classes during the summer intensives, when students from all over the world would come to study dance for six weeks.

The First Annual DTH Street Fair was presented on June 23, 1973, with food, bric-a-brac, face painting, plenty of dancing, fashion shows, and bodybuilders. These fairs became a way to showcase DTH and students from the summer intensive program and connect to the immediate community neighborhoods of North Harlem, also known as Sugar Hill and Hamilton Heights (HamHi). It is no small fact that the person who booked the bodybuilders

was a muscleman himself, a behind-the-scenes publicist extraordinaire and assistant to Arthur Mitchell, one Lorenzo James. This unassuming brawny young man put DTH on the glitterati map. He was connected in the show-business world and introduced jet-set celebrities to the cool new ballet company in Harlem. The public relations guru corralled the likes of the Hammersteins, the Fondas, Hilary Knight, Zelda Wynn, Halston, and Revlon; not to mention Montgomery Clift, for whom he served as personal secretary. James would broker luxurious evening gowns for the ballerinas to wear for black tie events.

Lecture demonstrations continued as a staple of outreach. As master of ceremonies, Arthur Mitchell captured audiences with his powerfully dynamic performance

Street fair attendees, c. 1973 (Photo: Marbeth, Courtesy of the Dance Theatre of Harlem Archive)

Arthur Mitchell as the master of ceremonies for a lecture demonstration at the Apollo Theater, 1976 (Photo: Marbeth, Courtesy of the Dance Theatre of Harlem Archive)

capabilities and connected them to real-life examples. For instance, he would demonstrate a catlike walk and connect it to a ballet exercise that strengthens the foot. George Gelles of the *Washington Post* wrote a glowing exposé on an Arthur Mitchell lecture demonstration for 15,000 school-district students. He gushed, "[Mitchell] dived into an explanation of the ABCs of classical dance. In a minute he had his audience enchanted; in an hour it was *his* for life."

In Washington, DC, there was a volunteer organization, begun in 1965, called Mimes and Masques Theatre for Youth. Student tickets to their shows were 50 cents and production costs were aided by foundation grants and community fundraising. Its aim was for children to see African American role models in the arts. Most had never seen a ballet performance danced by African Americans. The children could relate to Mitchell and his company. Mitchell declared in the *Washington Post*: "The children can see themselves . . . relate. They need to know there are professional black dancers and they need to see what we can do." Forever expressing the importance of classroom exercise and discipline in terms of developing a ballet dancer, Mitchell would use the analogy, "When you plant a seed, the seed becomes a bulb, the bulb becomes a plant, and then the flowers will bloom." It is no secret that a single theatrical experience for a child can light the flame of passion to become a dancer. Mitchell spread that passion to thousands. It was his mission.

ALLIED ARTS

In a 1972 DTH brochure, Arthur Mitchell stated, "without the school to provide it with dancers . . . the company could not exist; but without the company the school would be meaningless. The dancers must have an example put before them and must also be trained for a real purpose." That training came to include immersion in many of the arts.

From the notoriety of the Company's performance, and Mitchell's perseverance, the School blossomed with an influx of over 1,000 students, and the curriculum grew as well. From the beginning, he insisted that everyone learn everything. It was a philosophy he had throughout his life, perhaps echoing his survival skills as his family's surrogate father, and as a star member of New York City Ballet.

He set the scene at DTH by inviting the technical experts to give workshops, master classes, and six-week courses. His dancers were not to be satisfied with being only good performers but were to be exposed to as much as possible. He expected everyone, when not in the studio working, to be engaged in learning other aspects of production. Throughout the organization, the notion of "sharing the wealth" flourished. Stage managers, lighting designers, costume designers, and other technical personnel gave workshops, seminars, and lectures to students and Company members.

Formal auditions began in 1975 for those wishing to learn an instrument or sing. A student orchestra was formed.

Students in a guitar class (Photo: Marbeth, Courtesy of the Dance Theatre of Harlem Archive)

KAREL SHOOK'S DANCE PHILOSOPHY

BY 1975 KAREL SHOOK HAD PERFECTED HIS APPROACH TO TEACHING DANCE TO CHIL-
dren. There would be four interlocking areas: dance, music, fashion, and theatre. Courses from these four areas were offered to hundreds of students, from preschoolers to senior citizens. Shook thought that children react with fervor to structure in a framework that is "at once controlled, counseled, and liberating."

Seeing children as young human beings at their eye level, and speaking to them in plain authoritative language, would reveal sophistication beyond adult comprehension. He further said, "More than just the classes, it was a way of life. Besides proving that classical dance is un-ethnic, it is about love and all its myriad styles and manifestations. It is about the fulfillment of the deprived child and the contentment of the senior citizen." Once again it was Shook as prophet and sage who brought into reality both founders shared vision. In essence, "the dancing child is the happy child."

Karel Shook teaching class, c.1970 (Photo: Marbeth, Courtesy of the Dance Theatre of Harlem Archive)

Company members with full rehearsal schedules were encouraged to take classes to sharpen their skills in other styles of dance. Versatility was not a question; it was an imperative trait necessary for all dancers. For some that was easy, for others less so.

Intergenerational mentorship was an idea initiated to keep dancers connected and improving. Some dancers came to the Company as young as 14, so someone was needed to "keep an eye on them" and to provide an atmosphere of guardianship and coaching. Older Company dancers acted as fathers and mothers and adopted younger new members as daughters and sons. They affectionately called their mentees "splibs." Dancers would teach, rehearse, and drill each other in choreography in the halls, hotel rooms, airports, grassy fields, stairwell landings, and

Rachel Sekyi teaching class, 1995. (Photo: Marbeth, Courtesy of the Dance Theatre of Harlem Archive)

theatre lobbies. In dressing rooms, they would share the art of making up for the stage as well as creating the perfect bun, with a "smooth kitchen." (The "kitchen" is the hair that resides at the nape of the neck, a difficult area to keep flat and contained.) A perfect ballet bun is round and smooth, not too high or low, with no flyaways. According to DTH faculty member Rachel Sekyi (pronounced SEH-chee), the line of the cheekbone determines the bottom edge of the bun. Shook and Mitchell were unrelenting in ridding distraction and imperfection. Water, do-rags, and products of all sorts, including Murray's Pomade, gels, and Luster's Hair Lotion, were used—it was part of the art and it had to be taught.

Everything revolved around the notion that there was too much to learn and not enough time to learn it. It was expected that a dancer should not have any idle time, that learning would be a never-ending process. Every performance was an opportunity to grow. Effort made in the studio would be 100 percent every day, no sitting down—ever. And no marking—ever. Marking is a rehearsal strategy whereby the dancer loosely practices steps, just going through the motions. Mitchell felt that marking was a waste of time. He believed that dancing full-out in rehearsal built stamina and revealed performance problems. It also gave him the opportunity to adjust, correct, fine-tune, and chide. Most dancers followed the regimen wholeheartedly, excited about the possibilities of "being part of something much larger than yourself," a phrase that Mitchell repeated tirelessly. That was how one became an *artist* at DTH.

Zelda Wynn

MS. ZELDA WYNN (NÉE BARBOUR), THE WIZARDESS OF DRESS, FASHION, AND COS- tume, owned a shop on Broadway near 158th Street called Zelda Wynn that opened in 1948. Jazz icon Ella Fitzgerald was her first client. She then went on to design costumes for Dorothy Dandridge, Josephine Baker, Mae West, Ruby Dee, Eartha Kitt, Diahann Carroll, Cicely Tyson, Sarah Vaughan, and in the 1950s designed the first Playboy Bunny costumes for Hugh Hefner.

For a full year, Arthur Mitchell tried to convince Zelda Wynn to head his wardrobe and costume shop. She was constantly in demand. She had a second location on 57th Street near Carnegie Hall called Chez Zelda. She finally succumbed to Mitchell's request when he said, "You will start tomorrow, I need chiffon dresses, and next week you will be in Europe with the Company." She went on to be the grand matriarch of DTH as wardrobe mistress and master costume designer.

Following Shook and Mitchell's idea of the allied arts, Wynn eventually took DTH students under her wing. They created their own designs and apprenticed in the arts of tailoring and dressmaking. Her costume

Left to right: Karel Shook, Cicely Tyson, Eddie Morgan, Phyllis Butcher, and Zelda Wynn, 1978 (Photo: Thaddeus Govan Jr.)

shop on the premises of DTH soon became a hub of activity with choreographers, wardrobe personnel, assistants, and student apprentices, truly making DTH a community-based entity. She consulted with designers and choreographers, and supervised costume building and fittings for almost 100 ballets. Fashion shows featuring student apparel were held during the Open Houses and at the summer street fairs. Wynn held court facing the door of the wardrobe room. If anyone passed by her door without a proper greeting, she would confront them with a lengthy lecture on manners.

She was an assertive woman and was savvy to the DTH way of discipline. She adored Mitchell and for his birthday had two pairs of his dance shoes bronzed. Well into her 80s, she would take the subway to the studios and walk from the 145th Street station to DTH to work. She officially retired from the Company in 1997 but continued to teach sewing and design classes. It was not unusual to see her walking with the dancers, giving advice and feedback.

TOP: A Zelda Wynn dress design drawing (Photo: Courtesy of the Dance Theatre of Harlem Archive)

BOTTOM: Zelda Wynn sitting among her 2,500 seat covers for the Loew's Victoria Theatre in 1972 (Photo: Marbeth, Courtesy of the Dance Theatre of Harlem Archive)

THE SCHOOL GROWS

In addition to Mitchell and Shook, the rosters of teachers for School and Company were prestigious. It included Tanaquil Le Clercq, Melvin Purnell, Francois Brooks, Mette Spaniardi, Carol Sumner, Istvan Rabovsky, James Truitte, Pepsi Bethel, Thelma Hill, Pearl Reynolds, Mireille Briane, and many others. The learning experience was invaluable. Younger students paid $1 a week, 13-to-18-year-olds paid $2 a week, and adults paid $22.50 for ten classes. Students were accepted based on talent, desire, and need. Apprentices were paid three dollars per hour to participate in apprentice workshops.

As early as 1973, a program called the DTH Children's Workshop morphed into the DTH Junior Company, consisting of 35 children from ages 6 through 15. Its premiere was in Atlantic City, with a subsequent premiere performance at the massive Episcopal Cathedral of Saint John the Divine in Harlem. The successes of the School and Company spread rapidly through word of mouth and press reviews. "Mitchell's four-year-old dance company has already made its mark on American dance as one of the finest companies in existence," raved the *Twin City Observer* (6/6/1973). The dance community and lovers of

Stevie Wonder entertaining Company members, DTH students, and supporters c. 1976 (Photo: Allan Tannenbaum)

ballet soon became privy to the high standards and the talent of DTH's artists. Organizations such as Friends of Dance Theatre of Harlem were created in Washington, DC, Pasadena, Berkeley, Seattle, Portland, and London and became sister cities for the Company, with annual or biannual tour stops. There was cross-pollination of dancers from New York to Chicago, a beehive of energy and ideas. DTH became the dance world's darling. Even Stevie Wonder stopped in for a building tour just after the release of his classic 18th album, *Songs in the Key of Life*.

Marie Brooks was a master ethnic dance instructor for DTH and founder of the Marie Brooks Pan-Caribbean Dance Theater. In 1973 she selected 5 boys and 16 girls for a dance study and cultural tour in Trinidad. Educational adventures and experiences such as this were not unusual. Experience was cherished as a force to propel excellence. Nor was it unusual for DTH to award full or partial student scholarships for general classes and other activities. Funds were raised for a plethora of ideas and programs, unlike most traditional ballet companies, whose basic program was perhaps running a school, a yearly gala, and Company seasons. These early years were about furnishing the family home and, perhaps unknowingly,

making history.

School newsletters reflected the community atmosphere that was DTH. Performances and activities were announced as well as new births. Headlines from volume 2, number 2, April 1973: "DTH Spring Bazaar"; "Eyewitness News Interviews Ron Perry"; and under School Notes, "DTH student April Berry auditioned for Agnes de Mille and was accepted in her workshop company." An article stated that two new pieces were added to the repertoire, *Haiku (A Dream for Brown Eyes)* and *Ancient Voices of Children*. It had music by George Crumb and was originally choreographed by Milko Šparemblek for his own company in Lisbon, Portugal. Šparemblek restaged the ballet for DTH. Though Mitchell insisted that he himself would never dance with his own company, a newsletter item surprisingly stated: "Arthur Mitchell and Lydia Abarca performed the *Agon* pas de deux in a benefit for the Atlanta Ballet Company in March."

On March 26, 1973, Arthur Mitchell's *Rhythmetron* aired on Public Broadcasting Service (PBS), and by the following June, School enrollment had jumped to 1,225 students. Students came to study from all over the United States and as far as Curaçao, Nigeria, and Australia.

THE COMPANY GROWS

The first years of DTH were filled with engagements in libraries, colleges, dance councils, high schools, women's clubs, dance guilds, and arts centers. Even marathons were not excluded from exposure opportunities. DTH was community-based, so no performance opportunity was overlooked, no matter how small or large. From street fairs to the London Palladium, DTH traveled, performed, and announced to the world that artists of the highest caliber were being created.

In 1972 DTH performed with the Buffalo Pops

Orchestra. That same year marked an appearance on Broadway at the ANTA Theatre. This theatre on West 52nd Street was the Broadway outpost of the American National Theatre and Academy, which was located in Greenwich Village. The ANTA was renamed the Virginia Theatre in 1981, and 14 days after African American playwright August Wilson's death in 2005, it was named the August Wilson Theatre. It was here that the young DTH Company performed in the City Center American Dance Marathon '72. DTH shared a week with the

young company. It starred Tony Bennett, the Peter Duchin Orchestra, Aretha Franklin, Dizzy Gillespie, Luther Henderson, and the Edwin Hawkins Singers. Two Harlem Homecomings were held at the now-closed Loew's Victoria Theatre, adjacent to the famed Apollo on Harlem's 125th Street. The theatre was a mess and the seats needed to be reupholstered. West Point-Pepperell donated enough bedspread material to cover the 2,500 seats. Taking over two months, designer Zelda Wynn and her crew covered all the seats for the comfort of the well-heeled who were bused to Harlem from midtown Manhattan.

Gloria Newman Dance Theater and the Sanasardo Dance Company, marking DTH's first Broadway debut. A landmark performance for the young company, this monthlong multi-bill dance happening featured DTH's *Laurencia Pas de Six* with Lydia Abarca, Virginia Johnson, Gayle McKinney, Walter Raines, Paul Russell, and Derek Williams. It was choreographed by Vakhtang Chabukiani and restaged by David and Anna-Marie Holmes.

Harlem Homecoming was presented in November 1972 and another in 1973. The '72 benefit featured Leontyne Price and Lena Horne. The 1973 edition was an evening of ballet, blues, and gospel for the benefit of the

LEFT: Josephine Baker backstage with the Company men at the London Palladium, 1974 (Photo: Marbeth, Courtesy of the Dance Theatre of Harlem Archive)

RIGHT: Leontyne Price and Lena Horne rehearsing for Harlem Homecoming, with Company members watching, 1972 (Photo: Marbeth, Courtesy of the Dance Theatre of Harlem Archive)

A ROYAL VISIT

A HIGHLIGHT EVENT IN THE SUMMER OF 1974 WAS A ROYAL VISIT BY PRINCESS Margaret, Countess of Snowdon. The princess was invited by the American embassy to the DTH studios for a program of dance. No stranger to the arts, the princess was an accomplished pianist and the first president of the Royal Ballet. Antony Armstrong-Jones, the princess's husband, known as Lord Snowdon, was an avid fan of DTH. He went on to write extensively about the Company and conducted major interviews with Arthur Mitchell. Snowdon's questions dealt with tough and somewhat provocative issues for the time, such as ethnicity and sexism. Are boy dancers at school called "sissy"? What can be done about the stigma of effeminacy in male dancing? Mitchell subscribed to what we might call today the "don't ask, don't tell" doctrine. Only some years later, after gay rights blossomed, would the stigma be lifted.

Snowdon tried to catch Mitchell in a contradiction when he asked what the "racial split" was in the ballet school. Mitchell had said one-third were "white." Snowdon countered by quoting Mitchell saying that he wanted the first all "black" company, so why integrate? Mitchell responded by saying first he had to break down the idea that those of African heritage could not dance ballet. In the 1980s, Mitchell pondered the dream of gathering two dancers of every ethnicity that would form a multicultural uber-company, to be called Noah's Art.

With the royals after performing *Le Corsaire* pas de deux. *Left to right:* Lincoln Kirstein, Dorothy Hammerstein, Alva Gimbel behind dancer Paul Russell, Mitchell, Princess Margaret, dancer Laura Brown, Judith Peabody (*sitting*), Lord Snowdon, and Karel Shook, 1974 (Photo: Marbeth, Courtesy of the Dance Theatre of Harlem Archive)

BROADWAY AND BEYOND

The year 1974 marked DTH's first full season debut at the ANTA Theatre on Broadway. Clive Barnes, in the April 18, 1974, edition of *The New York Times*, set the stage for the Company's ascendance along with a stunning justification for multicultural ballet: "On Tuesday night, Arthur Mitchell's Dance Theatre of Harlem swept authoritatively into the ANTA Theater to begin its first Broadway season. The night was warm with love. The gala audience, for once black and white together, had rooted for Mr. Mitchell and his co-director, Karel Shook, for years. . . . Just as a James Earl Jones or a Brock Peters will think Shakespeare with a difference, and black playwrights will have different poetry, so our black dancers can take Balanchine and give him a taste of Africa—our Africa, the Africa of Harlem. . . . This was a coming-out party for the Dance Theatre of Harlem."

The 1975 New York season was ushered in with an all-star benefit gala held at Broadway's Uris Theatre in April. It was hosted by Marian Anderson, the first African American singer to appear at the Metropolitan Opera, and American actor Brock Peters (a member of the first DTH board of directors), best known for his role as Tom Robinson in the 1962 film *To Kill a Mockingbird*. The star-studded event included Aretha Franklin, Cicely Tyson, opera star Shirley Verrett, and bandleader Peter Duchin. The Company's season was performed at the Uris, and as a part of

Marian Anderson and Karel Shook onstage reviewing the text for the performance at the 41st International Eucharistic Congress of the Catholic Church, 1976 (Photo: Marbeth, Courtesy of the Dance Theatre of Harlem Archive)

Arts Exposure Week, seniors and children were admitted to performances for one dollar.

The DTH Orchestra was born with this event. Peter Duchin conducted the gala benefit performance and Tania León conducted the rest of the season. From this experience, the orchestra was then mandated to present concerts and divide into soloists, chamber groups, and small performing ensembles of all kinds. Members of the orchestra also served as adjunct music faculty in the School, and master classes in music were given.

In August 1976 another first was made at the 41st International Eucharistic Congress. These large stadium gatherings included thousands of Catholic clergy and laity bearing witness to the ritual of the holy bread and wine, or Eucharist. The Catholic Church commissioned a special dance work to be part of the celebration in Philadelphia. The ballet, choreographed by Mitchell, was called *Spiritual Suite*. It was a tribute to Dr. Martin Luther King Jr., and the music was based on three of the favorite spirituals of singer Marian Anderson, who narrated the text. Mitchell had to deal with conservative clergy who scoffed at non-Catholics participating, as the Second Vatican Council's openness to ecumenism would not fully blossom until the mid-1980s. Mitchell persevered, and the piece was performed.

EAGLE EYE

The Company was very strong with talent, not only as a whole, but strong in that each dancer had their own gift that was used in performance. This was the essence of Mitchell's genius: that he had a keen eye for individual talents, no matter what they were. He was known as having an "eagle eye" by the dancers because of his knack for noticing imperfect ballet. Whether it was a body line askew, a missed pirouette, an untucked ribbon, or just an overall lack of energy or concentration, he would see it. Backstage after every ballet, and sometimes during intermission, he would give notes, fix, remind, inspire, and often, reprimand. He had a young company, and it had to be not only good, but excellent, as perfect as possible. If a dancer had a skill that was particularly strong, Mitchell would find a way to use and feature it. This was epitomized by Paul Russell and Mel A. Tomlinson.

Paul Russell was an elegant classical dancer who had developed skilled virtuosic tricks (bravura). Russell asked Mitchell if he could perform the *Le Corsaire* pas de deux (1973) and worked with Karel Shook on developing a magnificent dance for two with bravura variations. Mel A.

Arthur Mitchell sporting his silver phoenix bracelet that dancers mistook for an eagle, rendering Mitchell's nickname, "eagle eye" (Photo: Courtesy of the Dance Theatre of Harlem Archive)

Tomlinson who later danced with Alvin Ailey, New York City Ballet, Boston Ballet, and North Carolina Dance Theatre, was extremely acrobatic. In *Manifestations* (an Adam and Eve story), Mitchell used Tomlinson's physique and talent (an extremely long neck, flexibility, and fearlessness) for the role of the snake. The score Mitchell used was originally composed for the Chicago Symphony Orchestra by Primous Fountain III.

Agnes de Mille called Tomlinson "the most exciting black dancer in America." Every role that Mitchell bestowed gave the dancers the opportunity to perfect the details of their performance. Tomlinson masterfully studied a real snake that he encaged and toted around, scaring fellow dancers. Known for his willingness to toil to the bone and his astonishing sense of humor, he later made a grand entrance at an alumni function dressed in his skintight and scaly *Manifestations* unitard.

Summer music and dance festivals in Europe are a long-standing tradition. The summer tourist season brings thousands of cultural arts performances into theatres, palazzi, streets, town squares, cathedral steps, and amphitheaters of all sizes. The summer of 1973 was one of many European festivals in which DTH would partake. The tour included Yugoslavia and Spain. From a nucleus of three young people with some dance experience, by 1973 Mitchell and Shook had grown a 25-member company.

After the critically acclaimed 1974 Broadway season at the ANTA Theatre, many high-profile engagements followed that were of historical importance. The Auditorium Theatre in Chicago, a major venue, saw the Company perform *Afternoon of a Faun*, dedicated to

NYCB principal ballerina Tanaquil Le Clercq, for whom the ballet was choreographed in 1953. There was a tour of Mexico where performances were presented out in the countryside and barrios.

Not only did the 1974 season include a Broadway debut and performances in Central America, but also a command performance for a king and three television specials in Belgium, London, and Manchester. In August, the company made its debut in London at the Sadler's Wells Theatre, breaking box-office records at 106 percent

Derek Williams and Gayle McKinney in Walter Raines's ballet *Haiku*, 1974 (Photo: Marbeth, Courtesy of the Dance Theatre of Harlem Archive)

capacity. The three-week engagement was sold out to standing room only and people lined up around the block for tickets. A continental tour followed, including a command performance for King Olav V of Norway. Then, in November, DTH returned to London at the invitation of Her Majesty Queen Elizabeth the Queen Mother to participate in *The Royal Variety Performance*.

In 1976, America's bicentennial year, a third Broadway season was given at the Uris Theatre. A return to Sadler's Wells took place that summer when the Company traveled to Newcastle and Manchester. In the fall the Company appeared in the Berlin Festival and was invited a second time to dance in *The Royal Variety Performance*, again a first, because it was unprecedented for the same company to perform twice in this production.

Her Majesty the Queen, in her Royal Palladium box seat. In the box above on the right is DTH Company manager Richard Gonsalves with famed ballerina and DTH faculty member Tanaquil Le Clercq, whom Gonsalves carried to her seat with accompaniment of the crowd, 1974 (Photo: Doug McKenzie)

BALLET BUILDING

Ruth Page, American pioneer of dance, created *Carmen and José* for DTH in 1972. It premiered at the Civic Theatre in Chicago. Page had a fondness for operatic theatricality and would turn opera stories into ballets. She choreographed the New York premiere of *Carmen and José* for the 1976 DTH season at the Uris Theatre in New York, setting the ballet in the Caribbean. Anna Kisselgoff of *The New York Times* called it a "ratatouille of ideas." She also credited Tania León as an arranger and composer of the electronic sequences. Page also staged *Carmina Burana* with Carl Orff's splashy setting of profane Latin poetry and costumes by André Delfau.

Walter Raines was the first company member to choreograph a new ballet, esoterically titled *Haiku (A Dream for Brown Eyes)*. The score was composed by Tania León. On April 24, 1974, Anna Kisselgoff from *The New York Times* wrote, "The policy of encouraging young unestablished choreographers within a company that is frankly aiming for establishment is unusual and even daring." *Haiku* had its debut performance at Connecticut College's American Dance Festival. Don McDonagh in *The New York Times* stated that "among the dancers particularly noticeable were Gayle McKinney, China White and Virginia Johnson. . . . Miss Johnson's long, lean form looks as if it had been designed for special creative expression." Raines also choreographed *After Corinth* in 1975, a ballet based on the Medea and Jason mythology. The ballet fused the Graham style with Balanchine's neoclassicism. Anna Kisselgoff in

The New York Times (5/2/1975) said, "Imitating genius is no easy task . . . Mr. Raines's courage should also be saluted."

Every Now and Then was another ballet choreographed by a Company member, William Scott. It was set to a Quincy Jones score. Clive Barnes in the March 3, 1976, The New York Times described it as "in the classic mold, with the women dancing in high-heeled shoes, which must be a first. It is a well-constructed, insouciant work that shows off its dancers—here cheerfully led by Sheila Rohan and Homer Bryant—with a casual feline grace."

TOP: Paul Russell and Virginia Johnson in Carmina Burana (Photo: Marbeth, Courtesy of the Dance Theatre of Harlem Archive)
BOTTOM: Elena Carter in Walter Raines's After Corinth (Photo: Marbeth, Courtesy of the Dance Theatre of Harlem Archive)

Geoffrey Holder

TOWERING IN TALLNESS AND *PLUS GRAND QUE LA VIE*, **THE MULTITALENTED PAINTER,** designer, actor, bass singer, and composer was born in Trinidad and Tobago. He is best known for his 7-Up "Uncola" commercials in the 1970s and 1980s; as Baron Samedi in the Bond movie *Live and Let Die* (a character also in DTH's *Banda*); and as the Tony award–winning director and designer of Broadway's original production of *The Wiz*. He met his wife and longtime DTH supporter Carmen de Lavallade as well as Arthur Mitchell and Alvin Ailey while performing in the Broadway show *House of Flowers*. Both were the subjects of the documentary *Carmen and Geoffrey* (2005). In 2018 de Lavallade and her son, Leo Holder, staged the revival of *Dougla* for DTH.

Bele was the first ballet Geoffrey Holder created for DTH. The score was by Holder and Tania León, and it had its opening premiere for Harlem Homecoming. Anna Kisselgoff of *The New York Times* said that *Bele* was filled with "unexpected beauty." The men strutted in lacy white bare-chested jumpsuits with white Panama fedoras; the bejeweled ladies wore chiffon dresses, draped over the knee, with high billowing collars.

The costumes *moved*—with ruffles, furls, and fans. Holder would say, "It's froufrou, dahling, just for you!" and the dancers would giggle. He would come to the studio and say in his booming basso-profundo voice, "Come to me, babies," and the whole company would run to his wingspan for a big group hug.

Bele would later be included in the television production of *A Streetcar Named Desire* filmed in Aarhus, Denmark.

Dougla, according to creator Geoffrey Holder: "Where twain meet, Hindu and African tangle, their offspring are called *Dougla*." It became DTH's signature work for decades. Choreographed, costumed, and designed by Holder, with a score by Holder and Tania León, it was on the bill in almost every city where the Company performed. It was one indicator of a dancer's versatility to dance other styles. Every dancer that came to the Company had to perform it. And perform it they did. . . .

An early photograph of the DTH Percussion Ensemble with Baba Don Eaton Babatunde, Terry Dubious, Mike Alyson, Mark Stephenson, and Rudy Bird (lead drummer) (Photo: Courtesy of the Dance Theatre of Harlem Archive)

As the adage goes, if something can go wrong in performance, it will. And it did—in New Mexico. The combination of altitude sickness, assorted illnesses from "drinking the water," and a slanted raked stage can create some interesting ballet. In *Dougla*, Walter Raines had choreography where he was to cartwheel into the wings for his exit. Like sending a bowling ball down the middle of an alley, such an exit takes a certain amount of aim. Mr. Raines did try his best. His foot, then leg, then torso tangled in the side curtain—spinning. It looked like a ballet dancer meets velour curtain in a food processor. During another scene in the ballet, the men entered carrying the women on their shoulders, and just like Amtrak train wrecks sometime occur, the men collided into a pile. A big pile. Center stage. Whoops.

A benefit of DTH's allied arts program was the many performing groups that the music department provided. One was the DTH Percussion Ensemble. Holder was keen on using Afro-Caribbean drumming. It is an unmistakable musical color that permeates the palette of much of his work, from *Banda*, *Dougla*, and *Bele* to his Broadway show *Timbuktu!* Considered by some as a vehicle for the talent of Donald Williams, *Banda* was made from the spiritual dust of the Caribbean. An unlikely subject for a ballet, the gods and goddesses of vodou were summoned. Of the multitalented Holder, critic Kisselgoff stated, "a showman . . . [he] never lets his audience down in the spectacle category." (*The New York Times*, 1/31/1982)

The Company in Geoffrey Holder's *Banda* (Photo: Leslie Spatt)

PINK TIGHTS IN BLACK TEA

A unique evolution in the young Company's history that became another historic first concerned color and costume. Classical ballet called for pink tights. It became traditional for women to wear pink tights in the early part of the nineteenth century. This risqué phenomenon mimicked pale skin tone of legs under gauzy overdresses.

This DTH legend unfolds with dancer Llanchie Stevenson suggesting to Mr. Mitchell that the dancers wear flesh-toned tights. From early on, there was experimentation to soften the shock of electric-pink tights on brown skin by soaking them in tea or dye. After matching her tights to her own skin tone, Ahmad put them on over her pink tights and showed them to Mitchell. He finally approved skin-tone tights in Oslo, Norway, on August 26, 1974, and the rest is history. The Company never wore pink tights onstage ever again—all because of pink tights in black tea.

For first DTH Ballet Mistress and Principal Dancer Gayle McKinney, the simple process of using natural tea leaves and dying pink tights in a black brew "was empowering . . . What was unique was that Virginia was one complexion, I was another complexion, and a different dancer would be a different complexion. And because we were doing that for ourselves, that made us feel very proud . . . it was really a caring, professional attitude about who we were and what we were doing." Skin-tone tights became a DTH trademark, emblematic of DTH's embrace of the individual, so that the uniqueness of each dancer was not lost. Each dancer received the attention they deserved—the audience would see the individual artist, rather than a mechanized chorus line of identical dancers. But it was much more than that.

Flesh-tone tights delivered a new approach to viewing ballet. This would impact the art of choreography, where choreography meets costume design. Instead of forming a single mass of bodies, the different colors created beautiful geometric patterns out of bodies. The individual was seen even when moving in unison, *tout ensemble*.

In consultation with designer Carl Michel (A/SP/A Michell), Mitchell continued to experiment on the costume design for *Swan Lake Act II*. One of the bold solutions was to use incremental shades, tones, hues, and tints of blue, for the tutus calibrating each color to the dancers' skin tones.

Tights and leotards in sepia skin tones allowed the entire body line to be seen uninterrupted. Mitchell said, "I choose to use flesh tone tights and shoes rather than pink because they harmonize so much more realistically with the dancers' various skin tones . . . it's the body line—the line—the line!"

At the time, tights were not manufactured in flesh tones. Zelda Wynn had to concoct ways to color pink tights in shades to match a multitude of complexions. It was not unusual to see large pots of boiling water in the wardrobe room and Ms. Wynn cooking up colors like a master chef in a kitchen. The process wasn't easy or always accurate. Later, Vernon L. Ross and Pamela Allen-Cummings in the wardrobe department tested and compiled color recipes on index cards. They documented and codified what they learned from Wynn. It was closer to an exact science. For new company members, a first stop was wardrobe, to pick up tights. If there wasn't a color match in the bag of options, it was back to the drawing board, and a new recipe would have to be created. Ross and Cummings became masters of using Tintex and Rit Dye for coloring tights to match skin tones. Makeup liquids, powders, and paints

Left to right, Derek Williams, Gayle McKinney, and Homer Bryant in Louis Johnson's *Forces of Rhythm* (Photo: Martha Swope, ©NYPL)

were used to blend tights to ribbons and shoes seamlessly. Hundreds of brands were tested to see which worked best.

The palette of flesh tones was a constant challenge for the lighting designers as well. Legs could look too red, blue, or ashy. Spotlights beaming too bright, too dim, or the wrong color could wreak havoc on the overall visual design. Balancing all of these elements became an art form in itself. It was developed, honed, and perfected, not exactly by the eyes of science, but by the exasperated voice of God in a rehearsal mic: "Her tights don't match her shoes! They're too red!" Mitchell was all about the details. Of utmost importance was teaching new members to dye shoes to match their tights. The dancers were originally instructed to use spray so that no part showed any pink or white, but the spray made shoes stiff, not an ideal solution. The seams and the under-toe pleats had to be filled with color. Inexpensive powdered makeup became the solution for blending tights into shoes. It had to be used carefully. If the powder fell onto the stage, it could make the surface slippery and dancers could fall—and they sometimes did. In addition, Mitchell was obsessed with the girls' shoes being quiet. He complained when he heard shoes tapping onstage. In ballets such as *Giselle* and *Serenade* he said it was a distraction and took away from the mystique that ballerinas were light and ethereal. He insisted for years that all the women wear Freed of London shoes because once broken in, they were the quietest. He commended dancers like Virginia because she never wore any other brand of shoes and never made a sound. Mitchell banned some brands because they were too hard and noisy, but changing brands during a season was difficult, so his rules were not always heeded. Hammering and crunching the toe box in the door jamb could be seen every day at DTH. Some dancers used rubbing alcohol to soften them or beat their shoes into submission on the cement sidewalk. Everyone had their own method of preparing shoes for performances.

Whenever a new shoe came to market, industry representatives would pitch them by giving free samples, with the hope that the shoe was right for the entire Company. But every foot is unique. Some dancers have high arches, strong toes, weak ankles, or need stronger shanks, sometimes made of steel. Some need high or low vamps, or lower side and heel cuts. Many different brands were worn, making it difficult to obtain any discounts from one company.

The production shoe budget was always astronomical for DTH. Shoes were rationed and dancers had to be creative to extend the short life of a pointe shoe. Some dancers resorted to pouring floor wax or shellac into the tip and then setting it in a warm oven. Another common method was to apply an extra layer of suede to the tip, using darning thread or glue. Even so, dancers often had to

supplement the shoe allotment by purchasing their own.

Aside from an early attempt in the 1980s, pointe shoe companies had not developed a flesh-tone shoe for the general market. Eric Underwood, a former member of the Royal Ballet and DTH, posted a video of himself applying makeup to his shoes on social media in 2016 that persuaded Bloch to produce shoes in his flesh tone. Underwood stated, "The simple acknowledgment that there's a need for a new flesh tone is groundbreaking in the world of ballet." Until all ballet shoe companies acknowledge the need to manufacture more shades of flesh-tone shoes, the problem will be far from solved, though an effort was made in that direction in 2020.

Alicia Graf Mack, Sonny Robinson, and Lenore Pavlakos Morales in George Balanchine's *Serenade* (Photo: Joseph Rodman, Courtesy of the Dance Theatre of Harlem Archive)

Nude Barre, an online retail site, specializing in undergarments in a variety of shades was founded in 2009 by DTH alum and model Erin Carpenter, who had difficulties finding dance undergarments that matched her skin tone. To fill this gap, Carpenter started her own online company selling a line of undergarments in 12 shades. This was a positive move to correct the disparity and neglect by corporations who refused to offer products for all skin tones.

Precious Adams, an 18-year-old from Detroit, became the first African American student to finish at the Bolshoi Ballet Academy, despite facing discrimination. Not only was she left out of performances, a teacher once told her to "try and rub the black off," and one teacher suggested that she try skin bleaching. Unaffected, Adams continued to work on her craft and secured a position with the English National Ballet and there, in 2018, she decided to wear tights that were of her own skin tone, instead of pink. With the support and permission of director Tamara Rojo, Adams broke a barrier—a *huge* barrier.

Predictably, and sadly, a social media user called it "a disgrace to the tradition of ballet." Though some traditions in ballet are empirical, the practice of *traditionalism*, though subtle and engrained, holds people bound to cultural bias as a norm.

These modest changes in cultural sensitivity that extended into the new millennium were grounded in the early 1970s. This was a time of great awakening for America, and enormous growth for DTH. The essay "A Seventh Year," by Lincoln Kirstein, is an important document outlining the skyrocketing success of the Company. He encapsulates, "The Dance Theatre of Harlem does not say what it means, it dances it. In seven years, it has provided a generation of strong dancers who, while still performing, attract others to its ranks proving the possibility that is. Wide open to similar dedication and delight . . . The triumph of Mitchell's troupe, of his school, of his service and its sources has turned a natural resource into a national treasure."

Pointe shoes being prepped for performance (Photo: Judy Tyrus)

The Seasons' Ballets

Le Corsaire pas de deux was staged by Karel Shook for dancers Laura Brown and Paul Russell. This was the first classical tutu ballet for the Company, a veritable turning point. Clive Barnes in the April 18, 1974, *The New York Times* wrote, "the pas de deux, from *Le Corsaire*, the Soviet exhibition number par excellence, [was] danced by Laura Brown and Paul Russell. It was a sensation. Miss Brown was clean, sharp and delightful, but the surprise came from Mr. Russell, who

bounded on and danced this role as well as I have even seen a non-Soviet dancer perform it." Another well known pas de deux was Romeo and Juliet, choreographed by Gabriella Taub-Darvash. Kisselgoff of *The New York Times* (3/6/1976) said, "Madame Taub-Darvash handled its special style with skill and flair."

Caravanserai was a ballet by Talley Beatty first seen with Donald McKayle's Inner City Repertory Dance Company. The ballet is based on a poem from Paramahansa Yogananda that begins, "The body melts into the Universe." Program notes described the piece as "an expression of the 'infinite joy' of the quotation. The dancers are in tattered rags, which perhaps represent the clothes of the pilgrims in an endless caravan whipped by sand, sun and rain. Solos, duets, trios, quartets, and ensembles interchange in

LEFT: Laura Brown in Karel Shook's staging of Petipa's *Le Corsaire*, 1973 (Photo: Marbeth, Courtesy of the Dance Theatre of Harlem Archive)
RIGHT: Paul Russell in Karel Shook's *Le Corsaire* (Photo: Martha Swope, ©NYPL)

a relentless impulse of tensions with few releases. A sense of mystery is established that defies interpretation."

John Taras, whom Mitchell had known from NYCB, had success with *Designs with Strings*, a ballet he choreographed for DTH. In the August 1976 issue of *Dance and Dancers Magazine* John Percival said, "Beneath its surface of simple pure dance patterns is our theme of adolescent love and heartbreak." This piece went by many names: *Design for Strings*, *Designs for Strings*, and *Design with Strings*. A handwritten letter from Taras to Ronald Dabney, director of administration for DTH, concerning a 1994 revival confirms that *Designs with Strings* is the correct title. Taras later returned to DTH to choreograph the highly acclaimed production of *Firebird*.

Gagaku are the musicians of the Imperial Household of Japan that accompany court dancers. Balanchine invited these musicians to NYCB many times. He commissioned Toshiro Mayuzumi to compose a ballet for symphonic orchestra in the Japanese court music style known as Bugaku. Remembering that Mitchell danced the lead role, Balanchine gave the ballet *Bugaku* to DTH as a gift.

When DTH began, some suspected that it would be just another company in the Balanchine orbit, only with African American dancers. Anna Kisselgoff of *The New York Times* emphatically stated that this suspicion couldn't be farther from the truth. Kisselgoff reasoned that it was Balanchine's aesthetic that actually freed DTH to be itself. In the March 6, 1976, edition of *The New York Times*, she wrote: "If there is a company that knows how to put the allegro in *Allegro Brillante*, one of George Balanchine's most dazzling ballets, it is this joyful ensemble." And in the January 25th, 1981 edition: "DTH dances Balanchine's *Allegro Brillante* superlatively, every bit as good as the City Ballet."

In the March 1976 issue, *Time* magazine stated, "In William Dollar's *The Combat* DTH achieved what some others are not yet quite up to: the melting intuitive linking of movements that occurs as dancers move beyond the science of ballet nearer to art." *The Combat* is a tragic love

Designs with Strings, the opening silhouette, c. 1974 (Photo: Martha Swope, ©NYPL)

story about mistaken identity, based on a passage from "Jerusalem Delivered" by Italian Renaissance poet Torquato Tasso. Costumes for *The Combat*, designed by Marie Laure and built by Zelda Wynn, were of exceptional beauty.

Choreographer is not the first word that comes to mind when one mentions the name Arthur Mitchell. Whether out of necessity or creative urge, he created more than 20 original ballets. He was fearless in using ethnic and mod-

ern steps to push the boundaries of ballet. Andrew Porter of the *New Yorker* (2/24/1973) stated, "In his *Holberg Suite*, a classical divertissement, and *Rhythmetron*, a classical 'Sacre' with ethnic accents, Mr. Mitchell shows himself a skillful and resourceful choreographer; his inventions stretch the dancers, but not beyond the limits of their technique."

Adagietto #5, a mainstay for the Company, was a popular pas de trois and a romantic crowd-pleaser worldwide. Set to Mahler's music, it was the prolific British

choreographer Royston Maldoom's second stint for the Company. According to Maldoom, it was "a romantic trio set to music by Gustav Mahler . . . choreographed as a

TOP LEFT: The Company in Talley Beatty's *Caravanserai*, 1974 (Photo: Anthony Crickmay)

TOP RIGHT: Company Dancers in William Dollar's *The Combat*, c. 1975 (Photo: Martha Swope, ©NYPL)

BOTTOM RIGHT: *Left to right:* Stanley Perryman, Susan Lovelle, and Alan Sampson in *Holberg Suite*, from P.BS's *Dance in America* (Photo: Courtesy of the Dance Theatre of Harlem Archive)

wedding present for two friends who, together with a third mutual friend, completed the first cast. It was something we did in a tiny studio in our spare time over weekends."

It was not unusual for dance pieces, some only minutes long, to be created for special performances. *Breezin'* by Arthur Mitchell was of this type, choreographed for an appearance at Avery Fisher Hall with Grammy Award–winning jazz icon and guitarist George Benson. Benson hit his apex of commercial popularity in 1976, when his album by the same name went certified triple-platinum.

Certain ballets became mainstays or signature works for the Company. In some cases, these works, like *Forces of Rhythm* and *Dougla*, were created for and performed by DTH. But between 1972 and 1976 the Company was performing four Balanchine ballets: *Concerto Barocco*, *Allegro Brilliante*, *Bugaku*, and *Agon*. Balanchine's *Agon* was set on the company in 1971 and was performed for the first time during the Festival of Two Worlds in Spoleto, Italy. By 1974, significant changes were noticed by Kisselgoff. In *The New York Times* (4/25/1974) she wrote, "There is no greater measurement of the way the company has improved than in the way it dances *Agon*. This is one of the most difficult works in the contemporary repertory and the highly talented Susan Lovelle, partnered excellently by Mr. [Derek] Williams, was absolutely brilliant in the pas de deux. An outstanding performance was given by Laura Brown, a very classical dancer; Miss [Gayle] McKinney and Ronald Perry in the first pas de trois."

TOP: Stephanie Dabney and Mel A. Tomlinson in the foot lift from Royston Maldoom's *Adagietto #5*, c. 1976 (Photo: Jack Vartoogian/FrontRowPhotos)

FOLLOWING SPREAD: The Company c. 1975 (Photo: Courtesy the of Dance Theatre of Harlem Archive)

CHAPTER 6

WORLD STATURE

The Seasons 1977–1985

Art is perhaps the most important conversation in all the Human Experience—
for art is the conversation of the soul.

—*Arthur Mitchell*

Joseph Wyatt and Elena Carter in *Paquita* (Photo: Courtesy of the Dance Theatre of Harlem Archive)

THE TIMES

- 1977: Patricia Roberts Harris, under the Carter administration, became the first African American woman to hold a cabinet position.

- A Pulitzer Prize Special Citation was awarded to Alex Haley, author of the novel *Roots: The Saga of an American Family*.

- Twentieth Century Fox presented Anne Bancroft, Shirley MacLaine, and Mikhail Baryshnikov in *The Turning Point*, written by Arthur Laurents, with choreography by Alvin Ailey and George Balanchine.

- According to the *New York Post* (6/11/1977), Gelsey Kirkland reigned as "the Swan Queen" at American Ballet Theatre.

- 1979: The Sugarhill Gang, named after DTH's Harlem neighborhood, recorded *Rapper's Delight*.

- 1980: Black Entertainment Television went on air in Washington, DC.

- 1985: Gwendolyn Brooks of Chicago became the first African American woman to hold the title of United States Poet Laureate.

ARTISTIC GROWTH
AND COMMUNITY

By 1977, Arthur Mitchell proclaimed that he had created a major dance Company and School with classes in music, sewing, and technical production; there was also in-house publicity, accounting, booking, and management. In 1979, the DTH School was among the first professional training schools in dance to be accredited by the Joint Commission on Dance and Theater Accreditation as recognized by the US Office of Education. This opened opportunities for students to benefit from federal assistance programs. By 1985 the School was packed with lush opportunities. There was a program on Saturdays for pre-dance conditioning, as well as teenage and children's preprofessional programs, and comprehensive dance classes for students with a high school diploma. Within these curricula, there were sections graded by age, as well as beginner, intermediate, and advanced. The Workshop Ensemble, which was given a generous three-year grant from the Eleanor Naylor Dana Charitable Trust, consisted of leading students who gave performances in the community. All this occurred despite the deep budget cuts made by the Reagan administration, which restricted the number of students that the DTH School could absorb.

The Workshop Ensemble, 1983 (Photo: Marbeth, Courtesy of the Dance Theatre of Harlem Archive)

A year later DTH solicited grants to renovate two buildings (the Aqueduct) located directly across the street from DTH for student housing—it never happened. Calling for conversion of 20 units to house 60 students, DTH claimed their operation touched 250,000 people a year, that there were 250 students in each session, and that 60 were preprofessional who moved to New York City to study. Some students were housed in people's homes. Open auditions would draw hundreds. The School also absorbed children from orphan homes. Leotards were given out to create uniformity in the studio. This equalization was a way to grant each student the power they needed to excel, to achieve their perfect *tendu*, to be a part of something great. The results spoke for themselves; young students from all backgrounds excelled in the studio, becoming accomplished dance artists.

Mitchell was known to move students up when they were ready. If a student could do in three months what others did in a year, he would advance them. New roles would challenge them and drive them forward. That the Company and School shared the main studios proved to be inspirational. Students were able to stand in studio doorways to witness the best dancers in the world, their role models, working toward perfection. Mitchell would offer open rehearsals for ballets that were in preparation, such as *A Streetcar Named Desire* and *Equus*.

The School's success can be measured by the success of the thousands of alumni who have excelled. That includes not only the dancers of African heritage in other major ballet companies of the United States and Europe, but also successful singers, at least three Tony Award-winning actors, stage techs, designers, arts administrators, and teachers, as well as doctors, executives, photographers, university presidents, lawyers, directors of ballet schools and museums, college professors . . . the list continues.

The people of Harlem became deeply involved in Mitchell's idea and DTH became a beacon of pride for the community. The mixture of art, dignity, and benevolence was a powerful tonic for those who chose to be a part of the organization. Mitchell said, "All that people needed in the community was the opportunity and someone saying, 'Come on, you can do it.' And that's all they needed." These positive affirmations reached far and wide. They could be very exciting—in 1984 students danced in the Metropolitan Opera's production of *Porgy and Bess*, for which Mitchell served as a consultant.

Because the School was in great shape, and all departments were thriving, Mitchell was free to choreograph. For him choreography was pure and immediate creativity with pure and immediate gratification, to make dance, to make something from nothing, to invoke the heart, mind, and soul. Mitchell knew theatrics and had the required skill set. He considered *Manifestations* representative of his style. Clive Barnes in *The New York Times* (4/20/1974) said, "He has a genuine choreographic gift that could perfectly well have been deployed with his parent company New York City Ballet." Though Balanchine and Mitchell choreographed the single engagement fundraiser, *Concerto for Jazz Band and Orchestra*, Mitchell never choreographed a season ballet for NYCB.

THE WIZ

IN THE LATE '70S *THE WIZ* **BECAME A SMASH HIT ON BROADWAY. IT WAS**
the retelling of the Oz story, musicalized with a funky soft-rock score and a multicultural cast.
Stephanie Mills played Dorothy and former DTH dancer Hinton Battle played the scarecrow.
Geoffrey Holder, who choreographed and designed for DTH, was the show's director and
costume designer. Subsequently, *The Wiz* was made into a movie in 1978. The choreographer
for the movie was Louis Johnson, who earned a Tony nomination for *Purlie*. Eleven dancers left
DTH to dance in the movie version alongside a luminous cast of stars.

Arthur Mitchell as a father figure was losing some of his children, so it would be expected
that he would be unhappy about the eleven leaving the nest to work on *The Wiz*. He was losing
some of his biggest stars, including Lydia Abarca, at least for a time. There were consequences
for DTH and those dancers—reentry to the Company came with stern caveats and auditions.
Shortly after the mass departure, Mitchell hired a new group of young apprentices, some as
young as 14. Of those, some went on to become principal dancers.

DOIN' IT, A MUSICAL REVUE

Mitchell had always dreamed of having a show on Broadway. *Doin' It*, subtitled *A Celebration of Dance, Music & Song*, was a fusion of the Company, choral, and music ensembles. (Mitchell's second attempt at Broadway was the DTH production of *St. Louis Woman* in 2003.)

In Philadelphia's *Sunday Bulletin* (8/13/1978), Sarah Casey Newman quotes Mitchell saying, "I want to do something that is totally ours, but still popular enough to turn on a mass audience." Sarah Casey Newman adds, "He hoped to blend the best of classical ballet, opera, and musical comedy into what he called musical theater." Mitchell continued, "The focus, the core is still classical ballet, but you have to get the people inside the theater before you can turn them on. Do you follow my thinking? I'm trying to appeal to the young."

It is precarious for a dance organization to justify a theatrical endeavor. The DTH family speculated that Mitchell wanted a vehicle that would run on Broadway and pay residuals that would fill the coffers of DTH. This model was a trend at the time, as exemplified by *A Chorus Line*, which paid royalties to Joe Papp's Public Theater, where it was born. Or perhaps there was a desire to put the *theatre*

into Dance *Theatre* of Harlem. Audiences enjoyed it, and the cast gained strength from performing *Doin' It*. Unfortunately, *Doin' It* didn't exactly do it.

The Philadelphia Tribune (8/18/1978) ran the headline: "Dance Theatre of Harlem Really Did Do It." Jovida Joylette reported, "Dance Theater of Harlem's male dancers . . . dispel the myth forever about the effeminate qualities of male dancers. . . . Dance Theatre's male dancers, while being fluid limber and graceful, are masculine, muscular, and strong."

Though it appears simpler than writing a musical, the art of revue is risky and complex. Without a universal singular subject, a unifying style, a solid clear thread, and cohesive structure, the piece can languish. *Bubbling Brown Sugar* and *Ain't Misbehavin'* were both successful hit musical revues with music from the Harlem Renaissance that played on Broadway during the years just before *Doin' It*, which may have tempted Mitchell. Though it had an extended three-week engagement in Philadelphia, *Doin' It* never saw the bright lights of Broadway, and fell out of sight in 1979.

FOR PRESIDENTS AND PRIME MINISTERS

PERFORMANCES FOR GOVERNMENT OFFICIALS BECAME CUSTOMARY for DTH. They gave the Company prestige, exposure, and credibility. They were thrilling for those performing and further established the DTH name. In 1977 the Company performed at Carnegie Hall in honor of Marian Anderson with Mrs. and President Jimmy Carter in attendance. In 1981, at the invitation of First Lady Nancy Reagan to the White House, Mitchell remembers: "The President attended our opening night in Washington, he came backstage

afterward and told us how much he enjoyed our performance, the energy and usefulness and particularly the discipline. He said that since his son had become a dancer, he is beginning to appreciate what it can do for you, boys, bearing a new authority in his manner. And he invited us to come and perform at his first state dinner."

In 1981 DTH performed at the White House in honor of British Prime Minister Margaret Thatcher's first state visit. *Forces of Rhythm* and *Allegro Brillante* were performed. In 1985, Nancy Reagan hosted opening night for the Company's Metropolitan Opera House debut and 15th anniversary celebration at Lincoln Center. The First Lady's benefit committee was star-studded: Adolfo, Michael Bennett, Placido Domingo, Gregory Hines, Joshua Logan, Rudolf Nureyev, Christopher Reeve, Schubert's Bernard Jacobs, and Gerald Schoenfeld.

The Company members shaking hands with First Lady Nancy Reagan and President Ronald Reagan after their performance, 1981 (Photo: Courtesy of the Dance Theatre of Harlem Archive)

CASTING LOGISTICS

By 1985 the Company had over 50 members; *Giselle* had a large cast of 46 dancers, and *Firebird* had 34. Ballet mistress and principal dancer Lorraine Graves became a master at piecing together the complicated casting puzzle. She had to make sure that the casting was logistically possible in terms of makeup and costume changes. Orchestrating and coordinating costumes with casting was masterfully handled by DTH's wardrobe team. In some cases, there was only one costume that several people had to wear at consecutive performances. The groin and underarm areas would be spot washed and blown dry with a hair dryer. If a dancer was particularly small or large in height or weight, they were thankful that they were the only ones

to wear their costumes. On top of these scheduling issues, Graves would also have to consider whether dancing multiple roles was too physically demanding for the artist and sometimes replace the dancer or go back to the drawing board entirely.

In Mitchell's rehearsals, if there was a role a dancer fancied, they could attend the rehearsals and learn the role. Mitchell with his "eagle eye" would notice who was working on roles on the side. Depending on where they were in the choreographic process, some choreographers, such as Glen Tetley, preferred to eliminate extra noise and bodies in the room, whereas Mr. Mitchell loved many casts working. The motto "everyone learns everything" worked

in Mitchell's favor especially when injuries arose. If there were injuries in the first three casts, a fourth cast would have to step up. Sometimes, to solve the casting dilemma, someone would just shout out: "Who knows the Green Girl in *Dougla*?!" This cast was not assigned or official, which provided the dancers an opportunity to prove themselves. Dancers were trusted and sometimes thrown onstage without any "in the space" rehearsal. It also kept the DTH ballet masters and mistresses very busy. These masterminds

included William Scott, Paul Russell, Gayle McKinney, Cassandra Phifer-Moore, Augustus van Heerden, and Charmaine Hunter.

Back uptown, the School and all its departments continued at full force. There were performances by all kinds of music and dance groups, including Ballet Hispanico. Fashion shows with dancers as models included the Bill Blass and Halston collections. Revlon gave makeup demonstrations. At one Open House, the Company danced Michael Smuin's ballet *Songs of Mahler* while the inimitable Jessye Norman sang the score. The DTH Chorus took on major choral repertoire, including *Missa Luba* and Orff's *Carmina Burana*. The music department presented chamber ensembles with varied instrumentation.

AWARDS

AWARDS AND HONORS WERE GRANTED WITH REGULARITY, IF NOT TO DTH, THEN TO Arthur Mitchell, who received hundreds. In 1987 Mitchell was appointed to the National Council on the Arts by President Reagan, and he received his ninth honorary degree from Harvard University. He was awarded in 1993 the Kennedy Center Honors for his lifetime contribution to American culture, along with Johnny Carson, Georg Solti, Stephen Sondheim, and Marion Williams. Mitchell attended the 16th year of the Kennedy Center Honors escorted by Virginia Johnson. At age 60, in 1994, the year of DTH's 25th anniversary, Mitchell won the MacArthur Fellows Award for choreography.

The Princess Grace Award, created by Prince Rainier III of Monaco in honor of his wife, Grace Kelly, is given to emerging talent in theater, dance, and film, awarding grants in the form of scholarships, apprentice-ships, and fellowships. The award has been bestowed upon DTH dancers Pierre Lockett in 1984, Gregory Jackson in 1986, Jenelle Figgins in 2014, and Chyrstyn Fentroy in 2016. The First Karel Shook Award, designed by Peter Bogardus, was given to Saul and Gayfryd Steinberg, major donors and supporters of the arts. The Karel Shook Award was given to Irene Diamond in 1992; Jessye Norman was presented with the award in 1993. The DTH Emergence Award was created to honor individuals who benevolently affected the arts. Some notable honorees were Dorothy Hammerstein, Joseph Liebman, Judith Peabody, Marian Anderson, Leontyne Price, Cicely Tyson, Lena Horne, Valerie Bettis, Walter Terry, Dr. Ruby Herd, and Zelda Wynn, among others.

The etymology of this award comes from Karel Shook's essay "The First Ten Years," quoting Joseph Lieb-man, who said, "Emergence! Out of darkness comes illumination. And radiant communication. And it is a cause for joy." Shook continues:

The Dance Theatre of Harlem is classical ballet that speaks with eloquence to all who have witnessed it, leaping across artificial barriers of race and ethnicity, of politics and place, of ways and words. The Dance Theatre has transcended all of these. Because this vivid, vital company speaks a special language, a lan-guage that our hearts understand well. And it has emerged into a world where achievement is passport, where talent is nobility, where meritocracy is the only structure acknowledged. Emergence. Because our Dance Theatre of Harlem has entered the boundaries of our souls. Has uncovered the sense of oneness that abides deep in us all. To experience them is to celebrate their beauty and their truth. And ours, as well. And it is time.

BENEFITS AND BENEFACTORS

Mitchell and his associates always fostered and encouraged adjunct ventures and proposals, keeping a sharp eye on what could be beneficial for students. The economic expansion of the mid-'80s brought arts endowments and trusts that were flush with capital. More funds were available for arts organizations not only to sustain operations, but also to enhance their portfolios. In 1983, after Arthur Mitchell and six Company members taught master classes and workshops at the University of Southern California, 22 of their students received scholarships to study at DTH.

The National Choreography Project of 1985, a pilot program designed to provide new opportunities for choreographers and new works, awarded DTH a grant to support the collaboration between postmodernist choreographer David Gordon and the Company. That same year, the Greater London Council awarded scholarships for three British dance students to serve as apprentices in the Company. This was to initiate a multiyear residency for DTH in London.

When funds diminished for a season on Broadway in 1978, he turned to other creative endeavors. Arthur Mitchell always seemed to find a way out. He, Karel Shook, and two board of education musicians, Robert Bass and Brenda Saunders, created an evening called *His Life is Everlasting*. Contralto Marian Anderson, Presidential Medal of Freedom winner and DTH board member, came out of retirement to narrate. Mitchell had formed a new 26-member chorus for the Easter evening fundraiser. It was held at Columbia University's St. Paul's Chapel.

The search for philanthropic support widened with the creation of the Friends of Dance Theatre of Harlem, Doctors for DTH, and Lawyers for DTH. In 1982, the National Endowment for the Arts awarded DTH with a grant of $800,000, the largest given. As a challenge grant, it was designed to stimulate contributions from the private sector.

Dance star Gregory Hines, and his daughter Dava, were host and hostess for a gallery cocktail

The Dance Theatre of Harlem Choral Ensemble, St. Paul's Chapel, 1978 (Photo: Jack Vartoogian/FrontRowPhotos)

he would bring combinations of styles together and present what would be the cutting edge for the masses. Delsener curated, with producer Ken Fritz, one of the first ever concert series with one popular artist, four nights in a row, at three very different venues in a single city. It was called George Benson X4. It began on May 6 at the Metropolitan Museum of Art, with Benson's guest Les Paul; May 7 at the Palladium Theatre, with guest Minnie Riperton; May 8 at Avery Fisher Hall, with "special guest appearance" by DTH; and May 9 at Avery Fisher with Grover Washington Jr. as guest. Mitchell choreographed no fewer than three pieces with music by Benson: *Breezin'*, *The Greatest*, and *El Mar*. Delsener, in the

benefit that raised thousands of dollars. Singer Lionel Richie gave a benefit concert and shared the proceeds with DTH. In 1983 Sammy Davis Jr. and Bill Cosby saluted DTH at their Broadway show *Two Friends*, the proceeds of which went to establish a scholarship in the name of jazz great Cab Calloway. The 1984 Second Annual Holiday Reception to benefit DTH was hosted by a cadre of luminous stars: Cicely Tyson, Mrs. Oscar Hammerstein, Candice Bergen, Adolfo, Darryl Strawberry, and others. Onetime Company member and Broadway star Hinton Battle hosted and Whitney Houston performed.

A marvelous standout event for DTH in 1977 was a performance with jazz-soul guitarist and singer George Benson, a triple-platinum Grammy Award–winning recording artist. When mash-up and fusion was at its infancy, one of its godfathers was concert promoter Ron Delsener. He gave us the Beatles, the Stones, Streisand, and the concerts in Central Park for one dollar. With an uncanny sense for marketing the different and esoteric,

event's printed program said: "It is one of the most unique ideas in contemporary music and we are very honored to be a part of it." *The Greatest*, a pas de deux choreographed by Mitchell, stayed in the repertoire for years and became a favorite in the Company's lecture demonstrations.

LEFT: *Left to right:* Karel Shook, Brenda Saunders, Robert Bass, Marian Anderson, and Arthur Mitchell taking a bow, 1978 (Photo: Jack Vartoogian/ FrontRowPhotos)

RIGHT: *Left to right:* Sandi Phifer-Moore, Hinton Battle, and Karlya Shelton in George Balanchine's *The Four Temperaments* (Photo: Marbeth, Courtesy of the Dance Theatre of Harlem Archive)

THE GEORGE BALANCHINE
TRIBUTE

Mitchell took a steady stream of gambits with his young company. The 1979 return to City Center was one of those. It would be a special season that saluted George Balanchine. Karel Shook seized the opportunity to put pen to paper for the New York City Center *Playbill*. In his article "DTH Salutes Balanchine," Shook credits and thanks Balanchine and Kirstein—first, for their foresight in making Arthur Mitchell a member of NYCB; second, for their unwavering support and advice; and third, for single-handedly creating twentieth-century ballet classicism from the "monoliths of 19th century romanticism." Shook claims that Balanchine's "vision and unrelenting effort have pulled together the threads of hundreds, even thousands of years—and woven them into a magic carpet of mysterious design upon which we, as dancers and spectators, can ride into worlds of inspiration and illumination that have not yet been fully explored."

Left to right: Arthur Mitchell, George Balanchine, Frederic Franklin, and Karel Shook, in a rare photograph together, 1980 (Photo: Courtesy of the Dance Theatre of Harlem Archive)

TOURS: TRIUMPHS, SURPRISES, AND MISHAPS

A splendid coup for the Company was the 1980 six-week tour of Australia, with performances in Brisbane, Adelaide, Sydney, and Melbourne. After the 23-hour flight, Mitchell promised the 46 dancers of the Company a day off to recover. But when he saw how puffy and stiff the dancers looked upon arrival, he rescinded the offer and announced that class and rehearsals would begin a few hours after landing. The dancers zombied into the studio. Once again, Mitchell took no chances on his Company looking less than perfect. The repertoire for the engagements was grueling and included *Serenade*, *Paquita*, *Swan Lake Act II*, *Troy Game*, *Mirage*, and *Manifestations*. In one theatre, there was no heat onstage, only in the dressing rooms with space heaters. Some dancers chose to hole up in their warm dressing room listening for their musical cues over the monitors. At precisely the correct second, they would do the 50-yard dash from the dressing room right onto the freezing stage, dance, then sprint back to warmth. Despite the icicles on the set, the critics acclaimed the dancing as "classical ballet with soul" and additional performances were added.

The six-week tour presented the once-in-a-lifetime opportunity for the dancers to perform in Hong Kong. The dancers were housed there in a chic hotel, whose surroundings offered shopping for silks, tailor-made suits, and local cuisine. Chefs would come from their kitchens to gape at the dancers, just as dancers gaped at their plates, never really knowing what they were eating. A rigorous program of demanding ballets was rewarded with a side trip to Kowloon, China.

In 1980 The Cultural Exchange Accord was signed by former Vice President Walter Mondale of the United States and Vice Premier Deng Xiaoping of China. In November of that year, Arthur Mitchell, Stuart Hodes, Bella Lewitzky, Michael Smuin, and Suzanne Shelton were sent to China by Charles Reinhart, who was president of the American Dance Festival. The delegation was one of the first five government-funded arts exchange groups.

Touring is exciting, but not without its pitfalls. At Sadler's Wells in London, the stage had a severe rake to it,

The Australian Elizabethan Theatre Trust, Michael Edgley International Pty. Ltd., J.C. Williamson Productions Ltd. and Sir Robert Helpmann present...

dance theatre of harlem

A THEATRE AUSTRALIA PROGRAMME

Ronald Perry on the program cover for Dance Theatre of Harlem's performances in Australia, 1980 (Photo: Courtesy of the Dance Theatre of Harlem Archive)

If the dancer was successful, it was considered a phenomenal feat on a rake, and all in the house and backstage would cheer and curtain calls would ensue, sometimes for almost the same length as the ballet itself. In a series of turns in the Sanguinic section of *The Four Temperaments*, one of the female dancers started off the turns fine. The choreography called for turns starting from stage left and exiting stage right, but because of the rake, she lost her compass and ended up going off stage left, from where she started, instead of stage right: difficult turns, wrong exit. She shook her hands in the wings, as if to say, "Oh my God, what just happened?" and then entered to finish . . . from the wrong side. Not much was said, because it was the work of the rake monster, after all.

where the stage is slanted on an angle upward and away from the audience. Some of the dancers were experiencing what they nicknamed "the rake monster" for the first time. When a dancer fell out of a turn or was a little off-balance, the dancers would say that the rake monster got them. To compensate, Mitchell ordered the dancers to spot higher on turns ("Look up!"); otherwise he assured them that they would fall. And some did. Dancers flocked to the stage wings to watch when *fouettés*, or any series of turns, were on display, as those in *Le Corsaire* and *The Four Temperaments*.

LEFT: The Company men in Robert North's *Troy Game* (Photo: Martha Swope, ©NYPL)

RIGHT: Arthur Mitchell working with students on the Beijing, Kunming, Chengdu, and Shanghai tour, 1980 (Photo: Courtesy of the Dance Theatre of Harlem Archive)

THE 1984 OLYMPICS

DTH DANCERS ALSO ASSUMED THE ROLE OF arts ambassadors. The Company represented the United States in the transfer of the Olympic flag and performed Balanchine's *Stars and Stripes* finale during the closing ceremonies of the 1984 XXIII Olympiad in Los Angeles, part of the Olympic Arts Festival. It was probably the largest audience exposure ever for DTH: thousands in the stands, millions watching on television. Though production at the stadium was very detailed to manage the hundreds of entertainers, it put the dressing rooms a far and muddy distance from the stage. Dancers had to cover their dance shoes with plastic bags fastened with rubber bands to make the trek and were only brought to the stage minutes before they were on. This Olympiad was the first open to women in cycling, rifle shooting, and canoeing, among other sports.

Arthur Mitchell calling out corrections during the onstage rehearsal in the Olympic Stadium, 1984 (Photo: Judy Tyrus)

In Tel Aviv, many dancers awakened early to go sunbathing before class. Little did they realize that at the evening performance their skin no longer matched their tights, throwing off lighting plans and making follow spots the wrong hue. Mitchell chastised the Company and banned sunbathing. Tel Aviv dance studios were boiling hot, but the views in the Roman amphitheater at Caesarea were stunning. At dusk, human-eating mosquitoes attacked through the dancers' tights for their dinner. Eddie J. Shellman shared the stage and a variation with a stray dog.

The year 1979 marked DTH as the first major foreign classical ballet company to perform in Dublin since 1957. In Ireland, men were enamored with the women in the Company (as in most places). They would dash out of the pubs with arms open wide and chase the female dancers down the street. There was also culture shock in Italy. Italian children would run up to the dancers and touch their arms when the Company was frolicking on the beach to see if their color would rub off.

Between Portland and Seattle, in May of 1980, the Company tour bus ran into the aftermath of the Mount St. Helens volcanic eruption. Though the air was highly toxic, Mitchell stopped the bus to get out and scoop up some ash for a souvenir.

The year 1985 saw the Company tour six European countries, and just after a load-out in Nervi, Italy, the theatre in which the Company had just performed burned to the ground. Similarly, after the Company performed at the historic and arresting Gran Teatre del Liceu in Barcelona, the auditorium and stage were razed by fire. Closer

to home, surprises could be harrowing. September of 1983 brought a major break-in at the DTH studios when thieves ransacked the offices. Company members were called in to help clean the disarray.

LEFT: "What's he doing!" While on tour, Arthur Mitchell stepped off the bus to scoop a cup of ash from the Mt. St. Helens eruption, 1980 (Photo: Joseph Wyatt)

RIGHT: Teatro Maria Taglioni in Nervi, Italy, before and after a devastating fire, 1985 (Photos: Judy Tyrus)

Despite mishaps, the Company's success continued to be meteoric. Box-office attendance was up; there were command performances for European royalty; White House guest performances sparkled; a New York season comeback was made; there was domestic and international touring. It would not be unusual for the Company to tour with up to 55 dancers, musical staff, and a full production crew. Even more, 1981 saw the timely arrival of the symphonic and Broadway pit conductor maestro Milton Rosenstock. With all gears working, one might describe the 1980s as the golden age for DTH.

TELEVISION

What further branded DTH's name was its exposure on television. In the 1970s there were three major networks: ABC, NBC, and CBS, and cable TV. PBS preserved, developed, and televised preeminent arts programming.

LEFT: Gayle McKinney and Roman Brooks in Lester Horton's *The Beloved* (Photo: Martha Swope, ©NYPL)

RIGHT: Stephanie Dabney, the original firebird (Photo: Martha Swope, ©NYPL)

PBS first televised their *Great Performances* series in 1972. In 1976 the spin-off *Dance in America* premiered. DTH appeared on the series in March of 1977 performing *Holberg Suite*, *The Beloved*, *Dougla*, and *Forces of Rhythm*. It was directed by Merrill Brockway and introduced by Robin Ray. It came in number one of the ten highest-rated specials in a four-week period in the Nielsen ratings.

The year 1982 saw the first performance of *Firebird*, choreographed by John Taras. *Firebird* premiered at New York City Center, completely reimagined and transported to a mysterious rain forest, with opulent sets and costumes by Geoffrey Holder, based on Haitian paintings. PBS

Virginia Johnson and Lowell Smith in Valerie Bettis's *A Streetcar Named Desire* (Photo: Leslie Spatt)

televised *Kennedy Center Tonight*, yet another TV show with DTH performing their greatest signature ballet, *Firebird*. Stephanie Dabney, Donald Williams, Lorraine Graves, and Sulpicio Mariano were the featured dancers, Holder was the designer, and Grace Costumes executed the costumes. The airing garnered a George Foster Peabody Award and Golden Eagle Award, among others. From 1982 to the 2000s, *Firebird* became a worldwide favorite and requests for it were constant.

PBS also presented the company dancing *A Streetcar Named Desire* with Virginia Johnson and Lowell Smith, the full Company in *Bele*, and *Sylvia Pas de Deux* danced by Judy Tyrus and Eddie J. Shellman.

Danilova and Franklin

Frederic Franklin and Madame Alexandra Danilova, he from Liverpool and she Russian born, were famous for partnering at the Ballet Russe de Montecarlo. *The New York Times* called them, "one of the greatest partnerships of 20th-century ballet." Kisselgoff in *The New York Times* (1/15/1981) said there was a nostalgic trend in the early '80s for Ballet Russe de Monte Carlo repertoire, and Frederic Franklin was still the go-to man to recreate it. His 1981 production of *Swan Lake, Act II* was "a very fine revival" as compared to the year before, which Kisselgoff found rigid. She said, "The mechanical and pure-dance manner that marred last year's performance is gone, as is the tendency to go from pose to pose rather than to link the steps properly. Miss [Elena] Carter is a very fluid dancer . . . her Swan Queen was beautifully danced and lyrical in tone."

Paquita, a ballet set in Spain with music by Minkus, was staged for DTH by Franklin and Danilova. According to Clive Barnes it was the touchstone of the Kirov style. With 15 women in tutus, *Paquita* was one of the first ballets in which more than a few women of the Company were completely exposed in performing classical ballet technique. The approach to dancing classical ballet in a tutu is different from dancing classical ballet in a dress or leotard. Mitchell would say, "You can't use the same legs in a tutu that you would use in a long dress." Of the piece, Kisselgoff of *The New York Times* (1/17/1980) said, "In the ballerina role, Elena Carter has a gentle style that compliments the technique that makes her one of the company's best dancers, while Joe Wyatt looked dashing as her partner and in the pas de trois with Yvonne Hall and Karlya Shelton."

An expression used among singers and dancers is "dress the instrument." Basically, this means dressing up when in public because the body is your instrument; it must be polished and presentable. Mitchell's directive to

The Company in *Swan, Lake Act II.* (Photo: Courtesy of the Dance Theatre of Harlem Archive)

Franklin had a photographic memory. He would set the steps and Danilova would impart the style, attitude, the tilt of the head, the flavor. They remembered everything, thousands of details. Neither of them looked at notes or videos. Mitchell would watch rehearsals to make sure that the dancers were totally focused and that they fully understood the magnitude of having these legendary dancers in the studio. Danilova and Franklin had total faith in the DTH dancers and recognized them as the best trained in the world. The choreography was not changed or simplified; it was taught the same way they had performed it with Ballet Russe. Peter Rosenwald, music and dance critic of the *Wall Street Journal*, stated, "For dancers of this generation to work with this legendary Russian Imperial Ballet dancer, now in her 80s, is an extraordinary experience. Mitchell said, 'If you are going to learn the classics, go to the source.'"

be presentable at all times was the DTH way; if a dancer came to the airport dressed down, he would say, "Don't come in here looking like who shot John."

The epitome of "dressing the instrument" were Danilova and Franklin. Danilova, known as "Madame D" by her charges, would arrive complete with peacock lashes, chiffon regalia with ballet-pink tights, matching character shoes, anesthetizing perfume—Chanel No. 5. Franklin would arrive as her dapper and devoted wingman, and never sat down. He was known for his effervescent personality, endless energy, and wisdom. The two not only gave the dancers a mountainous wealth of balletic knowledge, but they were also entertainment in themselves. The corps was enamored and absorbed by them. Dancers gazed in stunned submission.

LEFT: Alexandra Danilova refining the port de bras with Joseph Wyatt in *Paquita* (Photo: Marbeth, Courtesy of the Dance Theatre of Harlem Archive)

RIGHT: *From left to right*, Frederic Franklin, Karel Shook, Alexandra Danilova, and Arthur Mitchell (Photo: Marbeth, Courtesy of the Dance Theatre of Harlem Archive)

GLEN TETLEY

It was a part of Mitchell's artistic process to bring in friends and artists whom he worked with or knew from his earlier career. One of those personalities and friends was the choreographer Glen Tetley. Tetley harmoniously blended modern dance with ballet, creating his own unique style that was influenced by his studies with Hanya Holm, Martha Graham, Antony Tudor, and Margaret Craske. Tetley's *Greening, Voluntaries, Dialogues,* and *Sphinx* were his works that left a mark on DTH's repertoire and style. Peter Rosenwald, music and dance critic of the *Wall*

Street Journal, wrote in 1980, "In many ways the test of the Company's technique and their ability to master a difficult idiom comes in Glen Tetley's *Greening*. The pace is very fast, the steps complicated, the lifts articulated and precise. To perform it well takes talent. Virginia Johnson, Lowell Smith, Eddie J. Shellman, and again the lovely Lydia Abarca gave the best performance of the ballet this critic has seen."

LEFT: Eddie J. Shellman and Yvonne Hall in Glen Tetley's ballet *Greening*, c. 1980 (Photo: Marbeth, Courtesy of the Dance Theatre of Harlem Archive)

RIGHT: *From left to right,* choreologist Bronwen Curry, Karel Shook, and Glen Tetley, 1979 (Photo: Marbeth, Courtesy of the Dance Theatre of Harlem Archive)

Firebird

Using Stravinsky's revised and shortened 1945 score, Taras and Holder moved *Firebird* out of the mythical forests of old Russia and reset it in an imaginary tropical jungle. This ballet became DTH's signature piece. It struck a chord with audiences and was the most popular and most performed. It made Stephanie Dabney a star. Jennifer Dunning stated in her (6/22/1985) *New York Times* review "Ballet: Harlem Troupe in Giselle, Firebird, and Voluntaries," "Stephanie Dabney as the firebird flew across the stage . . . regal bearing and lethal legwork which included Plisetskaya-style back kicks in jumps." Three ballerinas learned the title role when the ballet was first choreographed, but for a year, Dabney danced only *Firebird*, no other ballets in the repertoire. Once Elena Carter and Judy Tyrus were cast, Dabney was freed to do other roles. Since its premiere, a total of nine dancers performed this challenging role.

The costumes Holder designed were elaborate. Head-pieces for the maidens were extremely complex, a feat of architectural engineering. Sprouting up from a double-decker tiara were five eight-inch-high wire antennae covered with large, faceted jewels. If there was ever a

A staged Firebird portrait with Company dancers Christina Johnson, Charmaine Hunter and Judy Tyrus (Photo: Martha Swope, ©NYPL)

thunderstorm in the theatre, these antennae would serve as lightning rods. Onstage at one evening performance, two of the double-decker tiaras accidentally got too close to each other and crossed paths, rapturously entangling each other, locking the two fair maidens head-to-head. Now these maidens, joined at the head, had no choice but to exit stage right, tripping on each other's feet as they went. They detangled their antennae offstage, laughing hysterically, then ran back onstage to finish the scene, blushing.

Mitchell believed that "reworking the classics can make them relevant without robbing them of their intrinsic qualities." Clive Barnes in the January 15, 1982, edition of *The New York Times* wrote that DTH's *Firebird* was "no reworking of The City Ballet production for it has the vitality completely its own. Indeed, it is one of the few

magic productions of the *Firebird* I have ever encountered, replete with a new fairytale enchantment and a firm sense of good and evil that gives the fairytale a charming profundity." Barnes gave the secret to reinventing a masterpiece: redefine it and give it just a tweak of relevance. He also stated, "that DTH was founded to prove that black was not only beautiful, but in dance terms, could also be classical . . . The need for proof is over." *Firebird* became a critical success that raised the bar in the ballet world.

Avon Products saluted DTH with a float in the Rose Bowl Parade depicting a firebird. Dancers Stephanie Dabney and Donald Williams opened the New Year's Day telecast with excerpts from the ballet. The float won the Mayor's Trophy award.

The cast of *Firebird* in the final tableau (Photo: Jack Vartoogian/ FrontRowPhotos)

Giselle

Fashioning a new piece from old material is precarious business. In the 1980s it became a trend to adapt period plays to other times and settings. For instance, setting Shakespeare's *Twelfth Night* in the 1940s swing era. Some rules apply in the making. The story line, plot points, and themes remain. In musical theatre, the main script idea stays; in a ballet, the dancing. Mitchell chose to premiere *Giselle* in London because he had heard that there was an acclaimed new adaptation of *Rigoletto* as a ballet exported to the states from Britain. He said:

I'm going to do Giselle, totaling it out of Austria and I'm putting it in Louisiana to make it relevant. The story, the time in history, the myths are very similar to those in the south. New Orleans was a Spanish and French city first, so it was more cosmopolitan, more European, and therefore ballet would be a natural for the people to do there. *Giselle* in New Orleans. The whole story then makes sense for us to dance. Giselle will be a freed black girl and she will fall in love with Albrecht, a Creole. At that time the laws were that you could not intermarry. When she finds out he is a Creole, her heart breaks, she dies and becomes a Willi.

Jack Anderson, in the June 19, 1985 edition of *The New York Times*, proclaimed, "Dance Theatre of Harlem's [*Creole*] *Giselle* may be one of the most important versions of a 19th century classic ever to have been offered by an American company, for it makes a clear distinction that is too often blurred in revivals . . . Mr. Franklin and Mr. Mitchell always carefully distinguish between stage production and choreography." The choreography was true to the original as set for the Company by Franklin. The period and location changed, as well as the character names and their family lineage. The story and plot points remained the same. DTH maestro Milton Rosenstock even used the 1841 orchestrations from the Paris Opera. The set and costume designer Carl Michel wrote detailed character sketches for the dancers, complete with French-Creole names. In his version, the first act takes place on the farm of Madame Berthe Lanaux, Plaquemines Parish, Louisiana.

Frederic Franklin coaching Virginia Johnson and Eddie J. Shellman for *Giselle*, 1984. (Photo: Marbeth, Courtesy of the Dance Theatre of Harlem Archive)

The parish is located some 30 miles south of New Orleans. It is the fall of 1841 and the completion of the sugar cane harvest is being celebrated. The young farm boys and farm girls, Giselle Lanaux and her friends, and all the neighbors of Madame Berthe have come to dance, a favorite pastime of all Creoles. Frederic Franklin on *Giselle*: "It's difficult throwing a big, narrative ballet at dancers these days. American dancers are not called on to do much mime. They have no real background in it and are uncomfortable doing it. This company has been responsive, but it takes a great deal for them to stand onstage and become personalities, become people. They've got to learn how to carry them, how to wear the costumes. In a ballet like *Giselle*, they can't leave everything to the principal dancers. It takes time and patience." The success of *Giselle* made it a major signature piece for DTH. In 1984, it won the Laurence Olivier Award for best new dance production.

TOP, LEFT: Costume and Scenic Designer Carl Michel showing a mock-up of the Act I stage design for *Giselle*, 1984 (Photo: Marbeth, Courtesy of the Dance Theatre of Harlem Archive)

TOP, RIGHT: Judy Tyrus and Joseph Cipolla in the Peasant Pas de Deux from *Giselle* (Photo: Leslie Spatt)

BOTTOM: Because the *Giselle* set at City Center blocked the backstage crossover, Charmaine Hunter, in her pointe shoes, costume, and eyelashes, had to exit the stage through a trapdoor, dash into an alley, and run around to the 56th Street stage door, through security, to make her entrance on the other side of the stage. (Photo: Marbeth, Courtesy of the Dance Theatre of Harlem Archive)

TOP: Lowell Smith, Lorraine Graves, and the Company in *Giselle* (Photo: Courtesy of the Dance Theatre of Harlem Archive)

BOTTOM: The Company at the end of Act I of *Giselle* (Photo: Courtesy of the Dance Theatre of Harlem Archive)

THE METROPOLITAN
OPERA HOUSE

The 1985 season at the Metropolitan Opera House at Lincoln Center was a watershed experience for DTH. Kathy Larkin in the *Daily News* quoted Mitchell as saying, "My God, 16 years ago, we started with two dancers and 30 children in a garage and now we are in the Metropolitan Opera! It's mind boggling. It's due to all the hard work, the staff, the friends . . . We've had such acclaim around the world. But there's nothing like being hot at home." And it was hot. Clive Barnes of the *New York Post* said that "*Stars and Stripes* suits the company like a firecracker on the Fourth of July."

The Met season marked the Company's premiere of Balanchine's *Stars and Stripes*. Balanchine had programmed it in the 1950s as a patriotic homage to the national spirit and John Philip Sousa. DTH performed an excerpt for the closing ceremonies of the 1984 Olympic Games in Los Angeles. Of the piece, Jack Anderson of *The New York Times* (6/19/1985) reported, "This is an almost shamelessly blatant applause-wooer. No wonder some ballet goers love it, while others consider it marvelous corn." Red, white, and blue bunting bedecked the Met's lobby, and a supersize American flag hung from the topmost

Judy Tyrus and Company in the first regiment of George Balanchine's *Stars and Stripes*, 1985 (Photo: Martha Swope, ©NYPL)

balcony in the auditorium. Joseph Mazo in *Women's Wear Daily* (6/19/1985) reported, "DTH dances *Stars* with a swinging, jazzy stride, a gentle sway of the hips and a happy bounce to its steps—which is the way the New York City Ballet used to perform the piece when it was first done. *Stars and Stripes* is a young ballet and DTH—all of 16 years old—performs it with all the brashness, the athleticism, and the dedication it should have."

Of the *Firebird* at the Met, the Canadian *Daily Gleaner* (7/27/1985) wrote, "Sets and costumes for *Firebird* by Trinidadian artist performer Geoffrey Holder drew gasps of appreciation from the sophisticated Met audience for the strong, exotic Caribbean beauty. Dance Theatre of Harlem is truly an extraordinary and powerful company. In fifteen years, Arthur Mitchell has achieved an impossible dream, and created a vision of overwhelming—beauty. He has received many awards including Britain's first Laurence Olivier Award, but his reward must be in watching the curtain rise on the company he has formed, and the talent that he has freed."

Major resplendent repertoire branded the Company onto the national dance psyche. Arthur Mitchell had announced from the stage that the Company received a grant of $142,000 from the city for its School activities. He thanked Mayor Koch by presenting him with a lifetime scholarship and the mayor replied that he valued ballet because "everyone in public office learns quickly to dance on their toes." (*The New York Times*, 6/19/1985)

The Met season included impressive program pairings: *Serenade*, *Voluntaries*, and *Firebird*; *Troy Game* and *Giselle*; *Piano Movers*, *Fall River Legend*, and *Stars and Stripes*; the premiere of *La Mer* with *Giselle*, and again with *A Streetcar Named Desire*. The program bill included some of the greatest ballerinas and danseurs in the world: Karen Brown, Stephanie Dabney, Lorraine Graves, Yvonne Hall, Virginia Johnson, Cassandra Phifer-Moore, Judy Tyrus, Charmaine Hunter, Christina Johnson, Joseph Cipolla,

Augustus van Heerden, Keith Saunders, Eddie J. Shellman, Lowell Smith, and Donald Williams. Jack Anderson in *The New York Times* (6/19/1985) called *Giselle* "one of the most important versions of a 19th century classic ever to be offered by an American company."

Piano Movers is a group work for 11 set to a Thelonious Monk jazz score in which the choreographer, David Gordon, promised dancers moving "in, on, and around a piano that doesn't get played." The premiere of this unusual ballet at the Metropolitan Opera House typified "the spirit of artistic risk-taking encouraged by the National Choreography Project, which in its first season matched eight adventurous choreographers with eight eager dance companies." Jane Rigney of the *New York City Tribune* (7/3/1985) stated, "This is a nice piece, but a bit insubstantial for my taste . . . although the women are in pointe shoes and dance on toe, the overall feeling is anticlassical. The ballet has kind of a relaxed atmosphere one might find in a smoky uptown bar." The ballet was performed in street clothes designed by Santo Loquasto.

La Mer was one of the premier ballets offered in the 1985 season at the Metropolitan Opera House; it included three symphonic sketches evoking different facets of the sea. It is Debussy's largest orchestral work of program music. As Debussy writes in a letter to his friend the musician André Messager in 1903: "I have always retained a sincere passion for the sea . . . I have an endless store of memories: to my mind, this is worth more than reality, the charm of which generally weighs too heavily on my thoughts." Jane Rigney in the *New York City Tribune* (6/3/1985) stated, "The work is lovely to look at thanks to the undersea effects produced by Paul Sullivan's lighting and also to the attractive bodies set off by the choreography's simple, form-fitting costumes (basically unitards). Williams and Dabney teamed for a sensuous pas de deux. Dabney, a dancer of astonishing range, has this season established herself as the strongest ballerina in the

Company . . . Lorraine Graves, another charismatic presence, was the queen of the mermaids, dressed in orange with a sunburst crown. The fiery Joseph Cipolla led the final scene, showing the ocean at its stormiest."

A ballet titled *Voluntaries* secured favorable reviews. A *voluntary* is a music term that is used in church organ music to signify a piece that a church organist would give, or *volunteer* to play, as a prelude to a service. Here, it is adapted as if the dancers would volunteer a dance. Jennifer Dunning, in *The New York Times* (6/22/1985), said, "This is a ballet whose skimming lifts and ardent, grounded pas de deux can suggest love, worship, and a longing for flight." She said of Donald Williams's dancing that he had "potent absorption . . . sailing through one clear jump after another." Of the pas de deux, Alan M. Kriegsman from the *Washington Post* (3/18/1988) remarked, "Yvonne Hall and Augustus van Heerden were so interpretively authoritative as the lead couple in the Tetley work that the elegiac fervor of their dancing wasn't marred by a few strained passages. They were ably abetted by Karen Brown, Keith Thomas, and Cubie Burke, as well as a strong ensemble of six couples."

DTH had pinnacled in the capital city of dance. The Met, known as New York's La Scala, is one of the most prestigious venues in the world. The performances here branded the Company as a major force in ballet. How much higher could the Company go? Dancing at the Met is to dancers what Carnegie Hall is to musicians. "It's like going to the graduation of your first child," said Cicely Tyson. "I'm so very, very proud."

Yvonne Hall, Augustus Vanheerden, Photo: Martha Swope © NYPL)

SCHEHERAZADE

IN 1981, KAREL SHOOK, WHO PENNED AN ARTICLE FOR Playbill Magazine titled *Scheherazade,* tells that the DTH production was set by Frederic Franklin "whose memory and musicality are infallible, and who had, as the Golden Slave, one of his most sensational roles." In recreating the *Arabian Nights* ballet for DTH, Franklin "decided to go straight to the original and stay there." Fokine's original choreography for *Scheherazade* was preserved by Serge Grigoriev who had a decades-long career as *régisseur* for The Ballets Russe, and in turn, the ballet was handed down to Franklin.

The original choreography stayed intact, so the burning issue was what to do with costume and set design. Franklin wondered what he would ask of designer Carl Michel if he were designing the ballet for today? The answer was that Carl Michel would be free to contemporize but keep the idea of sensuality and fleshiness. They wanted "to show the dancer's body in a different light and from a different point in time." Shook mentions in the article that in 1910 it would never have been tolerated to have dancers with their underwear or skin showing, as opposed to the modern flesh-colored body stockings and tights. Mitchell and Michel used sources from which Leon Bakst, the original designer took his inspiration—Persian, Arabian, Hindu art, miniatures, and paintings. This mammoth production was included in the 1983 tour to Tokyo, Kyoto, and Osaka, Japan. The set included a painted floor and the use of supernumeraries, male shirtless bodybuilders hired locally to appear in costume wielding huge paper maché swords.

Shook also wrote, "It returns to the living stage a masterpiece that could in time be regrettably lost forever; it is our first attempt at an all-out, full-scale production which is both spectacular and complex; it provides our dancers with the challenge of demanding acting roles, plus the opportunity to enter completely into another era of time and space." Anna Kisselgoff in *The New York Times* (1/18/1981): "...lush...superb...highly theatrical...the fact that the race issue—the accent on mixed pairing—has been made irrelevant in this production should not go unrecorded."

TOP: Lorraine Graves and Lowell Smith in Michael Fokine's *Scheherazade* (Photo: Marbeth, Courtesy of the Dance Theatre of Harlem Archive)
BOTTOM: Eddie J. Shellman and Company in *Scheherazade* (Photo: Courtesy of the Dance Theatre of Harlem Archive)

THE END OF AN ERA

The 1980s were peak years for the ensemble spirit of the Company. It was the fruit of twelve years of growth. Mitchell and Shook's way of developing a Company paid off. In the *Washington Star* (2/8/1981) Shook was quoted: "We didn't have to waste a lot of time eliminating the unnecessary from our training. I had seen what I wanted at Balanchine's school and have always worked for the technical discipline that will allow the company to dance together, but not be alike. Who wants lots of personality with no orderliness in the movement? On the other hand, we do not subjugate personality either." This is the crucible from which the ensemble style of DTH emerged. The classical ensemble style, "extended and stretched," as Kisselgoff would say, paired with the unique adaptations and reinventions from non-balletic source material, would become the DTH recipe.

The years 1977 through 1985 were DTH's first golden age, when magnanimous change and growth brought worldwide notoriety. Mitchell and Shook's hard work brought forth a company of professional dancers with a splendid repertoire. Magnificent signature ballets were created. Walter Terry, a dance critic for *The New York Herald Tribune* and the *Saturday Review*, in the 1982 January edition of *Playbill Magazine* said: "Their techniques, their skills, their range, their accomplishments have transformed them into an international ballet company of world stature."

A subtle but important change was noted in a feature article in 1983 in Playbill by Kisselgoff: "It might be a jolt . . . for those encountering the company for the first time this season to notice that there are now non-black dancers in its ranks. In Mr. Mitchell's mind, this change has less to do with ideology than with artistic considerations. The wider statement DTH has made in nearly 15 years is no longer dependent upon exclusivity. The goal now is further artistic excellence, one manifest in the new thrust of the repertory. Gone is the time when Mr. Mitchell and others created ballets especially for novice dancers." Mitchell as quoted by Ann Marie Welsh of *The Washington Star* (2/8/1981): "People aren't referring to us as a black dance company anymore. I think now we're just considered a good dance company."

In 1979, DTH's 10th anniversary year, Karel Shook wrote an article titled *The First Ten Years.* It is about the Company's first stunning decade of rapid growth and holds a special place in the DTH archive of written materials. Another of his writings, *The Aboutness of DTH,* further clarified the uniqueness of what the world was seeing in the small world of ballerinas and danseurs with African roots. Yet another rich accomplishment of Shook's was the publication of *The Elements of Classical Ballet Technique,* based on his teaching at DTH, published in 1982. In 1980 he received the United States Presidential Award for Excellence and Dedication in Education.

After a long illness, during a sabbatical where he was creating a new syllabus for the School, Karel Shook died on July 25th, 1985. He was sixty-five years old. A memorial service was held at the Cathedral Church of St. John The Divine in New York City. Arthur Mitchell gave the homily, Leavata Johnson and Veronica Tyler were the soloists, and the three movements of *Doina* were performed by the Company. Jennifer Dunning in *The New York Times* (2/24/1997): "Karel Shook, a white teacher who believed as Mr. Mitchell did, that black dancers . . . have a natural place in the serene realm of the arabesque and the entrechat."

The Seasons' Ballets

Forty-three ballets entered the DTH repertoire from 1977 to 1985. The protean level of dancing and versatility was exemplary. Anna Kisselgoff of *The New York Times* aptly codified DTH ballets into categories. It was during this time that these seven ballet types were performed, and the Company could nimbly jump from style to style. The categories were: *Balanchine Tradition, Ballet Russe Tradition, Black Heritage, Contemporary Fusion, Bravura, Modernist Revival,* and *Dance Drama*. Because of artistic blending and brewing, no codification can fully compartmentalize and exactly order the DTH ballets. Some may be included in two or even three of the categories. Nevertheless, here, Kisselfgoff's effort clears the way to fully understand the larger picture of the range and depth of the DTH repertoire, and the capabilities of the dancers. The first category is *Balanchine and Associates*. Here, Kisselgoff assigns ballets that were created by George Balanchine and those he influenced, including Arthur Mitchell and John Taras. The Balanchine style was attractive and inventive. It was art in the classical sense but reflected the contemporary American zeitgeist. It was uptown art rather than downtown music hall. It was the epitome of what would come to be known as authentic American Ballet.

Virginia Johnson had performed the *Tchaikovsky Pas de Deux*, a fine example of Balanchine's neoclassical style, in the DTH premiere with Paul Russell. It is an eleven-minute piece filled with fish dives, stage-length piqué turns, virtuosic partnering, and optional single double or triple fouetté turns at the discretion of the ballerina. It was revived in the next millennium under company direction of Virginia Johnson. *Serenade* was the first ballet choreographed by Balanchine in the United States, in 1934. It used Tchaikovsky's *Serenade for Strings* and was first presented by the students of the School of American Ballet

and soon after it entered the NYCB repertory. Performed by twenty-eight dancers in ankle-length blue romantic tutus in front of a blue backdrop, it became a staple for DTH in the 1980s and was performed worldwide. As a lesson in stage technique, Balanchine worked rehearsal mishaps into the piece. When one student fell, he kept it in the choreography. Another day, a student arrived late, and this became part of the ballet. Affirming it as a crowd pleaser, Robert Greskovic of *The New Leader NYC* (4/9/1979) stated, "A glimpse of human perfection." Clive Barnes of

Virginia Johnson in George Balanchine's *Tchaikovsky Pas de Deux* (Photo: Martha Swope, ©NYPL)

The New York Times (6/21/1985) said, "They give it with a lilt and romantic lushness some way removed from the more crystalline and balanced interpretation favored by the New York City Ballet. But a masterpiece can accept many interpretations and this more overtly emotional view of *Serenade* is perfectly valid, and here beautifully expressed."

The Four Temperaments is one of Balanchine's black and white minimalist ballets. The original costumes, designed in 1951 by Kurt Seligmann, proved to be problematic for the dancers in performance: flapping fabric, spiny spikes, heavy helmets, and fluttering flags. Balanchine stripped all these away. *The Four Temperaments* was performed in rehearsal gear: flesh-toned tights and black leotards on the women, and white T-shirts and black tights for the men. In essence, "lights and tights." The score was commissioned by Balanchine and composed by Paul Hindemith. Balanchine's most popular saying (adapted from a review he received) can be applied to these kinds of ballets: "See the music, hear the dance." Popular throughout America and

Europe, *The Four Temperaments* became a favorite among many DTH dancers. Clive Barnes in the *New York Post* (6/21/1985) exclaimed, "The DTH performance of it is one of today's great ballet experiences, miss it at your peril. . . . I can recall no other company—including New

TOP: *From top to bottom,* Yvonne Hall, Keith Saunders, and Elena Carter in George Balanchine's *Serenade* (Photo: Martha Swope, ©NYPL).
BOTTOM: The Company in George Balanchine's *Serenade* (Photo: Jack Vartoogian/FrontRowPhotos)

132

York City Ballet—ever conveying a greater sense of fidelity to the heart of this masterpiece."

Square Dance is George Balanchine's harder-than-hell ballet. With a cast of 12, and a score by Corelli and Vivaldi, traditional square dance patterns and formations with neo-classical steps were executed at break-neck speed. Balanchine originally included a caller prompting the steps, later cutting the idea. DTH restored the original version, and for the premier, the piece was called by Howard Rollins of the 1979 *Roots* miniseries, and later by DTH dancer Cubie Burke.

Another Balanchine influenced work, *The Greatest*, a pas de deux, was choreographed by Arthur Mitchell for Virginia Johnson and Paul Russell. It was performed at Avery Fisher Hall in 1977. The song, composed for the movie about Muhammed Ali, had lyrics by Linda Creed and music by Michael Masser. The piece was adored by audiences because of the familiarity of the pop-hit song

with which they would sing along with George Benson. The universal message of the song resonated with Arthur Mitchell and audiences alike: the love of children as hope for the world, who must be taught well, can walk with dignity, and achieve greatness.

TOP: *From left to right,* Laurie Woodard, Cassandra Phifer-Moore, Leslie Woodard, and Karen Henry in George Balanchine's *The Four Temperaments* (Photo: Leslie Spatt)

BOTTOM: Judy Tyrus, Eddie J. Shellman and Company in George Balanchine's *Square Dance* (Photo: Leslie Spatt)

The second Kisselgoff category is *Ballet Russe Tradition*. The repertoire from this tradition became manifest through the mega-talent and eidetic memory of Frederic Franklin. His talent and foresight in programming the right ballet at the right time was profuse. This repertoire strengthened and refined the corps in pure classical ballet. These ballets made ballerinas. They were the base and bones of working in a tutu. For example, in *Swan Lake Act II,* keeping the rule of leg and hand: if standing on the right leg, and the left is behind, then the right hand at the wrist is crossed front, over the left wrist. Embodying this style, in nuance and detail, was key to performing many pieces in the DTH repertory. Delibes' *Sylvia*, based on Tasso's play *Aminta*, is of the Ballet Russe ilk and was choreographed by Frederic Franklin. Danced by Judy Tyrus and Eddie J. Shellman, Anna Kisselgoff in *The New York Times*

(6/25/1989) wrote, "Both proved wonderful performers, with Miss Tyrus exhibiting an elegant quality in her arms and torso, classically measured to suggest a huntress of antiquity. Mr. Franklin's choreography begins with an ecstatic plastique style and ends as a traditional classical pas de deux. The final tricky fish dive was fantastically rendered."

Pas de Dix is a set of variations danced by ten dancers taken from the last act of *Raymonda*, a ballet that was choreographed by Marius Petipa. In Ballet Russe style, the variations in *Pas de Dix* were technically exacting. The men's variation was always a nail biter, a cause for anxious nightmares, because each man had to do double tours en l'air on a dime, multiple times. Some could pull it off with ease, while for some, praying in the wings with religious fervor was a common occurrence.

Lorraine Graves and Donald Williams in Marius Petipa's *Pas de Dix* (Photo: Leslie Spatt)

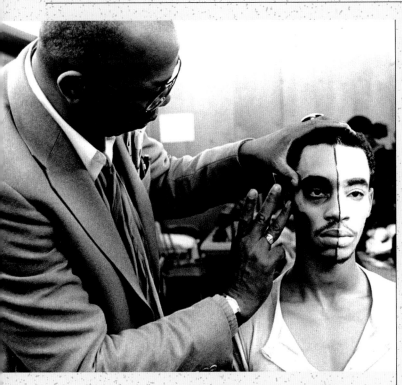

Kisselgoff's third category is *African Heritage*. Here, content is king and if the subject material of the ballet displays the social behaviors, norms, knowledge, beliefs, arts, and habits of an individual group or society, then it is of the "heritage" type. *Ode to Otis* (1969) could be classified as the first DTH work of African American heritage; *Dougla* would sit well in the category as well. These were the kind of ballets that set DTH apart from other classical ballet companies.

Banda, a Holder ballet, concerns Vodou, an African diaspora religion born at the confluence of Catholicism and French slave ownership during the early settling of the Caribbean shelf. It is the dance of Baron Samedi, a deity (Iwa) of cemeteries and eroticism, an aristocratic King of Clowns among many other things. His attributes are a scarf and a cane, symbols of life and pleasure. Kisselgoff in *The New York Times* (1/31/1982) credits Donald Williams, who dances Baron Samedi as taking an ". . . extraordinary pelvis-popping virtuoso turn—strangely

LEFT: Geoffrey Holder and Donald Williams working on makeup for Geoffrey Holder's *Banda*, 1981 (Photo: Marbeth, Courtesy of the Dance Theatre of Harlem Archive)

RIGHT: *From left to right, Eddie J. Shellman, Donald Williams, China White, and Peter Hunter in Carmen de Lavallade's Sensemaya* (Photo: Marbeth, Courtesy of the Dance Theatre of Harlem Archive).

mystical and erotic—as a voodoo god that makes Geoffrey Holder's *Banda* so sensational."

Sensemaya, the first choreographic effort for DTH by Carmen de Lavallade, had a short shelf life in the repertoire but is worthy of note. It tells the story of an ancient Mayan creation legend. Though de Lavallade's dance vocabulary was more modern than balletic (having an early association with Alvin Ailey and Lester Horton), Kisselgoff in *The New York Times* (02/24/1979) stated, "It is like a condensed ceremony. It is startlingly brief and makes its point with total directness."

The *Contemporary Fusion* category concerns the fusing of styles that gives the creator baselines from which to work while retaining the freedom to break rules. The fused elements could mock, expand, or create an entirely new style. The palette becomes broader, and the result, if the laws of consistency are followed, can be an exciting audience experience. Support for this kind of artistic exploration pushes the art form forward.

Choo San Goh, born in Singapore and former Het Dutch Nationale Ballet dancer, is most noted as choreographer with Mary Day's Washington Ballet, creating fifteen ballets including *Variations Serieuses*, danced by DTH with music by Mendelsohn. Of his ballet *Introducing*, also danced by DTH, Anna Kisselgoff of *The New York Times* (3/4/79) reported, ". . . danced to Stravinsky's *Ebony Concerto*, was a playful spin-off from Balanchine's 'Rubies' . . .

accompanying at the pipe organ. Mitchell combined cultural components to see if something magnificent would happen. It did. Not only was the music ethereal, but the white netting costumes made the dancers' legs disappear.

Secret Silence, 1979, choreographed by Spanish-Filipino-Swedish-American Carlos Carvajal with music by Daniel Kobialka, dealt with mystic themes. *Shapes of Evening*, also by Carvajal, a work for three men and three women, used the beauteous *Sacred and Profane Dances* by Claude Debussy. The choreographer created over 200 works for ballet opera and television. He also founded, directed, and choreographed over fifty works for San Francisco Dance Spectrum.

Troy Game choreographed by Robert North for 14 scantily dressed male dancers was a bevy of acrobatic articulated formations combined with slow-motion transitions. The score used *batucada*, a samba-style of group drumming from Brazil. Jennifer Dunning in *The New York Times* (6/6/1985)

[*Introducing*] is a further example of his craftsmanship and skill at showing off the abilities of young dancers."

Royston Maldoom's *Doina* is an example of high-stakes creative programming. *Doina* exemplifies the original "DTH recipe" at work: a classical ballet company of color dancing to a Romanian Arab-Persian musical genre probably derived from Eastern mourning and grieving songs that are modal and improvisational, played by Zamfir on pan flute with Swiss organist Marcel Cellier

LEFT: Eddie J. Shellman, China White, Ronald Perry, and Hinton Battle in Choo San Goh's *Introducing* (Photo: Courtesy of the Dance Theatre of Harlem Archive)

RIGHT: Choo San Goh rehearsing the dancers in *Introducing* (Photo: Marbeth, Courtesy of the Dance Theatre of Harlem Archive)

wrote, "The suite of athletic solos and group numbers can be looked at as a camp or as street-corner *Pilobolusing*." A crowd pleaser with massive sex appeal, *Troy Game* required big jumps, breakneck velocity, and high-octane stamina from the dancers.

It may be surprising that the sexual revolutions of the late twentieth century would make a mark on ballet. Most of the DTH repertory, if movie ratings were to be applied, maintained a solid G. However, some DTH ballets were a bit racy, such as Billy Wilson's *Mirage*. *The New York Times* review (3/20/1987) was succinct: "Mr. Wilson's subtitle for *Mirage* is *The Games People Play*, and these are wife-swapping games at a cocktail party . . . The action is now more tightly pulled together than ever, the comic timing to Gary McFarland's score very sharp. Everyone is terrific. Mr. Lowell Smith can do no wrong, and Miss Virginia Johnson, who is very good at jumping up on his shoulder, is now as witty as she is beautiful."

TOP: The Company in Royston Maldoom's *Doina* (Photo: Jack Vartoogian/FrontRowPhotos)
BOTTOM: The Company men in Robert North's *Troy Game* (Photo: Martha Swope, ©NYPL)

Another piece that elicited gasps from the audience was *Wingborne.* Jennifer Dunning of *The New York Times* (2/14/1983): "Loyce Houlton's *Wingborne* . . . doesn't require much but line, fluidity, and utter fearlessness. Yvonne Hall and Lowell Smith had all that as they twined, stretched and balanced through Miss Houlton's pas de deux . . . A lyrical exercise in Soviet-style partnering, its high lifts, with Miss Hall assuming all sorts of unlikely streamlined contortions, had the audience gasping."

Of *Songs of Mahler,* Jennifer Dunning in *The New York Times* (3/27/1993) wrote that the dancers looked at home behind the expansive New York State Theatre proscenium, and that Jessye Norman who sang from the stage was "glittering and glowing. Michael Smuin has created

TOP: The Company in Billy Wilson's *Mirage* (Photo: Martha Swope Associate, Blanche Mackey)
BOTTOM: Yvonne Hall and Lowell Smith in Loyce Houlton's *Wingborne* (Photo: Jack Vartoogian/FrontRowPhotos)

a playful, lyrically romantic romp that demands a high standard of academic dancing." The group of dances was staged by Paula Tracy.

The Kisselgoff category *Bravura* deals with works that display classical artistry and technique. Comparable to what the étude is for a pianist, a bravura piece is very difficult and proves artistic prowess. In ballet, this type of masterful piece can be exhibited through the pas de deux

structure: a couple dance an adagio, the male and female dance variations, ending with a coda. Bravura pieces have been performed throughout DTH's history such as *Le Corsaire* pas de deux and *Don Quixote*, both restaged by Karel Shook. *Sylvia* pas de deux would also fit comfortably in this category.

Early twentieth-century pieces of the modern era that are revived much later are a consideration for the category that Kisselgoff refers to as *Modernist Revival*. They are those mostly created in the 1920s to the 40s. Whether revived or adapted to celebrate nostalgia, reinvent the past, or to mine idioms that are out of style, they revitalize and preserve the essence and artistic gumption from balletic history.

Poulenc described his music for *Les Biches* as a "contemporary drawing room party suffused with an atmosphere of wantonness, which you sense if you are corrupted,

LEFT: Kellye Saunders, Robert Garland, and Leslie Cardona in Michael Smuin's *Songs of Mahler* (Photo: Marbeth, Courtesy of the Dance Theatre of Harlem Archive)

RIGHT: Eddie J. Shellman in Michael Fokine's *Scheherazade* (Photo: Marbeth, Courtesy of the Dance Theatre of Harlem Archive)

but of which an innocent-minded girl would not be conscious." *Les Biches*, or, *The Does*, are beautiful well-heeled females who gather in an aristocratic house. The contrast between Poulenc's modern music and classical dance technique created something new and different. When it was re-staged for DTH by Irina Nijinska (the daughter of Bronislava), labanotation (a way of notating dance) was used. Dancers viewed photographs, film clips and taped interviews with earlier casts. Playing with sexuality, the girl in the blue velvet waist jacket, white gloves, and white tights was danced by Virginia Johnson portraying a "page-boy." With all sexual ambiguities and good notices for the cast, Kisselgoff thought *Les Biches* "delightful."

Walter Terry, in the January 1982 edition of *Playbill*, called *Frankie and Johnny* "rowdy, funny, and unmistakably

LEFT: Eddie J. Shellman (in the air) and Company in Bronislava Nijinska's *Les Biches*, 1983 (Photo: Marbeth, Courtesy of the Dance Theatre of Harlem Archive)

RIGHT: Stephanie Dabney and Mel Tomlinson in Ruth Page's *Frankie and Johnny* (Photo: Marbeth, Courtesy of the Dance Theatre of Harlem Archive)

American." It is wrought from the old "my baby done me wrong" ballad that was based on a true story of a lover's spat gone badly awry. Ruth Page and Bentley Stone created it under the auspices of the Federal Theater's Chicago Works Progress Administration Dance Project. Page was on hand at the end of the DTH rehearsal period for polishing.

Set in a specific time with period costuming, the *Dance Drama* category allows dancers to act and react on stage. A dramatic ballet unveils a story with plot points and characters with episodes of rising action, climax, and falling action. The story, historical or otherwise, is acted with the body and the face, usually dramatized by sets, props, and costumes.

The element of drama runs deep in ballet, and some styles demand more of it than others. In Virginia Johnson's own words: "Dramatic ballets are what I love doing most.

To tell a story, to be a character, to become somebody else through the movement you do is like going on an adventure. You could be distracted by the character from the technical difficulties, and the technical difficulties could be met by fulfilling the character."

The original *A Streetcar Named Desire* was created by Valerie Bettis for the Slavenska-Franklin Ballet Company in 1952, and the 1982 production had been restaged especially for DTH. Mia Slavenska, famous in her homeland, Croatia, and Frederic Franklin in Britain, eventually had their own ballet company in Hollywood. They were the original cast members playing Blanche DuBois and Stanley Kowalski. The production was dedicated to Tennessee Williams in honor of his seventieth birthday. On the first performance of *A Streetcar Named Desire*, the Company received a telegram from Tennessee Williams that read, "Success and all that, but remember the road to success is

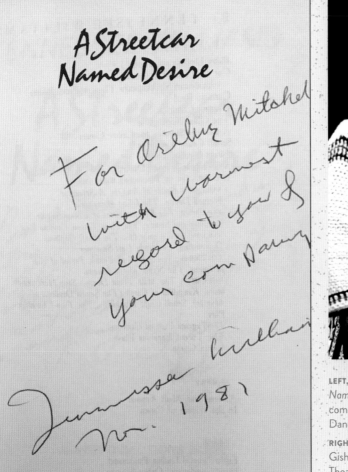

LEFT, TOP AND BOTTOM: Autographed copy of the book, *A Streetcar Named Desire* "For Arthur Mitchell with warmest regard to you and your company, Tennessee Williams, November 1981" (Photo: Courtesy of the Dance Theatre of Harlem Archive)

RIGHT: Choreographer Valerie Bettis, Frederic Franklin, actress Lillian Gish, and Virginia Johnson, c. 1982 (Photo: Courtesy of the Dance Theatre of Harlem Archive)

paved with mad ideas." Anna Kisselgoff said, "The story is very cleverly condensed, . . . in pure dramatic action—as in Stanley's pursuit of Blanche—Miss Bettis and the DTH dancers know how to pack a real wallop." *Streetcar* served as a perfect vehicle for the dramatic talents of Virginia Johnson, Lowell Smith, and the entire ensemble.

Othello dances the dramatic essence of the Shakespeare tragedy—the moment when Iago, the puppeteer of death, achieves his manipulations. "Virginia Johnson, as a translucently innocent Desdemona, is another company treasure. She, Sulpicio Mariano, as an oily, insinuating Iago, and Lowell Smith, as a noble but duped Othello, enriched the exciting, gestural drama of John Butler's 1978 Othello set perhaps too exactly to Dvořák music," said Barbara Figge Fox, *Trenton Times* (11/16/1983).

In 1892 the infamous Lizzy Borden was tried and acquitted for axing the heads of her father and stepmother in Fall River, Massachusetts. Though a true story, the ballet *Fall River Legend* explores the oppression and turmoil of ordinary living, and the passions that lead to violent resolution, rather than recreating the Lizzy Borden story. Lewis Segal in *The Los Angeles Times* (6/1/1989) gave this review: ". . . the dancers looked most impressive on Tuesday in the familiar production of Agnes de Mille's *Fall River Legend* . . . Certainly the urgent, carefully shaped performances of Virginia Johnson (Lizzie Borden), Cassandra Phifer-Moore (the Stepmother), and Lowell Smith (the Pastor) again reached the heart of De Mille's 1948 dance drama. Some revivals are valuable relics. Some are worthless curios. This one is a living monument."

Donald Williams plays the title role of Othello and Vince Collins as Iago in John Butler's *Othello* (Photo: Marbeth, Courtesy of the Dance Theatre of Harlem Archive)

Working in the studio with Agnes DeMille, a legend, was intense. Johnson says, "she was a dragon lady, but she was wonderful." DeMille prodded everything—the movements, music, dramatics, and the intensity—until it was flawlessly perfect. She demanded the highest respect for the work. Studio time could be unnerving. Johnson recalls: "She had had her stroke and could barely move, but she had this big ring; when she wanted you to stop, she would bang the ring on the mirror."

Fall River Legend, along with *A Streetcar Named Desire*, were the first DTH ballets that shifted into *dance drama* as noted by Kisselgoff, as opposed to "the plotless pure dance Balanchine ballets."

LEFT, TOP: *Left, from top to bottom:* man near piano unknown, Stephanie Dabney, Carol Crawford, Joselli Audain, Theara Ward, Milton Rosenstock, Sally Leland, Agnes de Mille, Tania León, in rehearsal of *Fall River Legend*, c. 1983 (Photo: Courtesy of the Dance Theatre of Harlem Archive)

LEFT, BOTTOM: The Company in Agnes de Mille's *Fall River Legend* (Photo: Jack Vartoogian/FrontRowPhotos)

RIGHT: Donald Williams in a *grande jete* with principal dancer Karlya Shelton being lifted by the Company men in Domy Reiter-Soffer's *Equus: The Ballet*, 1982 (Photo: Jack Vartoogian/FrontRowPhotos)

Equus: The Ballet, was derived from Peter Schaffer's 1973 psychological hit play on Broadway. Themes of ecstasy, magic, religious fervor, love, and fulfillment are explored. Anna Kisselgoff, in the March 1982 Issue of *San Francisco Ballet Magazine*: ". . . it is Mr. Donald Williams again, snorting and stomping as the best-known human horse [Nugget] in Anglo-American drama, who steals the show . . . Lowell Smith danced the role of Martin Dysart the psychologist, D'Artagnan Petty danced the role of Alan Strang, and Karlya Shelton was the stable girl, Jill."

Jerome Robbins' *Fancy Free* had a stellar bond with DTH. With just a few characters and one set, Robbins based his small-cast ballet on the controversial and racy painting *The Fleet's In,* by Paul Cadmus. It depicts rowdiness and bawdiness of navy men at liberty. Told in emotional vignettes, Robbin's masterpiece blended ballet, jazz, and popular styles of dance. It skyrocketed Robbins to fame and fortune.

Robbins wrote Arthur Mitchell a note dated October 16, 1984: "Arthur, *Giselle* was touching and charming! You really <u>should</u> do *Fancy Free* - your company would be a knock-out in it . . . Your kids would be terrific in it. Think it over - love - Jerry." On November 13, 1984 Mitchell responded: "Dear Jerry: Thanks for your note I am so very pleased you liked *Giselle* and appreciate [to] no end your letting me know. I would love to do *Fancy Free*! I agree that it would be terrific for us. Thanks for offering it and we'll stay in touch. Love, Arthur Mitchell."

The New York cast featured Bernard Mclain, Donald Williams, Cubie Burke, Tyrone Brooks, Charmaine Hunter, Christina Johnson, and Sharon Bogan. The production garnered rave reviews from Kisselgoff in *The New York Times* (3/11/1987), "Exuberant! Outstanding!" Jerome Robbins was in the audience.

Ronald Perry, an early company member, also had a stellar bond with *Fancy Free*. After being with DTH for eleven years, he joined ABT and there, in 1982, danced the Robbins masterpiece. Jennifer Dunning in *The New York Times* (4/22/1982) said of him that his, "soaring lyrical elegance was the high point of the evening." He then moved on to dance with Béjart and in 1988 returned to DTH to rejoin the Company. He taught in the School until 2017.

Graduation Ball is set in a Viennese finishing school for girls and concerns the students at graduation. With choreography by Nijinska-trained David Lichine and music by Johann Strauss Jr., it was staged for DTH by Terry Orr. Ballet Russe premiered the original ballet in 1940—a ballet with categorical cross-over.

THIS PAGE: Cubie Burke and Christina Johnson in Jerome Robbins' *Fancy Free*, c. 1987 (Photo: Martha Swope, ©NYPL)
FOLLOWING SPREAD: The Company in front of London's Covent Garden, 1981 (Photo: Catherine Ashmore)

CHAPTER 7

RIDING THE WAVE

The Seasons 1986–1996

You are not a line, not a phrase, not a paragraph,
not a page . . . but a chapter in history.

—*Arthur Mitchell*

Bethania Gomes in Taras's *Firebird* (Photo: EduardoPatino.NYC)

THE TIMES

- 1986: Martin Luther King Day was officially observed for the first time as a national holiday.

- The *Oprah Winfrey Show* began national syndication.

- 1987: The Queen of Soul, Aretha Franklin, was inducted into Cleveland's Rock & Roll Hall of Fame.

- Jennifer Jones became the first African American to be hired as a Rockette at Radio City Music Hall.

- 1988: The First World AIDS Day was celebrated.

- 1989: David Dinkins became the first African American mayor of New York City.

- The Berlin Wall fell.

- 1993: Dr. Mae Carol Jemison became the first African American astronaut.

THE SHOOK LEGACY

The School continued to be the bedrock of DTH. Shook left a firm foundation, especially in terms of curriculum and syllabus. After his death, a special notice was added to the printed programs: "Karel Shook, August 8, 1920 - July 25, 1985, internationally renowned ballet master and co-founder/co-director of Dance Theater of Harlem, was one of the few in the United States to foresee the enormous potential of black ballet dancers and give the training which enabled them to take their rightful place in the dance scene. From his studio came Arthur Mitchell, Alvin Ailey, Carmen de Lavallade, Geoffrey Holder, Billy Wilson, Mary Hinkson, and many others." The legacy that Shook left to DTH was monumental. What he left to the dance world, even more.

Shook had a remarkable sense of humor, but in ballet class he was all business. He was prone to outbursts if the music wasn't right or if a dancer wasn't paying attention. He walked around with a stick, but only to tap a tempo or guide a foot into proper position. Exercises were never complicated, and corrections were precise. In class he kept things very simple. It was all about repetition. Class was intense and built strength. Dancers believed in his methods.

Shook had a deep respect for musicians and had much to say about the keyboard accompanists who played class. To the pianist, for petite allegro, a step that uses music that should be light and snappy, he would shout, "You are killing them, the music is too heavy, change it!" About staff

Arthur Mitchell and Karel Shook (Photo: Courtesy of the Dance Theatre of Harlem Archive)

pianists in general he would say, "To me, the pianist is as important in the class as I am. If the music isn't right, nothing is right, there is no beat. I'm a stickler for a first-rate pianist and her musical choices." The "her" he was alluding to was likely Svetlana Litvinoff.

Litvinoff came to the United States in 1974 from Kiev. She performed throughout the Soviet Union and Europe and served as a dance accompanist for many ballet companies, including NYCB. She and her husband, also a pianist, decided to settle with DTH because Arthur Mitchell had shown them hospitality and took them in when they were young and struggling. Karel Shook took Litvinoff into a recording studio and there produced and published a vinyl LP of piano music for ballet class. During DTH's 50th anniversary Litvinoff celebrated more than 44 years accompanying generations of DTH dancers through their careers.

Dancers who were new to the company after the infamous *Wiz* exodus spent valuable and intense studio time with Shook. Class began at nine o'clock in the morning and the ladies had to wear pointe shoes, even if they never went up on pointe. Shook wanted the dancers to get used to working the shoe. The remainder of the day was spent learning a barrage of ballets. New dancers were not permitted to sit during classes and rehearsals; even stretching was considered resting and was not acceptable. Older dancers reinforced this with wagging heads, raised eyebrows, and glares.

Shook's death left a vacuum in many ways. Not only as founder and sage but also as chief advisor to Mitchell. Many who were involved with DTH in the early years would say that Mitchell was the front man and Shook the behind-the-scenes fixer. After his passing, DTH mourned but continued.

ALLIED ARTS AND MORE

In 1988, in *Smithsonian Magazine*, Arthur Mitchell rhapsodized, "What I'd really like to have, is an international school of the allied arts. I'd bring children from all over the world and call it Noah's 'Art' [sometimes referred to as Noah's "Ark"]. I'd put together a company with these young people and tour the world to show that regardless of race, class, creed, or color, it's the quality of what you do that's important." He often spoke in metaphors: "As I always say, you hit the high C or you don't hit the high C, whatever the color of your skin." Mitchell challenged everyone, from students to faculty to staff members and creators.

In 1987 students performed their first full-length ballet, *The Dancing Princesses*, at Aaron Davis Hall for their spring recital. Nancy Schaffenburg, school director, directed the production. The instructors provided the choreography and Zelda Wynn designed the costumes. DTH master

teacher Darryl Quinton danced the role of the soldier, and Wanda Dryer the witch. In 1990, the school also began participating in dance concerts to benefit the Emergency Fund for Student Dancers.

The Open Houses continued with regularity, still important to rounding out DTH as a local arts institution. In the late 1980s and early 1990s, by then a near 30-year tradition, the programming had evolved with the times: there were fewer fashion shows, more hip-hop and rap, and more appearances of Alvin Ailey students and the Alvin Ailey Repertory Ensemble (now Ailey II).

DTH has always had a relationship with Ailey; dancers and staff have cross-pollinated. In 1989 there was a special Open House performance that reflected the growing public awareness of people with physical or mental challenges. Suleiman Rifai, from Tanzania, a blind dancer with

ARTS EXPOSURE AND DANCING
THROUGH BARRIERS™

IN MARCH OF 1990, CITY CENTER SPONSORED THE YOUNG PEOPLE'S DANCE SERIES.
DTH participated by presenting educational experiences for thousands of public school children throughout the five boroughs of New York City. The end goal was to build next-generation dance audiences.
Likewise, a school outreach program with a significant history was DTH's Arts Exposure Program. It began
in 1974 and continued to evolve into a remarkable and marketable project. Originally it was created to
educate audiences about the world of ballet-theater, but it became much more. For many years, Mitchell would narrate the lecture demonstrations. Later, he would give the reins to Eddie J. Shellman, Sandy
Phifer-Moore, Keith Saunders, Luis Dominguez, Elena Dominguez, and others.

DTH's mission was to always have one hand in educating the public, and the other in dance production.
America has always valued education, and education for those with African heritage in America has always
been found lacking. Segregation, bigotry, inferior schools, gerrymandering, and microaggressions are only
a few of the issues that have hindered the education of African American children. For Mitchell, these
prejudicial barriers could be danced through. In John Gruen's book *People Who Dance*, Mitchell is quoted,
"You might say I am a political activist through dance. . . . The fact is, racism is still very high in this country, and one way to combat it is to follow in the precepts of Gandhi and Dr. Martin Luther King Jr.: face
the oppressor through peaceful means." These issues became even more vivid after the Company's tour
of apartheid South Africa, sparking the title idea for a new program, Dancing Through Barriers™ (DTB),
which originated in 1992. DTH describes the program as "the educational in-house division of DTH."
Scouting new talent was one of the program's valuable side benefits for DTH and its future.

Mitchell would say, "Don't even tell me kids don't want to learn about dance . . . I've seen what they
can do. They dance in the streets. They bop while they're sweeping the stoop. They have energy they
don't know what to do with." DTH became a haven for people to experience and learn dance, not only
the outward expression with the body but how to internalize dance somatically and also cognitively. These
grassroots educational programs and outreach experiences cemented the dance matrix into the collective
consciousness of the larger community.

retinitis pigmentosa, performed. He was from Alvin Ailey and their New Visions Dance Project for blind dancers, helmed by former DTH dancer Wendy Amos.

In 1990, at Howard University's Blackburn Center, Keith Saunders, DTH principal dancer and eventual Company ballet master, curated *Virginia Johnson Dances, Selected Photographs 1970-1990*. The exhibition was dedicated to Michael Scherker, the DTH archivist and founder of Preserve, an organization that gave workshops to arts groups on archival preservation.

The students' education continued to grow and change, as seen in the morphing of the Workshop Ensemble into Dance Theatre of Harlem School Ensemble. The Ensemble was first designed in 1982 to provide professional experience for the most gifted and promising students in the Professional Training Program (PTP). It

Members of one of the many DTH Ensembles, 1994 (Photo: Marbeth, Courtesy of the Dance Theatre of Harlem Archive)

provided entertainment in tristate communities that were without larger cultural venues, and also became a magnet for young choreographers eager to see their work danced. *Newsweek* called the School Ensemble "dazzling," and *The New York Times*, "exuberant." This was also the group that appeared in the Met's production of *Porgy and Bess* and at Lincoln Center's Out of Doors summer series. It also toured the Caribbean.

The practice in ballet of having a second cast waiting in the wings is born out of necessity. Ailey II, ABT II, and the DTH Ensembles are prime examples. Not only do these smaller companies ready the young dance artists to feed into the larger mother company, but they also can serve to fill the bill on side engagements, or "run-outs." At DTH "an ensemble" could be a cadre of Company members, students, preprofessional, or a mixture thereof. Mitchell championed the fluidity of mixing talent levels—it gave Mitchell the occasion to see what a dancer could do in performance, and it provided dancers the opportunity to prove their mettle.

BALANCHINE AND DTH

DTH's leg up for performing Balanchine's repertoire was Arthur Mitchell. He had witnessed firsthand "Mr. B" give, rehearse, and fine-tune the choreography, especially in pieces like *Agon* that he created just for Mitchell. Of the more than 400 ballets he created, Balanchine gave Mitchell a few for his young company. He knew Mitchell's mission. He knew his goals. He knew what Mitchell's company was ready to do.

DTH had several of Balanchine's works in its repertoire, but after Balanchine died, acquiring rights from the Balanchine Trust became more complicated and expensive. The trust insisted that the *répétiteur*, a former NYCB dancer chosen by Balanchine to "protect" the piece, cast, stage, and rehearse the ballet before its premiere. At times Mitchell disagreed with how a certain movement was being set by the *répétiteur*, especially those in which he originated a role, like *Agon*. It was not unusual for the *répétiteur* to have a version that they understood to be the original. There could be multiple versions of the choreography, but it wasn't necessarily true that the *répétiteur* had the "original" steps, only the version they experienced. Mitchell would remember Balanchine's motivations and hand them on to his progeny, sometimes reverting steps after the *répétiteur* had left. When the trust's representatives would come back to see the work, it is likely that they recognized the changes. Mitchell was treading on thin ice. However, he knew that steps without meaning or intent are just steps. This was an important part of the DTH style—there was never to be moving just for movement's sake, whether it was Balanchine's or anyone else's choreography.

Bessie Schönberg

BESSIE SCHÖNBERG, A RENOWNED COMPOSITION TEACHER FROM SARAH LAW-
rence College, caught the attention of Martha Graham and joined her company around 1929. She
danced in *Heretic* (1929) and *Primitive Mysteries* (1931). Her career was cut short due to a knee injury.
She shifted her focus from dancing to teaching, earning her degree from Bennington College. Schönberg began developing her own teaching style and became a highly influential figure in the study of
dance composition in higher education. Her innovative pedagogy purported that students who end-
lessly copied dance steps were not able to develop or understand their own unique way of moving. Her
reach went beyond the classroom. Many of her students went on to become prominent choreographers. In honor of Schönberg, the Bessie Award was established in 1983 by David White at New York
City's Dance Theater Workshop. She is known for saying, "the only thing dance should never be is
dull." In June of 1986, Schönberg directed and taught a series of workshops in choreography at DTH.
From this emerged new works in progress by six featured artists: Ron Alexander, Gail Kachadurian,
D'Juan McCrary, Walter Rutledge, Rachel Sekyi, and Hector Tello. Deborah Jowitt of the *Village
Voice* called her "a gardener of dance" blessed with "a champion green thumb."

Left to right: faculty member Mette Spaniardi, Bessie Schönberg, and dancer Lee Edwards, 1984 (Photo: Marbeth,
Courtesy of the Dance Theatre of Harlem Archive)

THE 1992 RENOVATION

Planning began on a major renovation and construction of a new addition to the DTH studios. A capital campaign was launched and solicited throughout 1993 for the 25th anniversary, celebrated in 1994. Through the kind donations of individuals and corporations, the property on 152nd Street was transformed into the Everett Center for the Performing Arts, named in 1993 after two major gifts from Edith Everett and her late husband, Henry. During the reconstruction, the School, Company, and administrative offices were moved temporarily to the Dalton School's Athletic Facility; the grant development office and marketing offices were moved temporarily to 30th Street in midtown Manhattan.

Studios one and two on the first-floor street level were not changed, though they had received sprung wooden floors over the years. An elevator was added, as well as a staircase allowing access to a new studio located on the third floor. It contains a catwalk observation deck reminiscent of the audience deck at the old studio in the Church of the Master basement. Second-floor offices outside studio three were added for marketing and development. Studio four was supposed to be the Company's main rehearsal space; oddly, it never happened. Studio three remained the Company's main space. Arthur Mitchell's office was decked out with a beautiful wooden spiral staircase from an old church pulpit and a private restroom with shower. The fire escape outside studio three that served as a smoking lounge was removed.

The bylaws of DTH wisely called for a library and archive to be maintained. The space opposite the elevator on the second floor was used for such, as well as for occasional music lessons, and housed a rich collection of books on dance, some very rare. Bequeathed initially from Shook and Mitchell's collections, many books were gifts and donations. It was a circulating library on the old Dewey decimal system maintained meticulously by volunteers and later by archivists. Handsome rosewood bookcases were installed to hold the collection.

TOP: The Arthur Mitchell weathervane on top of Dance Theatre of Harlem Studios (Photo: Robert Garland)

BOTTOM: Arthur Mitchell in the original photograph (Photo: Martha Swope, ©NYPL)

The basement was renovated, housing new dressing areas, company showers, two new bathrooms, a physical therapy room, a classroom, seating for waiting parents, and an extra room that eventually became an archival space. The sugar on top of the entire renovation was a weathervane perched on the northwest corner of the roof in the shape of a ballet dancer in a *pas de chat*. The figure is actually Arthur Mitchell and was designed from a photograph by Martha Swope. Later, the design image was used as the DTH logo. The vane turns with the wind.

THE VISUAL

There was a great amount of guesting out every year, where Company dancers would be cast in roles for the *Nutcracker* or other ballets. Guesting was an opportunity to get away and experience a new dance atmosphere during off times, and to make additional income. It was also revitalizing to dance with another company in new roles, in other ballets. Dancers had to obtain permission from Mitchell, which he granted unless there was a conflict with DTH performances. Some requests for guesting came through the front office, but most often dancers would find their own work. Mitchell advised dancers to never accept less than a certain amount of remuneration when performing as guests. He set a high bar, and the fees were substantial. He told dancers to ask for what they were worth. In this regard, he was on the side of the dancers looking after them as artists.

In 1991, the Royal Ballet's *Chance to Dance* and DTH's Arts Exposure Program joined forces for a historic collaboration to introduce more children of multicultural background to classical ballet and the allied arts. Anthony Dowell was the artistic director. In conjunction with the Royal Ballet's education department, the programming included lecture demonstrations, school matinee performances, and workshops given by dancers, musicians, makeup artists, and wardrobe personnel. Each year approximately 50 children were awarded scholarships. Dancers from DTH had the opportunity to perform as principal guest artists with the Royal Ballet in *Agon*, *Giselle*, and Peter Wright's *Nutcracker*. Through the years DTH sent artists including Christina Johnson, Ronald Perry, Eddie J. Shellman, Virginia Johnson, Judy Tyrus, and Donald Williams. Christina Johnson and Ronald Perry were the first dancers of African American heritage to appear with the Royal Ballet since Johaar Mosaval, a South African, was made full-time Company member in 1974.

When booked for the *Nutcracker* at the Royal Ballet in London, DTH dancers were asked to wear blond wigs and pink tights to fit into the production. Christina Johnson remembered, "When they showed us their wigs for us, we literally said, 'Oh no, that's not going to work.' You should have seen Ronald's face . . . They made new ones for us." The knotty issue of a person with deep-brown skin tone having to wear a blond wig brings to the surface many assumptions, one being that because of tradition, production designers never had to be concerned with multiracial casting. Another assumption is the nagging issue that the performers need to look uniform for the stage "picture." The flesh-toned tights that DTH dancers wore were not always welcome and became a lost battle with some artistic directors, who were not ready to switch from what was traditional to flesh tones.

In a like manner, issues of color also surfaced at home. Geoffrey Holder thought that Euro-American Joseph Cipolla did not blend in with the other dancers, so he was asked to darken his makeup on his face and body.

The notion of dancers appearing "out of place" is a

thorny issue for artistic directors and causes much damage and pain for dancers. When skin tone rather than dance talent is a deciding factor, the result is segregant protectionism—and the justifications range from ridiculous to blatantly bigoted. When the Metropolitan Opera's prima ballerina Janet Collins auditioned for De Basil at Ballet Russe, De Basil said he would have to create a particular role for her or whiten her face with paint. Russell Markert, who formed the New York City Rockettes in 1925, would not let his performers get suntanned because they would "look colored," the justification being that there should be "mechanistic conformity, fraternity, and cooperative spirit; they're supposed to be mirror images." His successor, Violet Holmes, in 1985 declared "The Rockettes are a precision line, and they are supposed to be mirror images onstage. One or two black girls in the line would definitely distract." This is justification by tradition—reiterating former policy and hiding behind historical rhetoric.

Other reasons blamed the "art" itself. George Balanchine: "I don't want to see two Japanese girls in my Swan Lake. It's not right. It's not done for them. It's like making an American blond into a geisha. It's a question of certain *arts* being things unto themselves. Japanese *art* is one thing; Chinese *art* is another. You cannot change what's inherent in a particular *art* form. As for my critics, these people . . . it's not their business to dictate to other people . . . They can say that a dancer is no good, but they cannot tell me what I should do." (It is ironic that Balanchine, in the ballet *Bugaku*, chose multiethnic dancers to portray Japanese women and men, and doubly ironic that Arthur Mitchell had performed the lead at NYCB, *and* that it was staged for DTH.)

Often it is heard that African American parents are resistant to their children spending 15 years in training to become a ballet dancer. This resistance may be contingent on affordability in the vicious cycle of poverty, but many DTH dancers did begin their training in childhood. Another misconception is that dancers of African American heritage start later, abandon ballet, and go on to modern or jazz.

Joseph Cipolla admiring his makeup with Donald Williams, 1980 (Photo: Marbeth, Courtesy of the Dance Theatre of Harlem Archive)

ON TELEVISION

DTH's television exposure continued throughout the 1980s and 1990s, with *A Streetcar Named Desire* airing in 1986 as part of PBS's *Dance in America* series. The production was subsequently nominated for three Emmy awards. In December 1987 *Creole Giselle* aired on NBC starring Virginia Johnson and Eddie J. Shellman. The following year *Creole Giselle* won first prize for the best TV production of a classical ballet at the first Grand Prix de Video, Nîmes, France.

Another new adventure for DTH was the release of a commercial VHS recording in 1989. The Company traveled to Aarhus, Denmark, to film *The Beloved*, *Troy Game*, *Fall River Legend*, and *John Henry* at Danmarks Radio Studios. Filming in Denmark was less expensive than filming in the States, and the studios were on the way to Norway, where the Company would be performing.

TOP: Arthur Mitchell with Zoe and Elmo (Photo: © 2021 Sesame Workshop®, Sesame Street®, All Rights Reserved.)
BOTTOM: The Company filming *Giselle* in Aarhus, Denmark, 1987 (Photo: Courtesy of the Dance Theatre of Harlem Archive)

In the 26th season of *Sesame Street*—the educational children's program created by Sesame Workshop, then known as the Children's Television Workshop—Arthur Mitchell and dancers from the Company and School appeared in several segments choreographed by Robert Garland. The pieces titled "Ruthie Wants to Join Dance Theatre of Harlem," "A Home in the Sky," and "None Some All" aired in episodes starting on January 3, 1995, and were later reused as inserts. This television exposure harmonized with the DTH mission of outreach and education, and further branded DTH as an American treasure, not only in the continental USA but also overseas, where it aired for over a decade.

THE MONEY PIT, LAYOFFS, AND CANCELLATIONS

Ballet companies are terribly expensive to maintain financially, as almost all of them are nonprofit and rarely make in ticket sales what it costs to break even. Salaries, costumes, sets, insurance, travel, and advertising incur considerable expenses, not to mention hiring a full symphony orchestra. Producing dance has come a long way from simply rehearsing a couple of ballets, renting a theatre, placing an ad, and watching the audience appear. Arts organizations go through high and low business cycles as others do, riding the waves of economic variables. DTH was destined to do the same.

In 1990, DTH underwent corporate restructuring. Faced with a $1.7 million deficit, DTH was forced to cancel its New York season and lay off dancers, technicians, and administrative staff for a six-month period. Mitchell bemoaned that for artistic directors, so much energy goes into fundraising and administration that their "burning desires are dampened." He also felt that "Everyone else thinks someone else should be doing the funding." Dolores Barclay of the *Denver Post* (2/2/1990) posited that "a decline in funding due to the economy, the mergers-and-acquisitions phenomenon and to a change in priority in some companies who now have an emphasis on the environment, education, and social causes at the expense of the arts." American Express and the Lila Wallace-Reader's Digest Fund stepped forward to fund DTH's debt reduction. Company classes and rehearsals began in the fall and touring resumed in January 1991. At a press conference for the grants, Mitchell snuck in the comment that he wanted to "secure a second base in a city like Washington, DC, for instance." He seized on the opportunity in case any fish wanted to bite.

Mitchell and the board of directors responded to the deficit with increased efforts to enlarge corporate support and strengthen their African American audience base. Three keystones were mentioned in restructuring: the quality of dance onstage, the quality of the school, and the quality of the social mission of cultural diversity. "Quality" was a business buzzword. The thinking was that quality gave value to a product or service, and profits would trickle down. DTH organized itself into seven departments: administration, finance, marketing, development, music, production, and school. The restructuring paid off. In 1994 DTH completed a $6 million expansion and renovation project, doubling classroom and administrative space, confirming the DTH commitment to providing access to the disciplined training necessary for a career in classical ballet.

However, financial problems continued. In February 1997, the Company was frozen by a three-week dancers' strike. The dancers' issues concerned scheduling: an extra hour of work had been added between breaks, rehearsal time had been added between matinee and evening performances, and rehearsals were called on days off. Another issue was the use of "floaters," dancers who were not DTH apprentices and not union dancers but were considered to be "receiving technical instruction." The final agreement included a two-year contract and a 5 percent salary increase.

THE DIGITAL AGE

The digital age began a new era in communications. Though basic, expensive, and nowhere near as powerful as today's iPads and iPhones, early computers, such as the IBM PC2, became the workhorse for many arts organizations worldwide. In 1986 DTH received major gifts from the Aaron Diamond Foundation, the Robert Wood Johnson Jr. Charitable Trust, and New York City Department of Cultural Affairs for a new computer system. Though word processors were little more than advanced typewriters, they allowed office workers to easily correct all their mistakes and cut and paste before printing the final copy. A real plus for arts groups was the feature known as *mail merge*, whereby after inputting hundreds of names and addresses and saving them on floppy magnetic disks, one could "merge" the data onto mailing labels and with the click of a return (the mouse was invented later), labels would spew forth from dot-matrix printers to be peeled and stuck on envelopes, flyers, and letters announcing performances, galas, or solicitations for funds—all by direct mail. Envelope-stuffing parties in the DTH development office would be held with all hands on deck. This group mailing phenomenon brought in audiences; group sales brought in groups, and in-house audience development was born. Only 20 years later, social media would become the new means of reaching people globally.

FRIENDS AND FUNDRAISING

Though computers became a major tool in all aspects of theatrical production, individuals who support the arts are still the bulwark. Through the years many groups were organized to support DTH. In 1982, the Friends of DTH was formed, unique in that it was powered by artists, writers, and photographers. One of their major achievements was publishing and selling a Fluxus-type art book, *Not Black Tie . . . Black Tights!* (1990) with Procter & Gamble as a corporate sponsor.

Annual arts budgets are mercurial because expenses exceed grants, donations, gifts, and ticket sales, which are unpredictable. In the 1980s DTH, like many other arts organizations, began to survey their audience for the purposes of market research and targeted marketing. Competition for expendable income was fierce. DTH could count on its large mailing list of family and fans, but board burnout, foundation grant fluctuation, and inconsistent ticket sales resulted in sporadic layoffs of Company members and staff. In 1995 the Company downsized from 52 to 36 members. This would happen again and again.

HIV/AIDS

In October of 1987, the AIDS Memorial Quilt went on display on the National Mall in Washington, DC, and AIDS became the first global epidemic ever debated on the floor of the United Nations. The jolt of HIV/AIDS for a young generation meant that love and sex equaled death. It placed a tragic and frightening pall on the entertainment and dance world. Most everyone in the arts knew of someone who died of AIDS. From 1981 to 2015, worldwide, 35 million people died from the disease, and 36.7 million were living with the deadly virus.

On October 5, 1987, DTH participated in *Dancing for Life*, described in the words of legendary choreographer and director Jerome Robbins as "an extraordinary collaboration, unparalleled in the world of dance. The entire New York dance world has come together as a community—and by its dancing, to help the funding for AIDS care, education, and research, express our support for increased activity by the government and public and private institutions involved in AIDS." With Robbins as artistic director, the fundraising evening at the New York State Theater featured 13 celebrated dance companies: Alvin Ailey, American Ballet Theatre, Merce Cunningham, Twyla Tharp, Laura Dean, Elliot Feld, Martha Graham, Joffrey, Lar Lubovitch, Mark Morris, New York City Ballet, Paul Taylor, and Dance Theatre of Harlem. Nancy Reagan was the lead chair. Dr. C. Everett Koop and Elizabeth Taylor, plus a who's who of New York celebrities, were in attendance.

Dancers and dance companies throughout the world, including those working behind the scenes, were affected by the epidemic, and DTH was not excluded. The layers of sorrow and sadness ran deep for all who perished, as well as their partners, family members, and coworkers. A dancer's body is their performing instrument and HIV/AIDS would destroy this most sacred of musical instruments. The disease did not discriminate. Dancers Responding to AIDS (DRA), founded in 1991 as a subprogram of Broadway Cares/Equity Fights AIDS, was one of many organizations that have raised millions of dollars for research and cures. Not until the second decade of the twenty-first century would those diagnosed with the disease be able to live a long life. The gay rights movement, America's success story of political activism, coupled with this profound cause, brought the LGBTQ community to the forefront of the American consciousness.

In 1989 Anthony Turney was appointed DTH executive director. A British expat and a nonprofit arts tycoon, he was responsible in 1996 for the final assembly of the AIDS Memorial Quilt on the National Mall, 42,000 panels seen by over a million pilgrims.

COMPANY TOURS

The global age for DTH was first characterized by the great number of performances on continental tours in the late 1980s and early 1990s. The year 1989 marked the 20th Anniversary National Tour, sponsored by the Chase Manhattan Bank, taking the Company to ten US cities. DTH also performed at venues in Provence, Tuscany, Spoleto, the Amalfi Coast, and at the London Coliseum, the Salzburg Festival, the Danish Aarhus Festival, and the 144-year-old Tivoli Festival. The Company performed for the first time on the continent of Africa in Egypt. There were performances in Alaska and the contiguous 48 states. Company tours to the continent of South America included Buenos Aires, Córdoba, Caracas, and Rio de Janeiro, all to sold-out audiences. The programming was packed to the gills with dependable winners: *Dougla*, *Voluntaries*, *Serenade*, *Le Corsaire*, *Troy Game*, *The Four Temperaments*, and the trustworthy *Firebird*. The Company was met with enthusiastic reviews almost everywhere it performed. But the most important global summiting for DTH were tours of the Soviet Union in 1988 and South Africa in 1992.

During these years, the United States was exporting democracy, and DTH was a part of the product, the perfect panacea: cultured, beautiful, entertaining fine art, all presented through the multicultural lens. DTH modeled cultural tolerance.

The pursuit of equality in ballet, the pursuit of cultural inclusion, depends on a bidirectional flow of awareness. The artists are aware of what barriers must be broken, and the establishment allows entry, acknowledgment, and acceptance. Bias and tradition run deep. The Russian, Egyptian, and South African tours were historic artistic and political events. In the birthplace of Russian ballet, where the audience was brass tough, they viewed DTH dancers in brown tights seamlessly performing classical ballet and other styles—a historic first and an extraordinary feat. In South Africa, some had never seen classical ballet, let alone a full multicultural Company dancing on pointe.

Each foreign country has their own brand of indigenous traditional dance, and idea of classicism. Professor Tarek Hassan, chair of the National Cultural Center of the Cairo Opera House, said, "We must all learn the win-win principle along the pluralistic road to growth and development for all, whatever their background, color or abode. We must learn to be able to link to all the great heritage of mankind each in our original ways without being excluded because of some illegitimately forced disadvantage." In essence, resistance to diversity undoubtedly obstructs the pursuit of equality.

THE SOVIET TOUR

The 1988 Soviet Tour included 32 performances of fourteen works in five weeks. A support committee was formed, made up of 26 megastars. From the theatre were Leonard Bernstein, Hal Prince, and Cy Coleman; from sports were Julius Erving, Magic Johnson, and Martina Navratilova; from the movies were Sidney Lumet and Kitty Carlisle Hart; and from TV Bryant Gumbel. Heather Watts, Suzanne Farrell, and Agnes de Mille gave guidance from the dance world.

Life on the road for a ballet company has its challenges—life on the road in Russia, even more. The Company toured with 44 dance artists, 13 workshop ensemble dancers, and 24 personnel in production, totaling 81 individuals. Black baseball warm-up jackets with the tour logo embroidered were worn by Company members.

The amenities in the hotels were subpar: hotel rooms painted brown with cigarette stench, brown running water that never cleared (and had an odor), and a "control room" instead of a concierge or meeting suite for the Company. The Company bunked in the Rossiya Hotel, which had 3,000 rooms. (The giant brutalist rectangle of concrete was demolished in 2006.) The Company would take their meals in cavernous empty banquet halls that could accommodate thousands. The *plat du jour* for most of the tour was potato, cabbage, caviar, and chicken kiev. Salads, a mainstay for dancers, were rare. Most everyone was either in the state of chronic hunger or ill from foreign microbes. Water and candy bars were shipped from Finland and the US. Dancers would wander from room to room asking their workmates if they had anything consumable and safe. Shopping sprees were less than ideal. But blue jeans from America were rare and in high demand, causing Russians to purchase them on the black market for hundreds of dollars. By tour's end, as they were paid in rubles, the Company had thousands left over that had to be spent—they were worthless in any other country. DTH folk returned with stuffed suitcases, trading their blue jeans for dishes, teacups, wine, Matryoshka dolls, and contemporary Russian art.

This was still the Russia of Stalin and Nikita Khrushchev, of spies, the KGB, and state-owned empty shops with long lines for necessities. Citizens had to be careful what was said in conversation as not to offend the party line or party members, for fear of being snitched on and possibly facing arrest. Company members were told to never walk around alone.

This was the period of Gorbachev's perestroika (meaning "listen"), or interior party reform; and glasnost (meaning "openness"), or exterior diplomacy. It was the beginning of the end of Cold War Iron Curtain communism; a mere seven years later US President Ronald Reagan would say, "Mr. Gorbachev, tear down that wall!" But old socialist ways were not yet changed when DTH appeared as the first and only ballet company to be selected to represent the United States under President Reagan's Soviet Exchange Initiative.

The Company played to sold-out audiences at the Kirov Opera House, Leningrad; Palace of Congresses Kremlin Theater, Moscow; and the Paliashvili Theatre, Tbilisi. There was a rare standing ovation at the Kirov. First Lady Nancy Reagan served as honorary hostess on opening night in Moscow, which was attended by President Mikhail Gorbachev and his wife, Raisa, with Mrs. Gorbachev returning the next night for a second performance.

The Palace of Congresses Theatre in the Kremlin was a glass and marble rectangle that seated 6,000 people. It had been built in 1961. As the Company rehearsed onstage, they would notice elderly "babushki" women sweeping the stage—their state job. There was no concern that they would get in the way, as the stage was the size of a football field. Dancer's entrances had to be retimed, as the distance from the wings to beginning position was a long hike that took more time and double the energy.

Because of very little advertising by the presenting organization, Goskontzert, the 6,000-seat house was not filled on the first night. But by the weekend, word of mouth had spread like wildfire and there were mobs around the theatre. Performances were sold out. The people of Moscow had not seen a performance of a foreign ballet company in 10 years, so there was a hunger for something new and different.

Audience etiquette in the Soviet Union came with its own challenges. Dress rehearsals were nearly full of people who could not get tickets for a scheduled performance. Audience members would enter through backstage entrances and find their way to a free seat, or just sit in the aisles. At regular scheduled performances, it was not unusual that the ticket gates were rushed, and people would enter without tickets. When the house lights went down, the people that had tickets in the upper balconies would stream down en masse to find better seats in the orchestra, where fights would break out over seat ownership. At performances after *The Four Temperaments*, the audience signaled its admiration with the Russian style of clapping, all in unison quarter notes at walking tempo. Vociferous applause drenched the Company after the curtain came down on *Firebird*. Shouts of "Bis!" could be heard.

Although DTH's diplomatic mission to the Soviet Union was to perform, schmoozing with ballet notables was a valuable perk (when backstage visitors were not covertly seeking information). Members of the Kirov Ballet interacted with DTH, sat in on rehearsals, and were astounded. They spoke of the velocity, exactitude, and accuracy of the dancers' meticulous technique. Julia Kazlova, a student at the Moscow School of Ballet, said, "These are techniques and talents we have never seen."

Mitchell took a carload of staffers to visit Balanchine's brother, Andrei Melatonovitch Balanchivadze. Judy Tyrus and Eddie J. Shellman were the dancers invited to go along. Russian hospitality, which meant serving everything in one's kitchen, was on show in an apartment that was filled with an odd assortment of not-quite-antiques, piano benches, and shaky chairs. Andrei's son and concert pianist Georgi Balanchivadze entertained by playing a Ravel tarantella.

No doubt, the DTH Soviet tour of 1988 was a huge success. DTH was inducted into the Kirov Museum's Hall of Fame. When asked by David Berreby in a February 21, 1990, interview in *Newsday* if American dance is better appreciated outside America, Mitchell responded that "over there the arts are an integral part of their lives, not dessert, not a little something extra, they understand that you've got to feed the soul."

The Company and staff in front of Saint Isaac's Cathedral in Leningrad, Russia. (Photo: Courtesy of the Dance Theatre of Harlem Archive)

EGYPT

It was pride that carried the Company to Cairo, Egypt, in 1990. The Main Hall of the National Cultural Center Opera House in Cairo is the largest, most beautiful, and most sophisticated of all theatres in Egypt and designed to seat 1,200. On the tour, both writer Stephanie Stokes Oliver and photographer Dwight Carter from *Essence* magazine traveled with the Company. The opportunity to travel to Cairo, Egypt, has a certain cachet much different than that of any other place on earth. That it is thought to be one of the first ever civilizations; that it left to generations its funereal monuments; that it bequeathed its hieroglyphic history in antiquity, so preserved, supersedes all travel expectations. Though very well received by Cairenes with

Dancers Richard Witter and Yvonne Hall in Geoffrey Holder's Dougla costumes at the Pyramid of Giza, 1990 (Photo: Dwight Carter)

DTH's steely repertoire including *Dougla*, *Firebird*, and *Serenade*, this tour would be remembered by some dancers for the allure of amazing sights and experiences. Dancers as subject are a chance for photographers to create art with perfect bodies, costumes, makeup, lights, a background, even a scenario. Setting up shots or shooting on location at a live performance can be artistically exhilarating, but static-pose shots are equally immersive for the photographer. Dwight Carter decided to take some DTH dancers to Giza to shoot in front of the great pyramids.

It was a Company day off, but six dancers knew that if they had not taken advantage of the opportunity, they would never have the chance to see the pyramids. In *Dougla* and *Firebird* costumes, Yvonne Hall, Richard Witter, Judy Tyrus, Lorraine Graves, Donald Williams, and Cassandra

Phifer-Moore awoke at 4:00 a.m. to be on the Giza Plateau before sunrise, as it was cooler then and the sunlight still mild. Carter set up the quintessential shots with expert foresight. Because ballet toe shoes don't do well in soft sand, he brought a wooden board that he masked with some rocks, so the dancers had a firm foundation on which to pose in their ballet shoes. He also had the brilliant idea to hire a camel to walk back and forth in the background between the dancers and the Great Pyramid of Giza.

Alex Haley, author of *Roots*, said, "It's significant that Dance Theatre of Harlem has come here for its first African tour because this is the place of the ultimate roots. I find myself filled with pride that the company is here, because this reminds us that our history didn't begin in cotton fields. The monuments in Egypt have Negroid features and have been here for thousands of years. The Nubians here are velvet black. That has to give you Pride."

THE SOUTH AFRICAN TOUR

It was announced on July 21, 1992, in the lobby of the United Nations that in September, the Dance Theatre of Harlem, with a Company of 52 dancers and a complete production and film crew, would appear in South Africa for five weeks. Twelve ballets would be performed. The tour had been made possible by the African National Congress (ANC), Pan Africanist Congress, the City of Johannesburg, the Market Theatre, the Ministry of Education, and the United States Information Service.

The immediate mandate was to perform at the unveiling of the newly refurbished Civic Theatre in Johannesburg. The invitation came formally and logistically from the Market Theatre, and more specifically from its artistic director, John Kani, the Tony Award-winning actor, director, and playwright who had seen DTH in 1975. The *New Nation* (9/4/1992) stated, "John Kani's career has been predicated on articulating the hopes and dreams of his people without compromising the division between progressive activity and apartheid stranglehold on cultural self-expression." Kani worked with the Johannesburg City Council to bring in DTH. South Africa's Nedbank would be a huge sponsor, among others stateside, including the City of New York and the Rockefeller Foundation. The tour costs totaled approximately $1.5M in risk capital. (The South African press reported that back-channel funding sources remained murky.)

Only two years earlier, the last South African apartheid president, F. W. De Klerk, put an end to discriminatory laws, lifted the ban on anti-apartheid groups like the African National Congress, and released civil rights leader and activist Nelson Mandela, who had served 27 years in Victor Verster Prison. The dismantling of apartheid occurred between 1990 and 1993, and according to Mitchell, it was agreed upon by all parties that in the hot political climate, DTH would remain neutral in all things.

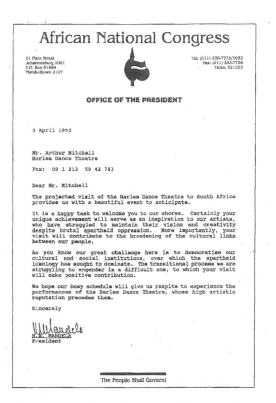

Letter of affirmation and welcome from Nelson Mandela to Arthur Mitchell, 1992 (Photo: Courtesy of the Dance Theatre of Harlem Archive)

Copies of warm endorsement letters were handed out at press conferences from Nelson Mandela and the Pan Africanist Congress Secretary for Culture and Sport. Mayor David Dinkins of New York City and Representative Charles Rangel also sent letters of affirmation.

Two groups from DTH advanced the Company to South Africa. The first group included Donna Walker-Kuhne, marketing director, who made the long trek with the Company's tech crew. Logistics for the performances and more than 200 workshops and classes with media coverage had to be arranged. From scheduling, photo shoots, television, and live production to props, equipment, and housing, everything had to be prepared in a working white paper for Mitchell's arrival. When asked about her feelings before arriving in South Africa, Walker-Kuhne said, "I felt a huge sense of responsibility. Diversity had to be in every aspect of the tour. The audience had to have access to the shows. I was very happy to represent DTH. In our first meeting there, full of white people, there was hostility. I had to use soft power to make them come around to think that it was their idea. I was the first black person to integrate the theatre; to walk across the stage, and when I did the technicians stood up (in shock). It made me sad. By the end of the first week, they were serving tea to me. The dynamics had changed."

The second group taught master classes, conducted workshops, and traveled to townships to lecture and engage with locals. The group included Frederic Franklin, Arthur Mitchell, Augustus van Heerden, Dean Anderson, Felicity de Jager, Cassandra Phifer-Moore, Virginia Johnson, Laveen Naidu, and Robert Garland.

Mitchell was adamant that DTH was there not to just perform, but more importantly to showcase their first-rate package of lecture demonstrations, master classes, and workshops. These educational experiences would expand into many South African townships. There would be visits to Mamelodi, Atteridgeville, Bosmont, and Soweto.

Production workshops in wardrobe practices and costume design were led by Frederic Franklin, who was 78 at the time.

In his South Africa workshops, Franklin gave the students his famous three keys to being a successful ballet dancer: "You must have the attack, the will, and the wanting." He also gave the keys for a good teacher: "You wait (observe), then give." And lastly, "Style is of the essence."

The two objectives of the tour were to demonstrate the level of excellence and cooperative spirit that can be achieved when individuals and especially children are given equal opportunity to excel, and to share world-renowned artistry with all members of South African society by providing educational outreach programs for children and professional aspiring artists. In the first speech of the tour, Arthur Mitchell said, "We at Dance Theatre of Harlem believe that the Arts embody an inherent healing power, and serve as a source of inspiration to all people speaking a universal truth of oneness . . . not division . . . I've come to give and to learn."

Alongside goodwill and benevolence, there was controversy. The embers of political unrest were still hot, and the fire from dismantling apartheid still flamed. DTH was met with two sorts of controversies in South Africa: those that dealt with money and those with communication.

Local arts groups felt slighted on both counts. The September 17, 1992, edition of the *South Newspaper* reported that "although reluctant to be quoted, some incensed local dance companies labeled DTH's attitude toward them as presumptuous. The local dance groups were enraged when they were not consulted about the Company working with them. There was no consultation on DTH having workshops with them, nor on the type of workshops they may have wanted." The Pact Dance Company director Esther Nasser posed the commonly asked question: Why did the Dance Alliance sanction the visit of a foreign company at such a high cost when local artists, and the

Alliance itself, were in desperate need of funds? When the Dance Alliance met at the Market Theatre in response, they said they were told that plans for DTH workshops were already under way. In the October 8, 1992, edition of the *Star Tonight!*, dance critic Adrienne Sichel reported there were still moans and groans about high ticket prices and the costs involved, but felt the teaching programs in the townships were invaluable. DTH's presence aimed to "bridge the cultural divide in South Africa." However, Sichel did mention that the press was not treated with exactly professional procedure. Program changes and cast changes were not given to the press and the information that was provided was confusing. This was unacceptable for a visiting company.

The cost of the refurbishment of the Civic was reported in 1992 at $66M. The center itself contains four venues including the theatre, named in 2001 the Nelson Mandela Theatre.

According to theatrical agent Yvonne Asherson, some in theatre thought that the spending was an "iniquitous extravagance at this time when the entertainment industry in South Africa is in crisis." She wrote that "a petition to

DTH conductors Tania León and David La Marche working with South African drummers (Photo: Marbeth, Courtesy of the Dance Theatre of Harlem Archive)

protest against the action has been drawn up. So, they are giving dance classes to South Africans, big deal. There are hundreds of dance companies in South Africa. We also have thousands of actors out of work, and dancers unable to keep body and soul together."

DTH needed to reach out to the local scene. The Company planned to visit 30 communities over four weeks and offered eight apprentice scholarships for dancers to come to New York for three years, with the stipulation that they return to South Africa and work for at least one year.

South Africa was isolated and in need of something new. Theatrical agent Moonyeen Lee in the *Weekly Mail* (8/7/1992) said, "It's not as if this is just a two-bit company. We are so starved for acts of this standard. If we keep stopping everything we'll never improve. We'll never learn anything." The *Star Tonight!* affirmed the notion in their September 9, 1992, edition. Reporting on opening night, "The starving crowd had not seen ballet in five years, it was a tough audience, some thought that *Dougla* was too ethnic and even offensive, the *Four Temperaments* thawed tension, and *Firebird* with Charmaine Hunter drew bravos." But the South African opening night audience sent their own message: there was no standing ovation for the first night performance.

Three dancers in the Company were from South Africa. One, Augustus van Heerden, trained at the University of Cape Town (UCT), but had to leave the country to dance because it was illegal for a citizen of color to appear onstage. The *Morning Star* (9/18/1992) stated, "Our immoral loss was the world's gain as evidenced by Van Heerden's fine-tuned lyricism and finesse in his professional debut on his homeland's stage in *The Four Temperaments*."

The second was Felicity de Jager, who was thrilled at the prospect of dancing with DTH in her hometown. She is also a UCT-trained dancer. She began her training at age six with the City Ballet School and was then

Tonight! (9/18/1992), reported, "Fellow South African Laveen Naidu, a member of the DTH Ensemble, more than holds his own among the stunningly athletic male dancers." The three South African DTH dancers were given wonderful reviews, with the critics assuring their readers that it was not out of patriotic bias.

The most seminal and inspirational occasion for those on the South African tour was meeting Nelson Mandela. The photo of him with the Company is iconic. He attended performances and sat with the people, not in the celebrity box, and without flourish. After the performance he said, "This is one of the most delightful evenings I have enjoyed. I have forgotten all of the troubles I have had in my life." The tour, despite controversy and glitches, was a great success, and John Kani said that the whole experience would usher in cultural freedom. Once again DTH lived out its mission so often stated by Mitchell: "unlike any other company, DTH is charged with three things: artistic, educational, and social empowerment."

recommended to Dei Kruin High School in Parktown. But she was unable to attend the school because of her color. Bernice Lloyd, head ballet mistress, instead coached her in a church hall in Parkview. After much fundraising in de Jager's community, she attended the National Ballet School of Canada in 1985. She was sent to a DTH summer intensive by her modern dance teacher Sylvia Glasser, and the rest is history.

The third DTH dancer with South African roots was Laveen Naidu, a future DTH executive director. The *Star*

LEFT, TOP: *Left to right:* Felicity de Jager, Augustus van Heerden, Winnie Mandela, Della Baeza, and Arthur Mitchell, 1992 (Photo: Marbeth, Courtesy of the Dance Theatre of Harlem Archive)

LEFT, BOTTOM: Felicity de Jager teaching a master class at Bapedi Hall in Soweto (Photo: Marbeth, Courtesy of the Dance Theatre of Harlem Archive)

RIGHT: *Left to right in the front:* Nelson Mandela, Arthur Mitchell, and John Kani, artistic director of the Market Theatre, Johannesburg (Photo: Marbeth, Courtesy of the Dance Theatre of Harlem Archive)

25th Anniversary

The barriers that Dance Theatre of Harlem has broken have been quite historical and that they haven't been broken by anyone else. So, we certainly have carved our place in history. . . . the next twenty-five years have got to be the most exhilarating time because of the foundation that has been laid." So said Donna Walker-Kuhne from the written transcript of "The Aboutness of Dance Theatre of Harlem: The 25th Anniversary: A Conversational Gathering," 2/15/1994, New York Library for the Performing Arts.

The 25th anniversary of Dance Theatre of Harlem celebrated giving audiences around the world the thrill of seeing live ballet while continuing to open the art form to embrace multiculturality. By 1994, Company dancers achieved the uncanny ability to smoothly transition from style to style. The scope and breadth of its vast repertoire ranged from Balanchine to Ailey to Soffer and Smuin. The mainstay ballets like *Dougla*, *Firebird*, and *Giselle* were now more than ten years old and had ripened and matured to perfection. Dancers like Christina Johnson, Charmaine Hunter, Endalyn Taylor, Cassandra Phifer-Moore, Tyrone Brooks, Keith Saunders, Robert Garland, and Augustus van Heerden, who had been dancing in these works for many years, served as role models for the younger

Tyrone Brooks and the Company in Alvin Ailey's *The River* (Photo: Martha Swope , ©NYPL)

dancers who had the privilege to learn newer techniques and approaches. Mitchell felt secure to further explore new theatrical gambits in dance. The Company had arrived, with more to summit.

The Aboutness of Dance Theatre of Harlem: The 25th Anniversary: A Conversational Gathering was a unique event held in February of 1994 to "give voice to memories and reflections on Dance Theater of Harlem's social, educational and artistic mandate; Dancing Through Barriers™; and DTH's birth, growth, and life." It was moderated by DTH's outstanding booking manager and longtime staffer Edward Schoelwer. Held at the Bruno Walter Auditorium at the New York Public Library for the Performing Arts, the audio recording was transcribed and remains a treasured item in the DTH archives.

LEFT: Tai Jimenez and Donald Williams in Michael Smuin's *Medea* 1992 (Photo: Carol Rosegg/Martha Swope Associates, Billy Rose Theatre Division, The New York Public Library)

RIGHT: Donald Williams and Tyrone Brooks in Domy Reiter-Soffer's *Equus* (Photo: Linda Rich Dance Picture Library)

AFTER HOMECOMING

The year 1986 brought a more meager season than that of the prodigious 1985 Met debut and was titled Harlem Homecoming, performed at Aaron Davis Hall on the City College campus, located 15 blocks south of the DTH studios at 137th and Amsterdam Ave. Arrangements were made for patrons to be bused uptown to 137th Street in Harlem from midtown Manhattan via four starting places: Grand Central Station, Columbus Circle, 86th Street, and Park Avenue.

Gordon J. Davis, DTH board president, lawyer, and a former New York City Parks commissioner, penned a telling article for the Harlem Homecoming program titled "Notes from the Dance Theatre of Harlem Boardroom (Or, How Will We Meet the Payroll This Week?)." "Yes, we play the world's great stages from the London Coliseum to the Met. As to the future, no doubt we will close this season with another string of great reviews, hot ticket sales, and looming deficits."

For this Harlem Homecoming season, the Independent School Orchestra (ISO) accompanied *Stars and Stripes* on opening night led by teacher/educator Jonathan Strasser, who played the role of the conductor in the 1980 MGM movie *Fame*. The youngest instrumentalist in the ISO was 10 years old, the oldest 18. This was great experience for the student musicians and an economical choice for DTH. It usually costs a king's ransom to hire a professional symphony orchestra for ballet.

The spring of 1987 brought DTH's 18th season, Harlem Homecoming II. Its 32 performances included the DTH New York City premiere of *Fancy Free*, set to the popular music of Leonard Bernstein, and *Phoenix Rising*.

Phoenix Rising was an enigmatic ballet—part Billy Wilson, part Arthur Mitchell, part Geoffrey Holder, seasoned with an Afrocentric score by Coleridge-Taylor Perkinson. With 35 dancers, it was conceptualized on Martin Luther King Jr.'s notion of leadership. As a triptych work in progress, the joint choreography embodied birth, death, and rebirth. Only part one was ever performed, with African priestesses and the birthing of a male. It exhibited Wilson's haute-revue choreography with Broadway formation patterning and hip-rotating dances. Holder's design featured backdrop graphics from his male nude figure book titled *Adam*, and his costuming featured "Nudity—partial or simulated," according to Kisselgoff in *The New York Times* (3/26/1987). Kisselgoff also hallooed, "Mr. Mitchell's company at its vibrantly elegant best . . . he can be shrewdly theatrical." A future dance scholar might try her hand at finishing this ambitious project, as musicians have tried to complete Mozart's unfinished *Requiem*.

Jerome Robbins (*left*) and Milton Rosenstock (*center*) are having a laugh, with a rehearsal pianist looking on. The inscription is to "Miltie" Rosenstock from Jerome Robbins, 1989 (Photo: Courtesy of the Dance Theatre of Harlem Archive)

In 1988, Martin E. Segal produced the first New York International Festival of the Arts with $8 million in private sponsorship. Arthur Mitchell was commissioned to create and present a ballet, *John Henry*. It premiered that summer at the New York City Center. Often paired with *Billy the Kid*, *John Henry* paid tribute to America's rich folk tradition, the stories that have buried within them the struggles for freedom and justice. Kisselgoff of *The New York Times* (6/30/1988) said that it " . . . roused cheering fans out of their seats during the curtain calls. Mr. Mitchell stayed in the spirit of things by throwing himself into a choreographed clog dance to acknowledge the applause." *Billy the Kid*, another balletic tribute to an American folk hero, choreographed by Eugene Loring with music by

LEFT, TOP: Yvonne Hall and Eddie J. Shellman in Arthur Mitchell's *John Henry* (Photo: Courtesy of the Dance Theatre of Harlem Archive)

LEFT, BOTTOM: Charmaine Hunter in *Polovetsian Dances* from *Prince Igor*, staged by Frederic Franklin, 1988 (Photo: Courtesy of the Dance Theatre of Harlem Archive)

RIGHT: Donald Williams in Eugene Loring's *Billy the Kid* (Photo: Martha Swope, ©NYPL)

Aaron Copland knitted the folk genre into ballet's weft and warp, yet another example of Mitchell's fearless brio. The Company also performed *Polovestsian Dances from Prince Igor*, staged by Frederic Franklin for the festival. This Ballet Russe plotless Fokine mood ballet with the *Kismet* music from the second act of Borodin's opera featured Lorraine Graves as an enchanting princess, and Hugues Magen as a commanding chief warrior.

Other artists contributing to the festival were Pina Bausch, Merce Cunningham, and the Jacques d'Amboise National Dance Institute. It promised "the best music, theater, dance and film of the 20th Century." The festival was produced again in 1991.

The year 1989 marked the ballet company's 20th anniversary. The Company returned to City Center with 54 dancers for a two-week New York season. *Giselle*, danced by Virginia Johnson and Eddie J. Shellman, was revived to glorious reviews.

Appearing at the gala performance was Kitty Carlisle Hart, the *To Tell the Truth* TV diva and wife of famed theatre director and writer Moss Hart; she was also a 20-year veteran of the New York State Council on the Arts. A 20th anniversary gift from Mayor Ed Koch was an inclusion of $2.5 million for DTH in the city budget. A surprise birthday cake was given to Mitchell, with the little school children in the aisles bearing helium balloons.

The year also included a two-week season at the Kennedy Center, and a tour engagement in Dennis Nahat's Cleveland Ballet season. At the time, in their 13th season, the Cleveland Ballet had 38 dancers and a $6 million budget. DTH's presence was of utmost importance since Cleveland Ballet had just initiated their Audience

Eddie J. Shellman and Virginia Johnson in *Giselle* (Photo: Courtesy of the Dance Theatre of Harlem Archive)

Development Task Force aimed at providing dance education and exposure opportunities in Cleveland's Afro-cultural communities, an area of expertise in which DTH was very adept.

The season of 1993 was momentous in many ways. The venue was the prestigious New York State Theater at Lincoln Center, now named the David H. Koch Theatre, flanking the Metropolitan Opera House and Avery Fisher Hall, now called Geffen Hall. Clive Barnes of the *New York Post* (3/18/1993) gave DTH a glowing review as "one of America's greatest companies." He also proclaimed that DTH "has succeeded in making black a primary color of classic ballet—an achievement as much political and sociological as artistic."

Two gala events were held, one in New York City and one in Washington, DC, to stabilize the financial challenges of the previous three years. Jessye Norman received the Emergence Award at the New York Gala.

The Kennedy Center announced an extensive community outreach program for 1993 with DTH, a three-year residency. It included training for 150 Washington-area students from 12 to 17 years of age, eight weeks for 40 advanced students, and summer study with the Company. DTH had performed yearly at the Kennedy Center since 1979.

In May of 1993 there appeared coverage in the *Washington Times* (5/2/1993) of the DTH Gala at the Kennedy Center Opera House. Kevin Chaffee led the social page with the headline "New Faces in the Audience." A quick scan of the bolded names heralded the new age of the African American philanthropist, a list that would expand into the new millennium only seven years later. The roster included Shahara Ahmad-Llewellyn and J. Bruce Llewellyn, General and Mrs. Colin Powell, Ron Brown, Sharon Pratt Kelly, Vernon Jordan, and Edward Perkins. In the new millennium, pro-cultural and African American financiers from Goldman Sachs would join the ranks.

In October of 1995, financial difficulties appeared again, and the Company was downsized from 53 to 36 dancers. There would be a 10 percent reduction in the teaching staff to take care of the 1,300 students. Lee Webb became the interim executive director, and in 1994 DTH had an $8 million budget. The following year there would be a $1 million reduction to get "the house in order." This was not the first time DTH needed to maneuver through financial hardship, and definitely not the last.

During this time, the concept of the Company as *family* began to change at DTH. Though the dancers were very close, by the beginning of the new millennium many of the veteran lead dancers had retired, leaving a polished and talented Company in their stead. This younger brood would be the last Company to be selected and coached by Arthur Mitchell. Until 2004, the Company performed DTH's large oeuvre-defining ballets. Later, there would be a smaller company, and fewer large-scale productions to tour. These significant and necessary changes to the Company's structure heralded a new age of fragmentation and fusion.

The Seasons' Ballets

New ballets premiered in 1986 that became stalwart touring ballets with favorable reviews. Billy Wilson's *Concerto in F* was a surefire crowd-pleaser with an adorable Gershwin score, and John McFall's challenging *Toccata e Due Canzoni*, with 21 dancers, provided plenty of applause payback for deft ensemble work. *Footprints Dressed in Red*, with music by John Adams, was choreographed by Broadway's *Lion King* choreographer Garth Fagan, who would whisk into rehearsal, kick off his shoes (revealing elaborately printed socks), and then proceed to grind into a demanding rehearsal. Company dancers did not find his style easy. There were many one-legged extensions with holds that took a great deal of control, as well as turns, spontaneous jumps from unusual positions, and unique overhead lifts. Asymmetrical costumes by Giovanna

Ferragamo had a futuristic look. Hairstyles were designed by the dancer and approved as long as it was an updo and not distracting or messy.

Special performances at City Center in 1989 featured an all-Nijinska program. Bronislava Nijinska, sister of the famed danseur Vaslav Nijinsky, choreographed *Les Biches*, *Les Noces*, and *Rondo Capriccioso*. Her daughter Irina was brought in to oversee the staging of this special program. It was the first tribute to Nijinska's work since her death and was held on what would have been the choreographer's 98th birthday.

Les Noces featured music by Igor Stravinsky. Mechanistic and ritualistic, it was ahead of its time when first performed by Ballet Russe in 1923. Howard Sayette, from Oakland Ballet, restaged it for DTH. With irregular mixed time signatures and odd polyrhythms, this ballet is

LEFT: Design drawing by Ferragamo for *Footprints Dressed in Red*.
RIGHT: Lorraine Graves and Lowell Smith in *Footprints Dressed in Red*. (Courtesy of the Dance Theatre of Harlem Archive)

perversely difficult. There was no room for error. Dancers had to be human metronomes. If one beat was missed, the dancers would pile up onstage.

Rosella Hightower, famed Ballet Russe de Monte Carlo ballerina, staged *Rondo Capriccioso*. *Rondo* was created by Nijinska in 1952 (her last work) for the Marquis de Cuevas Ballet and Hightower. Mitchell brought *Rondo* to DTH as a vehicle for Stephanie Dabney. Again, Dabney used her Firebird-like qualities—nervousness, unpredictability, and flightiness.

In 1990, Flemming Ryberg of the Royal Danish Ballet set Bournonville's *Flower Festival in Genzano* on a cast of eight. It was presented as a suite of dances without story and ordered with a pas de six, a pas de deux, and a saltarello (Italian jumping dance). It ushered in a new and challenging style addition to the DTH repertoire. *The Washington Post* (03/23/1990) divulged that Ronald Perry as the lead male had " . . . bounding beats and [Endalyn] Taylor's airy jumps were especially fine."

According to Jack Anderson of *The New York Times*

TOP: The Company in Bronislava Nijinska's *Les Noces*, c. 1989 (Photo: Courtesy of the Dance Theatre of Harlem Archive)

BOTTOM: Rosella Hightower coaching Stephanie Dabney in *Rondo Capriccioso*, c. 1989 (Photo: David Regen)

originally supposed to be about the DTH financial crisis and arts funding in general but instead ended up telling a story of cultural pride and prejudice. Walter Goodman in *The New York Times* (7/25/1991) said, "The hour provides glimpses into what Mr. Jennings calls the world of middle-class blacks. ('These are not the people you most often see making news,' he notes.)"

The 1992 season at the Brooklyn Academy of Music (BAM), after what Janice Berman of *New York Newsday* (4/30/92) would call "a financially induced three-year exile from New York," featured the New York premiere of Billy Wilson's ballet *Ginastera* and Glen Tetley's masterpiece *Dialogues*, both with a score by Alberto Ginastera. Of the Tetley piece, Berman continued, ". . . [there is a] palpable sense of intimacy; these dancers support each other

(5/7/1992), Michael Smuin's ballet *Medea*, set to a Samuel Barber score, is a "sensational" work. The title character was deftly portrayed by Lisa Attles, and this role was her breakout performance. When Smuin cast her, it was a wonderful surprise. "Lisa Attles was a commanding Medea. Only a fool would cause her temper to flare."

Yet another season was presented close to home, called Harlem Homecoming '91, again held at Aaron Davis Hall in June. Company performances were given in Bermuda at the Bermuda Festival in January, at the Spoleto Festival in July, and in Barcelona in September.

The year 1991 also saw a special ABC News program, *Peter Jennings Reporting: From the Heart of Harlem*. It was

LEFT: Donald Williams and Lisa Attles in Michael Smuin's *Medea*, 1992 (Photo: Martha Swope, ©NYPL)

RIGHT: Christina Johnson and Donald Williams in Glen Tetley's *Dialogues* (Photo: Martha Swope, ©NYPL)

on stage and off, and they're willing to show it. It is that quality that makes the Company so adept at performing the dramatic ballets that are a staple of its repertoire." She describes *Ginastera* as ". . . a marvelously flashy evocation of the atmosphere of flamenco dancing." *Dialogues* was revived in the 2017 season and re-staged by Augustus van Heerden. Company touring continued worldwide including Munich and Recklinghausen, Germany.

The year 1994 saw the Company again at the Kennedy Center for a two-week season in April, where a rich repertoire was performed that included Ron Cunningham's *Etosha*. Named after a national park in Africa, the fast-paced ballet called on dancers to take on the wildness of nature by vaulting, jumping, and leaping.

The run also included Mitchell's *Bach Passacaglia*, which had been co-choreographed by Rachel Sekyi, a former Company dancer who became one of DTH's preeminent ballet teachers in the School. Over the years she developed a reputation for having the exceptional ability to elicit extraordinary balletic technique from the very

young dancer. The performance of *Passacaglia* included School students under the tutelage of Sekyi and was performed in the season held at the New York State Theater at Lincoln Center.

TOP: Virginia Johnson and Hugues Magen in Wilson's *Ginastera*, with Company men cheering them on (Photo: Martha Swope, ©NYPL)

BOTTOM: Lisa Attles in Ron Cunningham's *Etosha* (Photo: EduardoPatino. NYC)

FOLLOWING SPREAD: The Company and Arthur Mitchell with DTH board member Gordon J. Davis, 1992 (Photo: Marbeth, Courtesy of the Dance Theatre of Harlem Archive)

CHAPTER 8

TOWARD A NEW MILLENNIUM

The Seasons 1997–2004

Certainly, it requires no stretch of the imagination to discern the significance of the recognition of your artistic being that has presented itself as a living reality and, therefore, of the inevitable design to fulfill an assigned historical task—of sharing your artistry, that special magic of reaching vast audiences that will without doubt reside in an international arena as its domain. It is my sincere hope to impart that my warmest and most heartfelt wishes to be with you wherever you are. The road traveled by the artist is too often a lone, solitary sojourn fraught with moments of anxiety and occasioned with endless hours of classes, learning, training, refining technique . . . the artist is universally, the backbone of one's culture and the prescribed task that presents itself is to translate artistically, statements that are not only aesthetically correct but also meaningful in the lives of people who comprise mass audiences—for those who can evidence the enviable ability to face this challenge resolutely and tenaciously and yet retain that special quality of resilience, warmth and dedication, the requisite definition of a fine artist become concretely manifest.

—Ellis Sheppard, a book inscription to Judy Tyrus upon her acceptance as a DTH Company Member

Kellye Saunders and Ramon Thielen in Augustus van Heerden's *Passion of the Blood* (Photo: EduardoPatino.NYC)

THE TIMES

- 1997: Carolyn Jefferson-Jenkins became the first African American president of the National League of Women Voters.

- 2000: President-elect George W. Bush nominated Colin Powell for Secretary of State and Condoleezza Rice for National Security Advisor, the first time either post had been held by African Americans.

- 2003: The US waged war on Iraq.

- 2004: Barack Obama was elected to the US Senate, becoming the second African American elected, and the fifth senator in US history of African heritage.

- Facebook was launched.

FRAGMENTATION
AND FUSION

If the past years were the global age of DTH, then the next eight years were the years of *fragmentation and fusion*.

In 1997, the digital music download file format known as MP3 became popular. This new format made millions of songs, from country to classical, instantly available to sample or download. These styles would be fused into thousands more new musical styles and subsequent recordings. The music industry fragmented in many ways, with far-reaching implications.

By 2003 with the creation of the iTunes Store by Apple, almost every musical composition ever composed could be heard, purchased, and downloaded online. YouTube would quickly follow. An enormous amount of music for ballet class could be downloaded and activated by a handheld iPod if a live pianist was unavailable. CDs could simply be burned for performances if a live orchestra was unavailable. Robert Garland became DTH's in-house CD burner, preparing tracks for performances and rehearsals.

Time-saving digitization was ubiquitous not only in audio but video as well. The new millennium, with digital home video cameras and later smartphones, gave everyone the ability to record dance, from little ballerinas in their basement studios to archival footage of Balanchine, all available on the World Wide Web. The web would bring more ballet information to more people instantly. Digital bulletin boards, newsgroups, email, and eventually blogs and social networking would give voice to dancers across the globe. Balletomanes and dance experts, from teachers to scholars, could discuss and share information about dancers of various cultures. Ballet companies curated their own websites; DTH built one as well.

Fusion itself is nothing new. Bach used the style of Vivaldi, Corelli, and other Italians to generate his music. The Beatles fused all styles of music to compose their mammoth catalogue of songs. Rock and roll had its roots in African American blues. In music history, styles would *slowly* evolve, style by style, age by age. Now, helped by the digital revolution, music and dance styles exploded at breakneck speed.

A FATHER FIGURE

As time marched on, so did the generations. Mitchell thought of himself as a father figure for "his children," and his "children" were maturing as well. Dancers were developing personal relationships, marrying, and having children. Baby formula was carried in the Company's touring crates and there were grandparents in tow. A third generation was moving in and up in the hierarchy of the Company. By 2001 a whole generation of dancers had been trained, and many founded their own schools and dance companies.

Mitchell as father figure was watchful when protecting his brood. Like a parent who experiences their child's first grave offense, so too would Mitchell have to deal with dancers (or their friends) in incidents concerning drugs, drinking, and all-night party behavior; "flinging and flailing" is what some Company members called it. It was not unusual for Mitchell to give specific advice to some

Arthur Mitchell wearing all black and choreographer Billy Wilson (whose children's godfather was Karel Shook). (Photo: Marbeth, Courtesy of the Dance Theatre of Harlem Archive)

dancers concerning their relationships. In-studio disciplinary lectures were common.

A difficult yet common issue was a dancer's weight. Occasionally Mitchell would tell a dancer that their weight gain was a problem. A warning would be issued and sometimes roles would be taken away. Weight was an ever-present stress for Company dancers. Some men would say that they would not lift a woman weighing over 120 pounds, a weight difficult for some dancers to sustain. If Mitchell saw a dancer with a cup of Häagen-Dazs Double Belgian Chocolate Chip with sprinkles, he would gesture to his own derrière, and the dancer got the message. Whether it happened publicly in the studio or privately in his office, it was uncomfortable for everyone when the weight issue was addressed. Some never recovered from the stinging echo of Mitchell's voice warning, "Don't come back from vacation looking thick!"

Of all the monumental hurdles within the life of a ballet dancer, the contract-end evaluation, a one-on-one meeting with the artistic director, was most unnerving and delicate. A dancer recalls Mitchell asking her, "Do you think you're beautiful?" "No, not particularly," said the dancer. Mitchell replied, "That's your problem. You need to believe that you are."

Mitchell read the press reviews. DTH was newsworthy and the reviews gave Mitchell and Company their credibility. When performances were well received, kudos were given. When reviews were unfavorable, Mitchell's demeanor shifted. If he entered the studio dressed all in black, dancers were cautious and attentive, murmuring "oh shit" under their breath, knowing he was going to be very—very—critical.

In a 2004 press interview Mitchell said, "This is my

life, I have no hobbies. I have no biological children, but those dancers are all my children in a sense. Some of them get obstreperous, and they want to fight the father, but that's the way it is. You know, I'm a war-torn battle-scarred gladiator. I've survived. I've been in the business 54 years. There is no trick, there's nothing that you think you can do, that I don't know or haven't tried myself. So just relax and dance."

GENERATIONAL CHANGE

In her *Washington Post* (4/6/1997) article "Family Dancing," Sarah Kaufman reported that Mitchell thought that the Company might fold when his dancers went out on a three-week strike. Mitchell said, "Why would I take someone that I've raised for 28 years and then decide to hurt them? . . . I can't seem to get an answer from anybody. It was like having your children turn against you. . . . But now, in hindsight, it's part of a growing process. It's like sometimes you've got to throw the children out of the nest, and they've learned how to fly." According to Kaufman it was not an "ordinary labor dispute . . . it was the country's first strike by unionized dancers. . . . This rebellion by his 'children'—as Mitchell is known to refer to his Company members—came as a stinging blow. Known for his strict devotion to professionalism, artistic perfection and erasing racial prejudice in the arts, Mitchell found himself cast, unbecomingly, as the callous boss."

In the end, management and the dancers settled on a 30-hour work week, as well as a two-year 5 percent salary increase and other benefits. But underneath, the strike was about more. Mitchell's flying-from-the-nest analogy was probably truer than he realized. The strike signified growth and change, as the dancers grew from being Mitchell's "children" into adult career dancers.

The mentor relationships of the past began to wane; gone were many of the allied arts taught alongside everything else; gone was the fact that DTH was the only integrated ballet Company in the US. Gone were the large number of enrolled students. By 1997, DTH, with its diminished number of dancers at 38 and staff at 26, could no longer tour its grand ballets like *Giselle* and *Fall River Legend*.

The first- and second-generation dancers, around age 40, were ready to retire. Virginia Johnson would say, "We were doing this thing together, out of the blue. Learning together. He was Dad. We were the kids. It was fun and there were lots of great things about that atmosphere. But that got diluted as the Company grew, and more and more dancers were not a part of that first family. It became more of a job than something you just loved. We knew we could sit down together around a table. A lot of the younger dancers did not have that direct relationship with Mr. Mitchell."

The relationship between Mitchell and the board also began to change. Board members were experiencing fatigue, and a sense of a strong logical plan for DTH was waning. Mitchell had seen firsthand what had happened at the Ailey Company when the board took supreme power. In 2001, Mitchell gave himself top billing above the Company name. The entity would no longer be called simply Dance Theatre of Harlem. It would be renamed *Arthur Mitchell's* Dance Theatre of Harlem.

Times were changing quicker than ever, and DTH was on the inevitable wave into the new millennium. A new generation of dancers was arriving. Fragmentation showed its face. Then it became the new normal.

Virginia Johnson

"Dramatic ballets are what I love doing most.
To tell a story, to be a character, to become somebody else through
the movement you do is like going on an adventure."

—*Virginia Johnson*

A NATIVE OF WASHINGTON, DC, Virginia Johnson began her training with Ferrell Smith. She studied with Mary Day at the Washington School of Ballet. After graduation, she became a university scholar in the School of the Arts at New York University before joining Dance Theatre of Harlem in 1968 as a founding member. Through the years, audiences were thrilled with her artistry and dramatic interpretations.

A certain comportment of privacy, discipline, openness, and confidence, among other things, is necessary for a fine artist to achieve lofty goals. Virginia Johnson embodied all of these. In her own words Johnson described why she danced: "I also believed in the ideal that I was trying to achieve, and pursuing that ideal was really why I did it. It's something that's always just beyond your reach. And that's what makes you get up in the morning and makes you keep pushing through hard times. You know there's something really beautiful ahead of you if you can just make your-

self do it." That ideal gave her freedom to develop and become one of the most celebrated character ballerinas in dance history. Quiet and focused at the small section of dance barre in studio three, distanced from the rest, but just next to Mitchell's front-of-mirror perch, she would interiorize her characters to the bone, creating the sturm and drang of Desdemona, Giselle, Lizzie Borden, and Blanche DuBois. As happens with actors playing highly charged roles, her day-to-day demeanor would change depending on the role's character. One dancer who shared a dressing room with Johnson admitted that she was scared to death. Why? She just had a chat with Lizzie Borden, an ax murderer!

At the close of the 1997 fall season, the DTH family paid tribute to Virginia Johnson. She had been a dancer with the Company for 28 years. At the event, she was feted by dance partners Lowell Smith, Eddie J. Shellman, and Donald Williams. They and others surprised Johnson with a tribute piece choreographed by Tyrone Brooks to Irving Gordon's "Unforgettable," as sung by Nat King Cole and his daughter Natalie Cole. Jennifer Dunning of *The New York Times* (9/23/1997) said, "It had something of Miss Johnson's distinctive lyricism and quiet radiance." Mitchell called her "my Virginia," and said she was "one of the truly great ballerinas dancing today." It was the only time that DTH celebrated a retiring dancer with a public performance.

Along with Eddie J. Shellman, Johnson, in her last year's dancing, had become a board member and was well-versed in fundraising—perhaps a harbinger of what was to come. After dancing 28 years as DTH's *prima ballerina assoluta*, Johnson founded *Pointe Magazine* in 2000 and was editor in chief for 10 years. In 2010, she became Dance Theatre of Harlem's second artistic director.

OPPOSITE: Virginia Johnson and Hugues Magen in John Butler's *Othello* (Photo: Martha Swope, ©NYPL)
THIS PAGE: Frederic Franklin, Judy Tyrus, Lorraine Graves, and Virginia Johnson at a reception following Johnson's final performance, 1997. (Photo: Courtesy of Judy Tyrus)

THE GARLAND STYLE

In the early 1990s, school director Walter Raines asked Company dancer Robert Garland to create a new work. With guidance from Bessie Schönberg, he created a work with an AIDS theme for the School Ensemble. Later, Mitchell gave him a chance to choreograph for the Company.

Garland's first Company ballet, *Joplin Dances* in 1995, was a fine choice for a first outing. Scott Joplin's music was used successfully in pieces by other ballet companies. Success could be assured with the perky piano score, and dancing ragtime on pointe was in keeping with the DTH recipe. The music could be performed live, using a single pianist who went on tour and played Company classes on the road.

In *Acid Dreams and Nightmares* (1996), Garland wanted to do an "Alice through the Looking Glass" theme. He used musique concrète by Harry Partch, in which Partch created his own timbres by inventing his own instruments. Garland's ballet used Partch's *Castor and Pollux—A Dance for the Twin Rhythms of Gemini* scored for Harmonic Canon II, Kithara II, Surrogate Kithara, Diamond Marimba, Bass Marimba, and Cloud-Chamber Bowls.

In the fall of 1997, Garland was appointed DTH's first resident choreographer. He worked with the Company and with young students from the School. In 1999, 24 students from the school studied and performed in Hong Kong in celebration of the Chinese New Year at the invitation of the Hong Kong Tourist Board. In a newsletter Garland

Cedric Rouse and Tai Jimenez in Garland's *Crossing Over*, c. 1997 (Photo: Nan Melville)

states, "My work with the students is especially exciting. I've been where they are and know what it takes to make it to the Company. I see myself as a bridge to the Company for the kids who truly aspire to join it." Garland would

continue to keep his finger on the pulse of the School with a sharp eye for gifted and talented young dancers.

Garland has described his style as *neoclassical urban contemporary*. This name was used to describe the choreographic choices that go into fusing disparate dance styles. Since Mitchell's *Forces of Rhythm* (1971), such fusion has been the secret ingredient in the DTH style. Garland's *Return*, a mix of ballet and popular soul music of the 1960s and 1970s, is an example of classical ballet technique fused with popular dance steps. It would become Garland's most performed ballet.

Influenced by Balanchine, Mitchell, and others, Garland carried the torch for the DTH style. Another influence for Garland was New York City Ballet principal Kyra Nichols. Garland worked with Nichols when

he co-choreographed *Tributary* with Robert La Fosse. Mr. Garland said of the ballet's lead female dancer, "She gave me back my art."

Garland's *New Bach* (using Bach's *Violin Concerto in A Minor*) represents classic Garland, working in classical context. Traditional ballet steps are carefully sprinkled with hip shifts, swiveling pelvises, revolving shoulders, boneless fluid arms, and never overdone. Exhibiting urban flair and street swagger, this was the perfect blend of ingredients for the DTH recipe. Garland's style was born from the Mitchell precept to create in the moment but rely on historic precedence. Though Mitchell had Balanchinian license to reinvent classicism, his dictum was "Don't be classical, be classic." Garland's *New Bach* was a part of one of Mitchell's resourceful initiatives that empowered DTH dancers to create new pieces; it was called Five Choreographers.

LEFT: Renee Bharath and Christopher Charles McDaniel in Robert Garland's *Hallmark* (Photo: Orin Zyvan)

RIGHT: Kip Sturm and Tai Jimenez in Robert Garland's *New Bach*, 2003 (Photo: Joseph Rodman, Courtesy of the Dance Theatre of Harlem Archive)

FIVE CHOREOGRAPHERS

A PRESS CAMPAIGN IN 2001 ANNOUNCED THE APPOINTMENT OF FIVE DTH IN-HOUSE
choreographers: Robert Garland, Laveen Naidu, Augustus van Heerden, Lowell Smith, and Arthur Mitchell. Adding ballets to a company's repertoire can be an expensive endeavor. Especially pricey are the creator's payments per performance, staging fees, rehearsal time, and music royalty payments. A live orchestra and score licenses add to the astronomical costs. Producing homegrown ballets with in-house choreographers could circumvent some of this, for example eliminating staging fees and associated expenses. However, this was not the main reason for Mitchell to nurture homegrown choreographers. It was a way to continue to grow the Company in new directions, and above all, continue to give opportunity to his artists and develop their talents. He wanted his people to excel.

Laveen Naidu was represented by *Viraa* (pronounced wee-RAH, the Sanskrit word for "brave"); Lowell Smith created *A Pas de Deux for Phrygia and Spartacus* with a Khachaturian score; and Augustus van Heerden's *Passion of the Blood* was a dance drama with Spanish music. Kisselgoff wrote that "not one of the pieces was dull, and their vitality sprang directly from the dancers' vibrancy and the imagination of their choreographers." Of Garland's *New Bach,* Kisselgoff in *The New York Times* (9/27/2001) gave the leads a sparkling review, "Donald Williams, wittily assertive in a noble style, and Tanya Wideman-Davis, eye-riveting in her robust but refined classical silhouette."

Choreography is a highly specialized art. In the early years of DTH, there was little work for balletic choreographers and even less for those concerned with Afrocentric style. It was an area of need and opportunity and Mitchell recognized that. He had encouraged Company members to choreograph starting with William Scott's *Every Now and Then* and Walter Raines's *Haiku* and *After Corinth*. But the 2001 September season at the New York City Center was no ordinary season.

Left to right: choreographers Augustus van Heerden, Lowell Smith, Arthur Mitchell, Robert Garland, and Laveen Naidu (Photo: EduardoPatino.NYC)

China Tour 2000

DTH toured China in November of 2000, performing in Beijing and in the Shanghai International Arts Festival. It was the first arts group from the United States to visit China since legislation establishing normal trade relations had been signed into law that preceding October. President Bill Clinton said, "Your invitation to participate in the Shanghai International Festival and to perform in Beijing are important milestones for your company and I can think of no better cultural ambassadors to represent the United States at this important international event."

The Company performed to sold-out houses at the Exhibition Hall Theatre in Beijing and at the Grand Theatre in Shanghai. Three performances were given in each city, along with an unprecedented number of educational Arts Exposure experiences. The last performance yielded a standing ovation, which was a rarity among restrained Chinese audiences.

DTH continued to see itself as a cultural ambassador and a "traveling university" to fulfill its mandate of educational, social, and artistic awareness. The tour celebrated the 20th anniversary of DTH's 1980 performances in Hong Kong and cultural exchange with China.

As in any tour to a foreign land, promoters and presenters have a special agenda of what they think will "sell" for "their" audience. Local Chinese presenters requested that DTH include *Giselle* into their repertoire because of the familiarity of the title. Other pieces that were performed were unfamiliar to Chinese audiences, so *Giselle* became the calibrating piece. At first, ticket sales lagged because audiences did not fully understand what kind of Company DTH was. In the end, the roster of performances included *The Four Temperaments*, *Giselle*, *South African Suite*, *Adagietto #5*, and *Firebird*.

On the road, especially outside of the United States, technical glitches can abound. On the technical side of the China tour, there were often electrical power surges that affected the lighting equipment and cues onstage—unwanted lightning effects. At that time, credit card use was tentative at best and there were no automated ticket outlets. However, thousands of audience members eventually gained admiration for the Company and marveled how seamlessly different styles of dance were fused with classical ballet. Performances were sold out.

Company Dancers in Balanchine's *The Four Temperaments* with Ramon Thielen, the first Hispanic principal male dancer with DTH (Photo: Joseph Rodman, courtesy of the Dance Theatre of Harlem Archive).

9/11

The dancers were in dress rehearsal at Purchase College in upstate New York on September 11, 2001, when they heard of the attacks on the World Trade Center (WTC) and the Pentagon. The Company was preparing for a performance for the Visa Presents Evening Stars program, a two-week summer bookend extension of the Evening Star Series, to be performed at World Trade Plaza in the heart of what would come to be known as Ground Zero. These performances were directed and curated by Liz Thomason for the World Trade Center.

On the return to the DTH studios, the Company bus was stopped at the Bronx side of the Macombs Dam Bridge near Yankee Stadium. Manhattan was closed to traffic. The Company proceeded to cross the bridge on foot into Manhattan and walk to the studio. The portable television in Arthur Mitchell's office had gone to snow, and only one phone line was working. All huddled around the phone, reminiscent of World War II families gathered around old radios, straining for new bits of information.

Liz Thomason had just finished breakfast at Windows on the World, the top-floor restaurant of the WTC's north tower. As she was leaving the ground-floor elevators, the first aircraft struck. When she was leaving the ground-level lobby, the second aircraft struck, and debris was falling around her. She survived. The DTH World Trade performance she was organizing, and for which the Company was rehearsing on that fateful day, was one of many beautiful American cultural experiences destroyed by terrorism.

That season's New York City Center performances were from September 25 to October 7. Monique McDonald sang "God Bless America" and Keith Saunders

announced that the board of directors had decided to rename the Company *Arthur Mitchell's* Dance Theatre of Harlem. NBC Channel 4 was named the official DTH media sponsor, donating more than $150,000 in public service announcements.

One year later, in 2002 in Manhattan's Battery Park, DTH performed Michael Smuin's *Stabat Mater*, also known as the 9/11 ballet. *Stabat Mater* was to have a score by Schubert, but the events of 9/11 made Smuin reassess. Instead, he chose to use Dvořák's towering, romantic lament for orchestra, chorus, and soloists, creating a piece of permanent loss and mourning. *Stabat Mater*, Latin for "mother standing," is a Catholic Lenten hymn, originally a Gregorian chant, whose many three-line, haiku-like phrases accompany the stations of the cross, telling of Mary's pain and sorrow as she stands by the gibbet on which her son Jesus is crucified. The *Stabat Mater* text has been set to music hundreds of times by many composers. After Smuin played the music over and over, he said, "I realized that I had found my response to all the death and pain of those terrible days."

Though the 2002 New York season was canceled, Open Houses continued as well as the summer street festival. DTH's 33rd anniversary was celebrated with two special Open House series performances in March and April. The following year the Open House Series performances featured the Red Hawk Native American Singers and Dancers with percussionist Edwina Lee Tyler. With the rise of megachurches in the 1990s, dance became very popular in evangelical Protestant worship services. DTH offered classes in spiritual and liturgical dance.

ST. LOUIS WOMAN

On July 8, 2003, at the New York State Theater, for Lincoln Center's Summer Festival, the most lavish and costly premiere production DTH ever produced played four performances. *St. Louis Woman: A Blues Ballet* would cost more than $1M for Mitchell to produce and would be one of the causes that led to disastrous consequences and shutdown of the School and Company.

Originally, *St. Louis Woman* was a short-lived 1946 Broadway musical whose lead role (offered to but turned down by Lena Horne) was played by Pearl Bailey, who conquered with the show's hit song "Come Rain or Come Shine." The musical was based on the novel *God Sends Sunday* by Arna Bontemps, and the book was adapted by Bontemps and Countee Cullen. The score was by Harold Arlen and lyrics by Johnny Mercer, one of the most famous songwriting teams in the 1930s and 1940s American songbook repertoire.

The DTH production of 2003 was choreographed and conceived by Michael Smuin who wanted to revive it seven years previously but could not get around its racist and caricature elements. Tony Walton, the prolific English costume, set designer, and director (once married to Julie Andrews), acquired the rights to *St. Louis Woman* in the 1990s and had discussed a collaboration with Smuin. Jack Wrangler, of the Johnny Mercer Foundation, approached Arthur Mitchell with the idea of turning the musical into a ballet in 2001. Wrangler was married to Margaret Whiting, who was 22 years his senior. Whiting, a popular singer and recording artist, would head the Johnny Mercer Foundation in 1994.

In 1997 Whiting starred in a Broadway revue, *Dream*, that contained all of Mercer's music, he being her lifelong mentor and career coach since she was 12. Whiting also toured *I Remember Johnny*, telling stories and singing the Mercer catalogue. One can see the ring

Caroline Rocher and Donald Williams in *St. Louis Woman*, 2003 (Photo: Joseph Rodman, Courtesy of the Dance Theatre of Harlem Archive)

of influence that brought *St. Louis Woman* to production. Walton knew Smuin, and Smuin knew Mitchell, since DTH had performed Smuin ballets. Walton owned the show rights, so Whiting and Wrangler completed the circle by offering Mitchell the adaptation rights for Mercer material. Mitchell would serve as executive producer. He had Walton designing the Matisse-inspired sets. Soon the rest of a Broadway ace team would be brought on board: Willa Kim on costumes and lighting by Broadway veterans Jules Fisher and Peggy Eisenhauer, also past collaborator with Walton.

Michael Smuin came with Broadway credits that included *Sophisticated Ladies* (1980), the smash-hit 1987 revival of *Anything Goes*, and the choreographic chops to do the show on pointe. He had been ABT trained, served as artistic director of San Francisco Ballet, and founded the Smuin Ballet. He knew dance, he knew narrative, and he knew theatre. The logo and poster graphics were by Hilary Knight, who branded *No, No, Nanette*, *Irene*, and *Sugar Babies* with his deft, lacy graphic designs, and maestro Joseph E. Fields, resident conductor for DTH, rounded out the A-team. Fields arranged and orchestrated the music from various Arlen sources, including an orchestral suite that was clipped from *Free and Easy*, the 1959 operatic version of the show. Fields also composed additional new music as the score required, that he described as new material derived from the feel of Arlen's harmonic style.

In the July 8, 2003, edition of the *New York Daily News*, Celia McGee reported that Mitchell said, "I'd like to see us bring the ballet to Broadway, having an added half hour in the works. Musical comedy is a great American art form. I'm just trying to push its envelope with ballet." It is no

Costume design drawings for *St. Louis Woman* by Willa Kim, c. 2003 (Photo: Judy Tyrus)

Broadway choreographers: Garth Fagan's *Lion King*, Matthew Bourne's *Swan Lake on Broadway*, and *Les Ballet Trockadero de Monte Carlo*.

If a Broadway show hits, or even plays a limited engagement to good reviews, the net box office take can be very lucrative, especially for a nonprofit. The residual touring income, recording rights, publishing rights, and even media rights can be substantial. Average grosses of a Broadway show can reach hundreds of thousands of dollars a week, while some earn more than a million.

St. Louis Woman could have been such a show. Mitchell and Smuin knew that they had to bring the running time up to at least 1 hour and 45 minutes. *St. Louis Woman* ran for about an hour at the Lincoln Center premiere. Mitchell admitted to the press that more material was planned. Charles Isherwood in the July 21, 2003 edition of *Variety* stated that "Dance Theatre of Harlem could have a breakout hit with this splashy new ballet." He reminded his readers that Broadway regulars gave the production a "dazzling polish."

The choreography incorporated classical ballet, tango, Charleston, jitterbug, and ballroom dance, all on pointe. It included a flash act by the Williams Brothers, a tap dance duo.

St. Louis Woman evolved gradually over two years, so the artistic team had the luxury of time. Smuin would come in every so often and spend two weeks working with the collaborators. Major artistic decisions were made, such as moving the choreography from the 1890s to the 1940s, the era in which Arlen and Mercer composed the music. The 1940s costumes would permit leg lines to be seen and not hidden under the ruffles and floor-length dresses of turn-of-the-century costumes. The racetrack setting was retained. A major decision by Smuin was to add a personification of Death and Death's acolytes, which included dancers Nikki Wilson and Ashley Murphy. Unfortunately, Smuin was not in good health at the time.

secret that Mitchell had another agenda as well: to have a production playing on Broadway that would financially support the Company back uptown.

All of the arrangements for *St. Louis Woman* were in place: the offer from Lincoln Center Festival, one of the greatest venues just a step from Broadway, the rights for the Arlen and Mercer score, the personnel, the artistic team, grant money, the challenge for the DTH Company of dancers, the conductor to arrange the music, an extra half hour of material waiting in the wings, the new concept of "a blues ballet"—what could possibly go wrong? It seemed a perfect fit.

In the late 1990s, Broadway saw a number of dance-driven shows that proved popular with audiences, and a few that were megahits: Bob Fosse's *Dancin'*, Susan Stroman's *Contact*, Jerome Robbins's *Broadway*, and Twyla Tharp's *Steppin' Out*. Other popular shows were by non-

Ikolo Griffin in Michael Smuin's *St. Louis Woman*, c. 2003 (Photo: Joseph Rodman, Courtesy of the Dance Theatre of Harlem Archive)

Mitchell had worked with Arlen's music before with *House of Flowers*. The decision was made to use three singers to perform some of the show's numbers, opening with "Blues in the Night," from Mercer and Arlen's 1941 movie score by the same title. Tony Walton built a loft in the set for the three singers.

Arthur Mitchell thought that people who saw *St. Louis Woman* on Broadway might then go to the ballet. But problems beleaguered the ambitious project. For a Broadway show to be developed, it is generally tried first in front of an invited audience with a very low budget to gauge its impact. Kinks are worked out. In this case, a million dollars was spent on production as if the show *were* on Broadway, even though it was not. DTH got stuck with the bill for sets that were too big to tour. The half hour of added material was never put in (there was no funding to do so), thus limiting the piece to a standard slot in the traditional ballet program. Ultimately, the production never entered into the realm of theatre—it was never scheduled or capitalized for a Broadway run or limited engagement. Funding was never raised for the millions *more* that were needed for a Broadway production. It barely remained in DTH's touring repertoire. DTH was inexperienced in playing the Broadway bet. For the few touring dates, Mitchell paired *St. Louis Woman* with one other contrasting piece, such as *Square Dance* or *Fall River Legend*.

Robert Greskovic of the *Wall Street Journal* (7/15/2003) said, "For all its riot of stage color, its hot tempers and its flashy social dancing, the effect is more numbingly jumbled than gripping and moving . . . unless some inspired show doctor can remedy the dramatically confused, shapeless, and visually unharmonized *St. Louis Woman: A Blues Ballet*, DTH would be far better off dropping the Broadway bait and sticking to more tried-and-true repertory . . . the problems of momentum and coherence of the Broadway flop appear more, not less, pronounced in this rendering."

Once it became clear that the show would not run on Broadway, it might have been possible to incorporate *St. Louis Woman* into the Company's repertoire. Unfortunately, *St. Louis Woman*, because of the size of its sets, could only play venues that had loading docks large enough to accommodate, such as the Dorothy Chandler Pavilion and the New Jersey PAC. There were only five such venues in the entire country. On the financial front, the dire needs of the organization forced Mitchell to sell his mother's home and use his apartment as collateral for a loan to help float the Company.

Sadly, in 2007 Michael Smuin succumbed to a heart attack in the studio while teaching class in San Francisco.

THE 2004 HIATUS

On September 18, 2004, Tasha Robertson in the *Boston Globe* reported that "The Dance Theatre of Harlem, one of the most acclaimed dance troupes in the world, plans to disband its 44-member Company and shut its doors for the rest of the 2004–05 season until its finances can be restructured." The Company was performing in Washington, DC, when the dancers received pink slips. The dancers scattered. The one-year hiatus painfully became a six-year hiatus.

On October 16, 2004, the DTH School closed its doors for the first time. The community was surprised and startled. *American Legacy* magazine reported that the causes were patrons with insufficient resources, loss of funding, and a lapse in payment for liability insurance. For thirty-five years DTH had been a beacon in the Harlem community and the effect of the closure on its artists, teachers, staff, and neighborhood would be tragic.

Undoubtedly this would be the lowest point for DTH under the reign of Arthur Mitchell. There were as many theories for its demise as there are grapes in Burgundy. Was it a lack of vision? Mismanagement of funds? *St. Louis Woman*? Artistic hubris? A weak board of directors, donor burnout, the economy, 9/11? Maybe one, probably all.

Forces outside of DTH cannot be ignored. Presenters on the road could no longer afford to produce large dance productions with full sets and lighting packages, let alone a full orchestra. Most dance companies were making their bread and butter by performing in new, small arts centers in small American cities. Playing in larger venues could only be profitable if the ticket prices were lower or the programming was dynamic. Dance companies were forced to reimagine themselves for future survival.

The mood at the DTH studios became bleak and unsettled. There was no plan B. DTH was flat broke. In the arts section of *The New York Times* (5/26/2004) Robin Pogrebin quoted Congressman Charles B. Rangel, who represented Harlem: "I get the impression that Arthur Mitchell believes he can handle this thing by himself, I don't know if he appreciates the need to get professionals. It's very difficult to talk to artists about bookkeeping."

In the December 2, 2004, edition of the *New Voice of New York*, it was reported that Laveen Naidu and Arthur Mitchell had worked with nonprofit fixer Michael M. Kaiser of the Kennedy Center in developing a plan to revitalize DTH. Together they spearheaded a fundraising effort that yielded over $1.6M. They raised additional funds of $1.2M from private donors, including an anonymous patron who contributed $500K, suspected by *The New York Times* to be Mayor Michael Bloomberg. Kaiser is also credited with turning around the fortunes of the Alvin Ailey American Dance Theatre and the Kennedy Center.

Kaiser knew that an executive director was needed to counter the strong-willed Arthur Mitchell. A *New York Times* (12/17/2004) article titled *A Match for a Strong-Willed Dance Legend*, by Linda Richardson, stated, "One wonders whether Arthur Mitchell, the theater's founding artistic director, with a reputation for keeping a tight rein on the organization, will loosen his grip enough to allow the [newly appointed executive director] Mr. Naidu and former director of the company's dance school to really call the administrative shots." Laveen Naidu responded with, "Absolutely yes, that's the bottom line. Now we have a different governing structure. The only way this institution survives is through this. It has to happen." In December of 2004 the School reopened, but the Company's comeback remained uncertain.

In the September 30, 2004, issue of *Time Out New York* magazine, Mitchell was quoted as saying that he needed to relinquish power but insisted "it's not about giving up control—it's sharing." *Time Out New York* found it bizarre that, at the news conference that announced the suspension of operations of DTH's Company, Mitchell digressed repeatedly, changing the subject from financial hardship to George Balanchine, Josephine Baker, and his tenure with the New York City Ballet. It appeared that Mitchell was in denial. He thought some money would be found somewhere and appeared to be in shock that Kaiser was restructuring with high-stakes fundraising. He probably thought that no matter what, he would retain his power, and just like before, the Company would return and ballet life would continue as usual, on a $3 to $7 million budget. That didn't happen. The power shift was real. The new restructuring had given outright control to the new board and executive director.

Mitchell eventually surrendered administrative duties and focused solely on artistic decisions. Negotiations and backroom discussions followed, property on the block was sold off to reduce the deficit, and there was debt forgiveness. Brought in by Kaiser, Catherine Reynolds was elected board member in February 2005. As DTH board chair, she launched the Ensure the Legacy campaign with a gift of $1M from her foundation earmarked for the return of the professional company. Sally Ann Kriegsman, a dance historian and former director of Jacob's Pillow, quoted in the *Boston Globe* (9/18/2004) said of DTH's financial problems, "It has struggled throughout its entire existence to keep afloat, and any time a company has to disband, you lose momentum, you lose dancers. . . . But Arthur Mitchell is so extraordinarily inventive and indomitable, and he has such courage and commitment and passion for this that he will do everything in his power to keep the company as a flagship company for this country."

Despite the years of success, hard work, and struggle, no horoscope could change the fate of the Aries master. With the Company and School, he trusted his instincts. His highly talented dancers were his insurance and collateral. But there was an elephant in the room. He was approaching his 80s, and people around him were looking at things differently.

The Seasons' Ballets

The Company's 1997 performance of Billy Wilson's *Concerto in F* in The Kennedy Center's 25th Anniversary Television Special was nominated for a Primetime Emmy Award for Outstanding Achievement in Cultural Programming. *Kennedy Center Tonight: Stravinsky's Firebird by Dance Theatre of Harlem*, another television broadcast, was the recipient of the George Foster Peabody Award.

Also in 1997, the dancers embarked on three different trips to Europe. They toured cities in Germany, Austria, Italy, Greece, and Spain. The season's final performance at Aaron Davis Hall included Garland's religious memoriam *Crossing Over*. DTH commissioned Vincent Sekwati Koko Mantsoe, "a fresh voice," to create *Sasanka*, performed barefoot, combining Balinese and Japanese movements into what Clive Barnes in the *New York Post* (9/11/1997) called "a classical mold."

The summer performances featured the 65th anniversary season of Jacob's Pillow, the wooded Berkshire Mountain dance retreat founded in 1932 by Ted Shawn. The Company had not performed at the Pillow since 1973. Mary Grace Butler of the *Berkshire Eagle* (8/8/1997) stated, "Dance Theatre of Harlem is better than ever . . . . the company brings with it all the style and fire and life that we have come to expect."

Fifteen years previously, same-sex partnering would have been shocking on the ballet stage, especially by men, but in *Adrian (Angel on Earth)*, by John Alleyne, audiences were jolted but accepting. The summer season was capped in September with the Company performing at Aaron Davis Hall celebrating Harlem's 360th Anniversary.

September 1999 saw DTH's 30th anniversary season at City Center and was packed with revival ballets. The repertoire also included premieres of Robert Garland's *Return* and Dwight Rhoden's challenging *Twist*, and the premiere of the expanded version of *South African Suite* with added

LEFT: The Company in Vincent Mantsoe's *Sasanka* (Photo: Joseph Rodman, Courtesy of the Dance Theatre of Harlem Archive)

RIGHT: *Left to right:* Duncan Cooper, Thaddeus Davis, Mark Burns, Donald Williams, and Cedric Rouse in John Alleyne's *Adrian (Angel on Earth)* (Photo: Marbeth, Courtesy of the Dance Theatre of Harlem Archive)

choreography by Mitchell, Van Heerden, and Naidu. The Soweto String Quartet that provided the accompaniment for *Suite* was in residence at DTH and then toured with the Company for the year. The blockbuster season continued with an incredible number of ballets, including *Prodigal Son*, *Bugaku*, *Banda*, *Ginastera*, *Manifestations*, *A Song for Dead Warriors*, and *Sasanka*. The Company also returned to Australia and appeared in the Melbourne Festival as a keynote attraction. It had been almost 20 years since the Company set foot on the continent.

The ballet *Sphinx*, choreographed by Glen Tetley, was restaged for DTH in 2001. Anna Kisselgoff in *The New York Times* (10/4/2004) called the cast "downright splendid." The ballet originally created for American Ballet Theatre in 1977 showcases a cast of only three dancers. The Oedipus-inspired story is a fundamental example of fusion. Kisselgoff goes on to say, "It is tailor-made for the Dance Theater of Harlem cast: Caroline Rocher gives this sphinx with human desires an astounding sensuality; Ramon Thielen is particularly intense as Anubis, the jackal-headed God of the Dead; and Duncan Cooper is the macho Oedipus."

DTH returned to Harlem's Apollo Theatre for two weekends in May of 2002. The repertoire included many signature works including *Ribbon in the Sky* pas de deux, originally choreographed by Mitchell for Motown's 30th-anniversary television special in 1990. DTH returned to the United Kingdom in 2002, performing in Manchester and at London's Sadler's Wells Theatre.

LEFT: Andrea Long and Duncan Cooper in Dwight Rhoden's *Twist* (Photo: Martha Swope, ©NPYL)

RIGHT: Caroline Rocher and Donald Williams in Glen Tetley's *Sphinx* (Photo: EduardoPatino.NYC)

In 2004, Balanchine's *Apollo* was restaged for DTH, coached by Jacques d'Amboise. Originally titled *Apollon Musagète*, it is the oldest ballet in New York City Ballet's repertory, originally choreographed in 1928 for Ballets Russes. Jann Parry from the *Guardian* (4/4/2004) said, "These days, dancers are taught to let the choreography to Stravinsky's score speak for them. [Rasta] Thomas, though, spells out the boy's first stumbling steps and barely controlled bursts of energy. . . . His Apollo is imperious from the start . . . Tai Jimenez as Terpsichore, a very feminine muse of dance, complements his masculinity. . . . As their legs fan out in arabesques, the shades of their tights matching their different skin tones, DTH's casting makes vivid sense." This would be one of the last times that audiences would see Dance Theatre of Harlem with a cast of more than 50.

TOP: *Left to right:* Andrea Long, Kellye Saunders, Rasta Thomas and Tai Jimenez, in George Balanchine's *Apollo* (Photo: Linda Rich, Dance Picture Library)

BOTTOM: The Company in Billy Wilson's *Concerto in F* (Photo: Martha Swope. @NYPL)

FOLLOWING SPREAD: A Company portrait before the long hiatus (Joseph Rodman, Courtesy of the Dance Theatre of Harlem Archive)

PART THREE

CHAPTER 9

EMERGENCE

The Seasons 2005–2010

I will always be proud of the growth DTH has accomplished and the inroads we have made in society and life. I am most proud of the individuals who helped make DTH one of the greatest artistic organizations of its kind.

—*Arthur Mitchell*

Professional Training Program students. *Left to right*: Kimberley Ho-Tsaï, Ashley Mayeux, Lacey Thomas, and Lindsey Donnell, c. 2010 (Photo: Judy Tyrus)

THE TIMES

- 2005: YouTube was created.

- Nancy Pelosi was the first woman to be elected as the Speaker of the US House of Representatives.

- 2008: The stock market crashed amid global financial stress.

- November 4, 2008: Barack Obama became the first African American president of the US.

- 2009: Eric H. Holder began serving as the first African American attorney general.

- Michael Jackson, icon of pop, died in June.

- Sonia Sotomayor was sworn in as the first Latin American Justice of the Supreme Court.

- 2010: Kamala Harris became Attorney General in California, the first African Indian American woman to serve in that role.

THE FALLOUT

In April 2005, a program called *Masters of African American Choreography* at the John F. Kennedy Center for the Performing Arts in Washington, DC, was the last performance of the DTH Company before it was announced that it would go on hiatus. The hiatus would last six years. It was ironic that the first and greatest multicultural classical ballet company in America's history met its denouement in the nation's capital. It would be the last time for many years to come that audiences would experience DTH on a grand scale with more than 40 dancers in the Company.

How could an internationally acclaimed ballet company, at one time ranking as one of the top five ballet companies in the world, survive financial ruin? A pall of speculation and grief hung over 466 West 152nd Street. Money and resources had been devoured and only a skeletal staff remained. By 2006 there were no funds left to book future engagements. The strongest asset of sustainability was the School. It had always been the lifeblood of the organization. During the difficult times of hiatus, the School continued.

When all the engines were fired up and running at peak capacity, Dance Theatre of Harlem was pure energy. When the Company did well, press was good, and bookings were up, the School echoed the Company's success and became stronger as well. However, with the organization on life support, the Company on hiatus, and less for students to see and aspire to, enrollment dropped, and the situation became precarious. Some life support came from tuition and reliable grant sources. But financial issues still plagued the institution. In 2008 there was a 20 percent reduction in salaries across the board. The warehouse had to be downsized. Consultants were brought in for institutional restructuring. In contrast, the DTH marketing tagline in 2009 was "Celebrating 40 Years of Passion, Power, and Perfection."

THE SCHOOL'S THE THING

The hiatus placed pressure on the School to drive more enrollment and keep the DTH spirit alive. The Dancing Through Barriers™ program continued. The Professional Training Program (PTP), which aligned with New York City and State Learning Standards, was established.

In January 2006, an Open House honoring the legacy of Dr. Martin Luther King Jr. was cohosted by Ruby Dee and Arthur Mitchell. The event was dedicated to actor Ossie Davis, Ruby Dee's late husband. School Director Ronald Alexander was succeeded by Endalyn Taylor in 2007. She produced *The Ugly Duckling* based on the classic tale by Hans Christian Andersen for the annual spring performance. That same year, a new program for schools called the Firebird Curriculum was created using DTH's signature ballet *Firebird* as its thematic basis.

The new curriculum fused dance, critical thinking, health, and wellness. The wholesome organic food movement, popular at this time, was promulgated to develop strong, fit dancers through diet. Inviting Pilates instructors and nutritionists into DTH—an approach not always found in other dance schools—echoed the "allied arts" from earlier years. This initiative was meant to combat anorexia and bulimia, the scourge of ballet artists in the later part of the twentieth century.

DTH's relationship with the Kennedy Center continued in 2006 with *Protégés*, where the International Ballet Academy Festival hosted DTH dancers Jamie Kotrba and Ashley Murphy, who danced an excerpt from George Balanchine's *Concerto Barocco*. The festival was designed to showcase the talents of students from the oldest classical dance schools, national styles, and the future look of ballet. In 2007 and 2008 DTH faculty participated in the Kennedy Center's Arts 20-week residency program.

National audition tours were held for students ages 8–24, and over 50 percent chosen were granted scholarships or financial assistance. In 2008, 417 students enrolled in the school from all five boroughs of New York City, from five states, and from five countries. Resurgence began.

DTH teacher Nikki Hefko guiding a young DTH Student, c. 2010 (Photo: Judy Tyrus)

HIPLET: BALLET AND RAP

DTH SCHOOL DIRECTOR ENDALYN TAYLOR FUSED RAP AND BALLET IN A 1990s PIECE KNOWN
as the DTH RAP as a way to teach students the positions of the arms and feet.

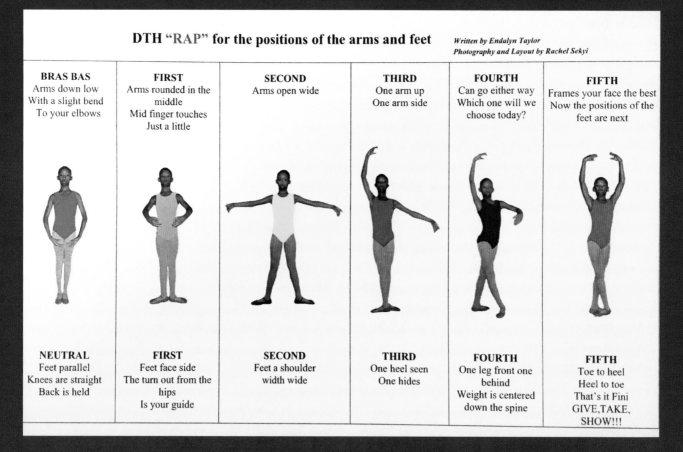

DTH "RAP" for the positions of the arms and feet
Written by Endalyn Taylor
Photography and Layout by Rachel Sekyi

BRAS BAS	FIRST	SECOND	THIRD	FOURTH	FIFTH
Arms down low With a slight bend To your elbows	Arms rounded in the middle Mid finger touches Just a little	Arms open wide	One arm up One arm side	Can go either way Which one will we choose today?	Frames your face the best Now the positions of the feet are next

NEUTRAL	FIRST	SECOND	THIRD	FOURTH	FIFTH
Feet parallel Knees are straight Back is held	Feet face side The turn out from the hips Is your guide	Feet a shoulder width wide	One heel seen One hides	One leg front one behind Weight is centered down the spine	Toe to heel Heel to toe That's it Fini GIVE,TAKE, SHOW!!!

It was bound to happen. In the early mash-up years of the new millennium, former DTH principal dancer Homer Hans Bryant, Artistic Director and Founder of the Chicago Multicultural Dance Center (CMDC), started to experiment with hip-hop moves on pointe; this eventually led to a new contemporary urban style known as Hiplet™ (2009). Bryant told the Hiplet story in posts on Instagram and in a BuzzFeed video. Later, ABC's *Good Morning America* featured his dancers performing the steps. Hiplet went viral. While some felt it a trendy gesture, others realized that it was a legitimate way to push the ballet envelope, technically and culturally; it was another way to provide youth in ballet a mode of learning and expression. CMDC is the only dance studio in the world that teaches the trademarked Hiplet technique.

HIATUS GAP

The DTH hiatus from 2004 through 2012 left the ballet world with a void but gave its dancers the unexpected opportunity to work outside the Company. DTH had been a reliable home for dancers from many backgrounds for many years. Now the dancers had to find new homes and prove that they were fine artists. Some dancers went on to other companies and gave up dancing on pointe. Dance was becoming mainstream on television, though mostly contemporary, hip-hop, and ballroom dancing, not ballet.

The damage from the hiatus reached even farther. Where would the role models be for young hopefuls who had the ballet dream? At the DTH School, a whole generation had less to aspire to. There were fewer young students gazing at their ballet heroes and heroines at the blue doors outside of Studio Three. For seven years without the Company as a role model and career destination, some dancers had to make the choice to pursue other styles of dance, join other companies, or simply not dance at all. Without DTH, for some, the opportunity to dance classical ballet had nearly vanished.

Several DTH company members auditioned for ABT and NYCB but were turned down. Tai Jimenez and Xzavier Cave auditioned for Boston Ballet and were the only DTH dancers at the time to transition into a major ballet company. Ms. Jimenez was accepted into Boston Ballet by Finnish artistic director Mikko Nissinen. Gia Kourlas in *The New York Times* article *Where Are All the Black Swans?* (5/6/2007) reported Nissinen as saying, "As an artistic director you seldom bring somebody in who is 35, but my reasoning was that she represented what a mature ballerina *is*, with a really ideal work ethic. I have an up-and-coming generation of very talented ladies, and I wanted them to have an example of what it means to be professional."

Alicia Graf Mack took an open class at ABT, and at five foot ten, she was told she was too tall. After she auditioned for NYCB, the company responded that there were no open positions. The Alvin Ailey company contracted Graf in 2005, and there

DTH School students having a peek into Studio 3 from the "blue doors" (Photo: Courtesy of the Dance Theatre of Harlem Archive)

she became a critically acclaimed star. The versatility, strength, and overall talent of DTH dancers made them a good fit for the Ailey company. Other DTH dancers hired at Ailey, including Antonio Douthit-Boyd and later Akua Noni Parker, gave Ailey an edge, as noticed by John Rockwell of *The New York Times* (1/12/2006): "Its dancers are better than ever, with the marvelous athleticism, vivid personalities and sleek sensuality the company has long fostered, now infused with the presence of starry newcomers, Alicia Graf Mack above all."

DTH dancers were hired to perform at the Joyce Theater with the 14-member Fugate/Bahiri Ballet NY. When Mehdi Bahiri discovered that Dance Theatre of Harlem dancers were being laid off, *The New York Times* (03/07/2005) article "A Dance Diaspora" quoted him as saying, "I jumped." Allyson Ashley, Duncan Cooper, Melissa Morrissey, Fidel Garcia, Stacie Williams, Kip Sturm, and Donald Williams rounded out the company.

Another seed planted after the hiatus in 2004 was the creation of the Collage Dance Collective (CDC) founded in New York City by DTH alum and Trinidadian American Kevin Thomas, with Marcellus Harper serving as executive director. As a teenager, Thomas realized there were few culturally diverse ballet companies but was inspired to pursue his dream after seeing DTH dancer Ronald Perry. Eventually Thomas became a principal dancer with DTH. Realizing the potential for dance in Memphis, with its diverse population and large pool of talent, he relocated the Collage Dance Collective there, and also founded the adjunct Collage Ballet Conservatory in 2007. French Guiana American Kimberley Ho-Tsaï and African American Rickey Flagg II, both DTH alums, became CDC company members in the acclaimed and culturally inclusive home for dancers, and more followed.

Other dancers auditioned and took positions with companies all over the country. Natalia Johnson and Iyun Harrison performed as guests with Ballet Lubbock. Adriane Richburg, Claudio Sandoval, Preston Dugger III, Akua Parker, Ikolo Griffin, Paunika Jones, and Taurean Green continued performing with dance companies throughout America. A few dancers carried their talent overseas, including Leanne Codrington, Caroline Rocher, William Smith, and Ramon Thielen. Two super talents were able to break into musicals: Rasta Thomas appeared on Broadway in *Movin' Out*, went on to found the Bad Boys of Dance, and became the artistic director of the ShowBiz National Talent Competition. Dionne Figgins went on to amass huge theatre credits over the years on Broadway, including *Memphis*, *Hot Feet*, and *Motown: The Musical*.

Sadly, some dancers had to give up dancing and worked in other fields. In an article in *The New York Times* (7/3/2005), DTH executive director Laveen Naidu stated, "Not everyone rebounded in the field of dance. Six or seven amazingly talented women are working in retail. There are only so many places for African-American women who are classical dancers."

Many artists created their own organizations and businesses fashioned from the skills and disciplines they acquired at DTH. Although this had been an ongoing phenomenon since the late 1980s, in the 2000s DTH alumni went on to start their own dance projects, from storefront studios and related allied arts institutions to full-fledged school and ballet companies. Ballethnic Dance Company was founded in 1990 by Nena Gilreath and Waverly T. Lucas II, both former members of Dance Theatre of Harlem. Since 1995, Iris Cloud's Dance for Joy Ministries trained and mentored thousands, from toddlers to adults; Homer Bryant founded his Chicago Multi-Cultural Dance Center in 1992; in 2003 Luis Dominguez became artistic director of Lexington Ballet; Nikki Hefko became artistic director of the New Orleans School of Ballet; and in 2006 the Dance Institute of Washington was founded by Fabian Barnes. The list is long, impressive, and growing.

THE DTH ENSEMBLE

To keep artistic continuity, and to keep DTH in the public eye, Arthur Mitchell and Laveen Naidu decided to assemble a small group of dancers that could perform at colleges, performing arts centers, and smaller venues. The new ensemble was composed of dancers from the School and a few from the former Company. This new group was named the Dance Theatre of Harlem Ensemble and retained the moniker "Classically American." Keith Saunders served as ballet master. On tour, the ensemble offered performances, school residencies, lecture demonstrations, classes, and workshops. It would also provide dancers as role models for students in the DTH School.

In 2009 *Instep* magazine reported, "The Ensemble embarked on their successful eight-week Dance for America Tour playing to sold-out houses, standing ovations, and rave reviews. . . . Over 40,000 people in 19 communities enjoyed their artistry. The tour featured the premiere of DTH's new interactive performance, a presentation that showcased the Ensemble's neoclassical repertoire and offered audiences a behind-the-scenes look at how the art is created from the studio to the stage."

In June 2010, the DTH Ensemble appeared at Jacob's Pillow Dance Festival. Claudia La Rocca in *The New York Times* (6/26/2010) noted the mix of professional and student dancers that made up the Ensemble: "The Ensemble, directed by Keith Saunders, is something more than a preprofessional operation but not entirely professional. It's a somewhat awkward limbo; some of its members, who range in age from 19 to 27, are clearly student performers, while others would surely graduate to the main Company. That they stayed in the Ensemble is perhaps testament to the strength of the legacy of Dance Theatre of Harlem . . . Or, it's a stark reminder that opportunities for those performers are still shamefully scarce."

Between 2005 and 2009 DTH paid down most of its debt primarily from donors and charitable foundations. By 2009, DTH had a small surplus, a hopeful sign, but nowhere near the financial base required to support a full company. The new board of directors had expanded to 25 members and applied hands-on oversight and management of all financial matters. Though the DTH Ensemble benefited from Mitchell's guidance, after 2008 he was seldom in the building and had less involvement in DTH's organizational activities.

Dancers Renee Bharath, Ingrid Silva, and Shoko Tamai with Keith Saunders as MC during an Interactive Presentation (Photo: Orin Zyvan)

MAKING A
NEW COMPANY

The first transition of artistic directors at DTH was uneasy and strained. Mitchell was granted the honorary title of artistic director emeritus. He chose Virginia Johnson as his successor. "Virginia is the ideal person to ensure the artistic legacy of DTH when I step down," he said. At his departure in 2009 he stated, "There's a lot more in there," indicating that his mind was still sharp, and he still wanted to work. He was asked by the New York City Ballet to consult on diversity, and traveled around the country visiting

Virginia Johnson in the studio with Nardia Boodoo (Photo: Judy Tyrus)

ballet schools, sharing his work and insuring his legacy. He taught master classes at NYCB and gifted his archives to the Rare Book and Manuscript Library at Columbia University.

In January of 2010, Virginia Johnson stepped into the role of artistic director of DTH, coming from a successful stint as founder and editor-in-chief of *Pointe Magazine*. The transition of power from Mitchell to Johnson was understated. Mitchell's office was packed up; there were no fanfares or big parties. Arrangements were kept private and proved difficult for Mitchell.

The years following Johnson's arrival as DTH artistic director were not without misfortune. Roof-related flooding called for the replacement of a sprung dance floor in studio three at a cost of $70K. A leaky skylight waterlogged a concert grand piano. There was a total breakdown of the HVAC system during the hottest July on record. The burgeoning archives were in imminent danger of being lost or destroyed. Funds were sought for their preservation, but misfortune aside, resurgence was in the air. DTH would continue to develop its own artistic personality and style through talented artists and carry on the Arthur Mitchell legacy. All had to keep on keepin' on.

Johnson knew the ropes and the responsibilities of being an artistic director, and she wisely focused on building a new team. Her leadership style differed from Mitchell's but was just as fervent. She needed individuals who could endure long hours in the trenches to build a new Company. Keith Saunders, with a long history at DTH as a principal dancer and Director of the Ensemble, was made Company ballet master, assisted by his wife, Kellye

Saunders, also a former Company principal, who was known for being detailed and methodical.

No doubt there would be comparisons between Johnson and Mitchell. Mitchell had an ability to identify a dancer's strength and use it. He was known for giving his dancers a chance, even if doing so was risky. This is how his dancers grew as artists. Johnson's approach was more experiential, even scientific.

An integral part of an artistic director's job is casting. Film director Elia Kazan stated that "successful directing is 90 percent casting." Johnson faced a challenging situation. She would eventually have to hold auditions. There was no longer the luxury of time for artistic grooming that had been crucial to Mitchell's approach. Because the Company would be smaller, the large ballets such as *Serenade* could no longer serve as a training ground for young dancers. Dancers hired would have to come to the Company fully equipped with top-shelf skills, talent, and versatility.

It was a big bill to fill. It was important for Johnson to have the Company continue performing classical and neo-classical work, as well as Balanchine, contemporary, and ballets about the African American experience. This was Johnson's idea of "reimagined dance for the twenty-first century." There would be more demands on the dancers. The new DTH recipe had to be tested, onstage, with smaller forces, and a new generation.

Master Teachers and Choreographers

Throughout the history of DTH, Arthur Mitchell brought in master teachers to give Company classes and instruct in the School. Mitchell wanted his dancers to have a multitude of styles of dance under their belts, not just jazz, tap, and West African, but the subgenres of classical ballet as well. He recruited teachers who were well-versed in the choreographic style that the Company was doing at the time. He understood that his dancers could not just jump into *Giselle*. The list of master teachers and choreographers that Mitchell provided for his dancers is impressive, including Jerome Robbins, Gregory Hines, Jacques d'Amboise, Jawole Willa Jo Zollar, Allegra Kent, and many more. They were eased in by observing, teaching Company class, and holding conferences with Mitchell. Each choreographer had their own unique dance language and

vocabulary. In a short amount of time, the dancers would have to absorb and process new techniques and styles. Garth Fagan, for example, whose style was not based on ballet technique, presented a unique challenge.

Some guests were friends or associates of Mitchell, while some were introduced by existing faculty. One new connection was Michelle Lucci. In the 1980s, she and her husband, Ted Kivitt, had been associated with the Milwaukee Ballet; she was a principal dancer, Kivitt the artistic director. Kivitt was an ABT principal dancer known to execute the phenomenal number of eight double *tours en l'air* without preparation; he had also served on the committee with Arthur Mitchell at the National Endowment for the Arts. In the late 1990s, in Baltimore, Nicholas Litrenta wished to mount a production of *The Nutcracker* and contracted Michelle Lucci to choreograph. In a

Gregory Hines teaching a master class in tap dance to DTH School students (Photo: Marbeth, Courtesy of the Dance Theatre of Harlem Archive)

feverish last-minute search for a cast, through an acquaintance, Lucci had been told that DTH dancers were on Christmas break. Lucci cast Laveen Naidu, Keith and Kellye Saunders, and Endalyn Taylor, all DTH Company dancers. Her *Nutcracker* opened with a culturally integrated cast. Lucci was eventually introduced to Mitchell by the four DTH dancers who had danced in her production, and she went on to teach at DTH.

Each teacher brought with them a certain unique "something" that DTH dancers could absorb. And if the dancers were not fully focused or "getting it," Mitchell would be right there in the studio, interrupting with his coaching: "You guys are not watching her! Don't stand behind her, watch from the front. See that! See what she's doing? Look at that!—go ahead, do it! Ruh-iyte! . . . that's right!" Later, Virginia Johnson carried on the tradition by bringing in ABT's Alexei Ratmansky, Ethan Stiefel and his wife, Gillian Murphy, as well as Jacques Cebron and others.

As the new millennium rolled out, a new kind of ballet teacher surfaced. Most college dance programs before the 1950s were housed in physical education departments and gymnasiums. The 1960s saw college dance curricula move into the drama department. The following 50 years of growth began turning out teachers who had earned master's degrees, if not PhDs, in ballet pedagogy, dance research, advanced technique, musculoskeletal sciences, somatics, and other related studies. The DTH School recruited some of these wunderkinds to teach, namely Adelaide Strellic and Alexis Arlene Andrews among others.

TOP: Jawole Willa Jo Zollar, founder of the Urban Bush Women Dance Company, teaching class as part of DTH's Masters and Mentors program, 2006 (Photo: Joseph Rodman, Courtesy of the Dance Theatre of Harlem Archive)

BOTTOM: New York City Ballet former principal dancer Allegra Kent teaching ballet as part of DTH's Masters and Mentors program, 2006 (Photo: Joseph Rodman, Courtesy of the Dance Theatre of Harlem Archive)

GENTRIFICATION

By 2010 Hamilton Heights had begun to shift rapidly. Neighboring universities expanded greatly and there was an exodus of students from the now unaffordable neighborhoods in lower and midtown Manhattan. The predominantly Caribbean and African American neighborhoods of Northeast Harlem became fashionably known as Hamilton Heights, or HamHi for short. New restaurants opened on Broadway above 135th Street, and all those who came to DTH to work, study, or see a performance could stroll the neighborhood for a variety of dining options. Airport shuttles brought their services to the neighborhood. Community alliances for the arts were formed. Harlem One Stop, a pioneer email-based newsletter, went viral and began to attract greater New York audiences to venues and events in Harlem.

During this time, Saint Catherine of Genoa Catholic Church, a DTH neighbor, began to host music concerts. Harlem Collective, a block away, opened rent-by-the-day offices for entrepreneurs. Murals were painted on buildings by the Audubon Mural Project, and the playground right next to DTH was totally rebuilt and updated. There were those who felt that the area was transformed for the wealthy, while others felt that the multiculturality was just right. Nevertheless, gentrification breeds displacement. From 2000 to 2005, despite the renaissance, 32,500 African Americans moved out of Harlem and 22,800 Euro-Americans moved in. Many children born and raised in Harlem could no longer afford to stay in their neighborhood.

New York City has a tradition of naming its streets after organizations or people who have made a significant contribution to the community. On August 12, 2006, 152nd Street between St. Nicholas Avenue and Amsterdam Avenue was officially and ceremoniously named Dance Theatre of Harlem Way by Councilmember Robert Jackson. A proclamation was made by the New York State Senate Democratic leader David A. Paterson celebrating the 2006 DTH Street Festival and declaring August 12, 2006, Dance Theatre of Harlem Day.

Dance Theatre of Harlem Way street sign (Photo: Courtesy of the Dance Theatre of Harlem Archive)

EVENTS

Events during the hiatus were fewer than when the Company was in residence, but some were notable. In June of 2006 Aretha Franklin performed with the DTH Ensemble at the Apollo Theatre for a much-needed and successful fundraiser sponsored by Time Warner Entertainment Company.

A unique event dubbed the Gathering served as a reunion for past and present generations of DTH alumni. Held in 2007, the three-day event included a reception at the Romare Bearden Foundation Gallery, a picnic in Riverside Park, and a photo exhibition honoring the prolific life of photographer Marbeth Schnare, whose photos show the grit, glamour, and gumption of the many years in which she photographed DTH.

Works in Process (2006) brought DTH full circle at the Guggenheim Museum of Modern Art, where the Dancing Through Barriers Ensemble participated in a series that explored artistic creation. That same year a performance in honor of Arthur Mitchell was given at the White House and aired on PBS. In 2007 the 22nd anniversary of Career Transitions for Dancers was celebrated, honoring Bebe Neuwirth, Anna K. Palitz, and the Jerome Robbins Foundation. The DTH Ensemble danced excerpts from *Return* for this event.

The passing of *The New York Times* and *New York Post*'s beloved critic Clive Barnes was a great loss to readers and the Company as well. Barnes was a supporter of DTH from its inception. In one of his first reviews of the Company, he wrote, "Black is beautiful, classic ballet is beautiful, so why are the two so rarely found together?" In all of his press reviews he attempted to answer that question and advance the discussion of Afro-cultural ballet in America. He called Mitchell's work "a controlled avalanche." He was married to Royal Ballet dancer Valerie Taylor-Barnes, a former faculty member at DTH. He penned many books on theatre, and his opinions were well-respected, honest, and fair.

LEFT: Aretha Franklin and Arthur Mitchell (Photo: Joseph Rodman, Courtesy of the Dance Theatre of Harlem Archive)

RIGHT: Photographer Marbeth Schnare in a rare self-portrait (Photo: Marbeth, Courtesy of the Dance Theatre of Harlem Archive)

Exhibitions

Exhibitions were an opportunity for DTH to educate audiences about its important history. In 1990, at Howard University's Blackburn Center, Keith Saunders, DTH principal dancer and eventual Company ballet master, curated *Virginia Johnson Dances, Selected Photographs 1970–1990*. The exhibition was dedicated to Michael Scherker, the DTH archivist and founder of Preserve, an organization that gave workshops to arts groups on archival preservation.

Another was installed at the Cornelius Vanderbilt Whitney Hall of Fame at the National Museum of Dance in Saratoga Springs, New York, in 1999. The exhibition, titled *Arthur Mitchell: From Harlem with Love*, curated by Edward Schoelwer, featured archival materials that told the story of the Dance Theatre's founding and life up to its 30th anniversary.

In 2009, to honor DTH's 40th anniversary, the Lincoln Center's New York Public Library for the Performing Arts proposed a retrospective that would chronicle DTH. *Dance Theatre of Harlem: 40 Years of Firsts* was co-curated by former principal DTH dancer Judy Tyrus and New York Public Library curator Barbara Cohen-Stratyner. The exhibition opened at the Vincent Astor Gallery and ran from February 11 to May 9, 2009.

When Arthur Mitchell approached archivist Judy Tyrus to curate this new exhibit, he said, "You are a

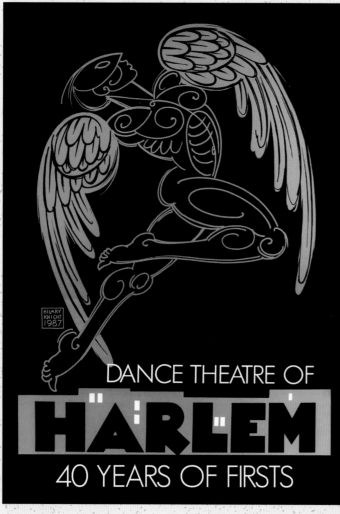

Postcards created by the California African American Museum and the New York Public Library for the Performing Arts (Photo: Dance Theatre of Harlem Archive)

principal dancer. You have done much harder things than this." In the fall of 2008, conversations between Mitchell and Tyrus set the stage for months of organization and research.

The exhibition was culled from a dusty warehouse space and from rooms at DTH that were debris fields, musty and shambolic. Cardboard box contents were dangerously and chaotically commingled and included fragile reels of film, rare audio tapes, early video formats, unprotected photographs, costumes, founding documents, and ephemera of all kinds. All were excavated.

Artistic gems that surfaced included a three-dimensional hand-carved puzzle by artist Frank Bara to celebrate DTH's 20th anniversary, and a handmade quilt by the New York City Chapter of Women of Color Quilters titled *Tableau*. The quilt featured six iconic ballets from the

repertoire, that became cornerstones of the exhibit. In tandem with the exhibition, the New York Public Library producer Alan Pally presented several panel discussions, including one featuring Karen Brown, Suzanne Farrell, Frederic Franklin, Kellye A. Saunders, and Alastair Macaulay, chief dance critic of *The New York Times*.

In 2010, two DTH alums, California African American Museum (CAAM) executive director Charmaine Jefferson and CAAM deputy director Woody Schofield, initiated the second installation of *40 Years of Firsts* at the

The Archive room before and after organizing. (Photo: Judy Tyrus)

California African American Museum. From there, the exhibition was built to tour, and went on to subsequent installations at major museums in Detroit, Houston, and many other cities. Lectures, panel discussions, and children's workshops were organized in conjunction with the exhibition, which was seen by over 110,000 visitors. Ted

Canaday of the Charles H. Wright Museum of African American History wrote that "*Dance Theatre of Harlem: 40 Years of Firsts* captures the majesty of the choreography, the beauty of the costuming, the dancers who defied gravity and stereotyping, and Arthur Mitchell's own wide-ranging accomplishments."

In 2010, Michael Armstrong (DTH board vice president) and his wife, Lori Hall Armstrong, hosted *An Evening with Dance Theatre of Harlem* in the Linda Kelly Theater at New Rochelle High School. The Armstrongs also sponsored the creation of a new exhibition titled *Harlem? Harlem!* at the Museum of Arts and Culture, curated by Judy Tyrus.

CLOCKWISE FROM TOP LEFT: *Dance Theatre of Harlem: 40 Years of Firsts* exhibition at the California African American Museum (Photo: Gene Ogami); The handmade quilt and poster wall in the *Dance Theatre of Harlem: 40 Years of Firsts* installation at the California African American Museum (Photo: Gene Ogami); Two young girls studying the tights and shoes display (Photo: Courtesy of the Dance Theatre of Harlem Archive); The shoes and tights display in the *Harlem? Harlem!* exhibition at the Museum of Arts and Culture, 2010 (Photo: Judy Tyrus)

FUNCTIONS AND FUNDRAISING

The spring of 2007 brought a Fete Noire and Silent Auction celebrating the silver anniversary of *Firebird*. Sade Baderinwa, anchor of WABC Eyewitness News, guest hosted, and R&B recording artist Freddie Jackson performed. In 2009 Cicely Tyson was cohost to an in-house performance entitled *Honoring the Elders*. In attendance were Mayor David Dinkins as well as other notable politicians, including Percy Sutton, Malcolm X's attorney, a Freedom Rider, and the longest serving borough president of Manhattan. As a surprise to Arthur Mitchell, veteran DTH dancer Dean Anderson gathered and rehearsed 26 former Company and Ensemble members to perform excerpts from *Dougla*.

The tenth anniversary of a dance series known as E-Moves at Harlem Stage brought Virginia Johnson out of retirement to dance in a segment titled *Legacies Interrupted*. Claudia La Rocco in *The New York Times* (4/27/2009) wrote, "Hope springs eternal for this forty-year-old troupe, which offered just that to black classical dancers at a time when few other opportunities existed. (Too few still do.) . . . 'What is left when the shoes are off and the waist thick?' Ms. Johnson asked in a voice-over. Plenty, it seems."

Left to right: Arthur Mitchell, First Lady of New York City Mrs. Joyce Dinkins, Ernestine Bell Temple, Karen Sutton, Basil Patterson, Charles Rangel, Mayor David Dinkins, and Cicely Tyson (Photo: Courtesy of the Dance Theatre of Harlem Archive)

THIS SPREAD: The Dance Theatre of Harlem Ensemble shown here in a revival of Billy Wilson's *Concerto in F* (Photo: Rachel Neville)
FOLLOWING SPREAD: The Dance Theatre of Harlem Ensemble, 2009 (Photo: Joseph Rodman, Courtesy of the Dance Theatre of Harlem Archive)

CHAPTER 10

A NEW COMPANY

The Seasons 2011–2015

Ballet is a language. It is an art form about transformation,
it can take you to a place that's unexpected.

—*Virginia Johnson*

THE TIMES

- 2011: The Occupy Wall Street movement trumpeted that 1 percent of the country's population owned as much wealth as the entire middle class.

- The new Martin Luther King Jr. memorial was dedicated in Washington, DC.

- 2012: President Barack Obama broke ground for the National Museum of African American History and Culture on the National Mall.

- 2013: The #BlackLivesMatter movement was formed in response to the acquittal of Trayvon Martin's murderer.

- 2014: Police brutality dominated the news with the murder of Eric Garner.

- 2015: Terror attacks included the shooting at Emanuel African Methodist Episcopal Church in downtown Charleston.

- Misty Copeland became the first African American woman to be promoted to principal dancer in American Ballet Theatre's 75-year history.

NEW PROGRAMS

Johnson was determined to rebuild the Company "one ballet at a time." She began developing satellite programs with the new Company in mind. In 2011 she launched Harlem Dance Works 2.0, a choreographic laboratory that served as an incubator for new ballets. (It was revived in 2019.) Though there were many popular and critically acclaimed ballets in the Company repertoire, Johnson initially chose not to select them. It was her choice to start fresh, be innovative, find a new path.

LEFT: Invited artists Laura Feig, Jamal Story, and Darius Crenshaw in a Thursdays @ DTH showing of Tanya Wideman-Davis and Thaddeus Davis's new work in progress, later titled *past-carry-forward*, 2011 (Photo: Judy Tyrus)

RIGHT: Invited artists Darius Crenshaw and Misty Copeland performing an excerpt during the development of John Alleyne's *Far but Close* in Thursdays @ DTH, 2011 (Photo: Judy Tyrus)

As part of Harlem Dance Works 2.0, dancers Misty Copeland, Darius Crenshaw, Jermel Johnson, Stacie Williams, Matthew Prescott, Laura Feig, Jamal Story, Ramon Thielen, Duncan Cooper, Ashley Tuttle, Andrea Spiridonakos, Adji Cissoko, and Tiffany Glenn were invited to dance. Daniel Beaty (a spoken word poet) and Daniel Bernard Roumain (a composer) were also brought in to create a new work. There were showings at DTH in August and December of 2011. An offshoot during this time was Robert Garland's new pas de deux, *M and M Variations*, performed at the Vail International Dance Festival and the Gala of Stars in Cincinnati, Ohio. It was choreographed for Misty Copeland and Matthew Prescott.

Thursdays @ DTH was an added offering that provided the opportunity to test choreography, hone performance skills, build audiences, and engage donors. The tradition of hosting Open Houses continued, renamed Sunday Matinées.

Slowly and cautiously, DTH began to grow anew. John Alleyne's *Far but Close*, Helen Pickett's *When Love*, and a restaging of Ailey's *Lark Ascending* were some of the ballets later premiered by the Company.

THE FOURTH GENERATION AND SOCIAL MEDIA

The transition of DTH leadership brought a gentler perspective with new motivating forces. The aura in the studio and type of dancers shifted. The first generation of DTH, those who danced from 1968 to about 1977, were of the boomer generation. These dancers had the courage to put on the tights, accept tough criticism, and revolutionize ballet in the face of both open and veiled hostility.

Ashley Murphy and Jehbreal Jackson in a studio performance of Helen Pickett's *When Love* in Thursdays @ DTH, 2012 (Photo: Judy Tyrus)

They led the bold experiments, from testing shoes and the color of tights to trying new choreography.

The second wave, roughly from 1978 to 1992, built upon the foundational strength of the previous generation. Brown tights became the norm, and the "theatre" of Dance Theatre was put to the test. The dancers had to hone their acting skills. They were expected to be extremely versatile and strong. Mitchell led everyone toward the outer reaches of their capabilities. An apprentice program appeared.

The sterling repertoire of diverse and challenging works rocketed the Company to world prominence.

The third wave, from about 1993 to 2004, was represented by dancers who were independent and self-assured. Whereas the previous generation of dancers utilized the advice and direction from the generation before them, these dancers were less keen to seek mentorship from senior dancers. They watched respectfully but wanted more independence. As Mitchell began traveling less with the Company, the Company received less attention from Mitchell. That included his wisdom and "eagle eye"—not so much for the seasoned dancers, but for the younger dancers who needed his polish and critique. More responsibilities were given to the ballet masters to cast and rehearse.

The fourth generation, known as the millennial generation (from roughly 2004), included the Ensemble and rebooted Company. These dancers had to arrive ready to perform. There was no time, staff, or funding to cultivate and mold dancers. They expected a space free from abuse and body shaming. This environment contrasts with the studio ethos and culture of the 1950s, 1960s, and 1970s, when dancers were sometimes subject to the harsh criticisms of tough directors. It is this generation that the digital revolution fully engulfed, and from them, Virginia Johnson built her Company. The focus was no longer on a single man who made history but was now also on a woman who made history with him, and who would continue the legacy with these new and vibrant artists.

Cultural issues had surfaced, not only at DTH with Johnson's rightful celebration of women choreographers, but in American society as well. Millennials who came of age in the early 2000s had their own views about what was happening in the great big mash-up of culture we call America, and particularly in American dance. Social media became an all-consuming behemoth. Millions of instant communications between dancers and the public flooded the internet.

By 2010, social media accounts were being launched and promoted that gave DTH a far-reaching tool for audience engagement. Company members found followers on Facebook, Instagram, Twitter, and blog accounts that hosted vivid photo albums and videos. Social media became the default way to connect with fans. Users could become a part of the DTH family instantly by liking and sharing photos from onstage and backstage, getting tips from Company dancers directly, and keeping up with the DTH calendar of events. Eventually Judy Tyrus was assigned the task of managing social media accounts.

Dancers took marketing into their own hands and built massive audiences for themselves and the Company—all without marketing and advertising expenses. Social networking built excitement for shows, provided deeper behind-the-scenes interactions with performers, and helped ticket sales. Dance and technology intermingled and created enormous potential as a place to incubate and develop work and get real-time feedback. The studio accompanists sat down at the piano and placed an iPad on the music rack that held the sheet music for thousands of ballet pieces. And with just a tap of the finger or a blow of the breath on the screen, the page would turn.

MOVING FORWARD

In January of 2012, DTH held its first national audition tour to find dancers for the new Company. Virginia Johnson was looking for quick studies and versatile dancers. In the very next month Johnson decided to present four performances at New York's Joyce Theatre. This group of dancers comprised members of the DTH Ensemble, briefly renamed DTH II, as well as some former Company members and new dancers. This was an opportunity for Johnson to see her dancers onstage and debut as artistic director.

Since 1982, the Joyce has been home to more than 400 dance companies from around the globe, including Complexions, Garth Fagan Dance, and Ronald K. Brown's Company Evidence. The billing page for the DTH performance placed Virginia Johnson and Laveen Naidu's names on the same line, signaling a sharing of power, a major change from the Mitchell years. Under the direction of Keith Saunders as ballet master, the ballets performed were *Six Piano Pieces*, by David Fernandez; *In the Mirror of Her Mind*, by Christopher Huggins; the New York premiere of *Contested Space*, by Donald Byrd; and *Glinka Pas de Trois*, the first Balanchine ballet restaged by the new Company. With music drawn from Glinka's opera, *Ruslan and Lyudmila*, this tough piece starred Michaela DePrince and Ashley Murphy in the 2013 season and won them rave reviews.

Johnson commissioned a short film to be shown at all performances. Titled *En Avant*, by Gabriel Lamb, it underlined her new role as artistic director and described the legacy of DTH and the making of the new company. Gia

LEFT: *Left to right:* Michaela DePrince, Samuel Wilson, and Ashley Murphy in George Balanchine's *Glinka Pas de Trois*, 2013 (Photo: Judy Tyrus)

RIGHT: Samuel Wilson and Alexandra Jacob in Donald Byrd's *Contested Space*, 2012 (Photo: Rachel Neville)

Kourlas, in *The New York Times* (2/8/2012), said of the film and the Company, "The message was obvious: Let's move forward, but what the film made poignant was the transcendent rigor and beauty from the early days. Once the

Company is up and running, the most important question may not be whether ballet needs a Black company, but whether the Dance Theatre can reawaken the individuality it once had. There was nothing like it."

THE NEW COMPANY

After the Joyce engagement, the Company was booked to start performing in October. The pressure was on. It would be a slimmed-down version, but nevertheless, Dance Theatre of Harlem would again have a *Company*. With style and grace, Johnson and her team rolled up their sleeves and began the monumental task. Formal auditions were held, and dancers were allowed to post their work online. If selected, they were called back for an in-person

audition—a painful process for some former DTH dance artists who were not chosen. Ed Schoelwer, DTH's long-time booking wizard, needed to perform his magic quickly to find venues for the Company's tour. Advertising, photo shoots, press, and preproduction had to be organized straight away. Budget constraints would later reduce the number of dancers from 18 to 16.

Once the dancers were hired, the new Company

Jenelle Figgins (#12) and a rainbow of dancers audition for the new Company in 2012. Figgins would soon be hired as a full Company member (Photo: Judy Tyrus)

bonded in two intensive workshops in 2012 and again in 2013. Ashley Melone, founder and resident director of the Vineyard Arts Project (VAP), brought the dancers together. VAP provided accommodations and rehearsal space, and allowed studio time to create new work. Robert Garland began to choreograph *Gloria*, and John Alleyne *Far but Close*. Thaddeus Davis and Tanya Wideman-Davis choreographed the new ballet, *past-carry-forward*, during the Company's residency with assistance from Tommy DeFrantz as the production dramaturg. During one of the showcases of new works, Melone said the performances "brought the house down every night. The energy as the audience left was inspiring and contagious."

TOP: Ashley Murphy and Da' Von Doane dancing a pas de deux from John Alleyne's *Far but* Close, 2012 (Photo: Matthew Murphy, Vineyard Arts Project)
BOTTOM: *Left to right:* Anthony Savoy, Gabrielle Salvatto, Chyrstyn Fentroy, Samuel Wilson, Jenelle Figgins, Da' Von Doane, Ashley Murphy, Jehbreal Jackson, and Emiko Flanagan in Davis's *past-carry-forward*, 2013 (Photo: Rachel Neville)

Finally, on April 10, 2013, the "hiatus years" ended. Rather than appearing at New York City Center, DTH moved into the Rose Theatre at Jazz at Lincoln Center, at Columbus Circle. The Company numbered 18 dancers, less than half of what it had been before the hiatus. The new tagline was "Believe Again."

The repertoire included styles from Balanchine to Garland. Reviews of the new Company were uneven. Brian Seibert, in *The New York Times* (4/11/2013), said, "*Agon* is terribly exposing—technically, emotionally—and the exposure . . . did not flatter the dancers. . . . There were bright spots." In the following day's edition (4/12/2013) he wrote, "*Coming Together* . . . is a thrill ride." *Agon*, Mitchell's cardinal signature piece, linked the legacy of the old guard to the new. It had been 56 years since its historic premiere at NYCB.

LEFT: Gabrielle Salvatto and Fredrick Davis in an *Agon* preview, 2013 (Photo: Judy Tyrus)

RIGHT: From left to right, Da' Von Doane, Jenelle Figgins, Anthony Javier Savoy, and Dylan Santos in Nacho Duato's *Coming Together*, 2013 (Photo: Rachel Neville)

After the Rose Theatre performances in 2013, national touring continued with some of DTH's well-established return engagements, including the Kennedy Center's series Ballet Across America III. The 2014 season, also at the Rose, marked the company's 45th anniversary season with the tagline "Live the Moment."

The new Company was on a trajectory of rebuilding and growth. The trimmed size of 18 dancers was feasible, and its life continued with the day-to-day rigors of ballet assemblage: morning class, hours of rehearsal, choosing repertoire, planning and booking performances, and touring. However, further changes were inevitable.

One change had to do with rank. Traditionally, in ballet, dancers are elevated in the company at the discretion of the artistic director. At DTH, the designations or ranking system—corps de ballet, demi-soloist, soloist, and principal—had not limited the dancers to roles in these groups. If one was a principal dancer, it didn't mean that they were cast only in principal roles. For example, in the matinee performance one could dance the title role of *Firebird*, and in the evening dance in the corps de ballet in *Firebird* as a maiden. Conversely, dancers in the corps de ballet performed principal roles. The new Company under Johnson eliminated a ranking system. All were billed as "dance artists" and everyone had to dance at all levels. The questions then become: Does a company with traditional performer rankings define it as a major ballet company? And one without, not?

A paradox in twenty-first-century ballet was the cross-pollination of Russian dancers entering the workforce in America. Mitchell never felt the need to bring in principal guest artists to sell tickets. Because of his consummate sense of loyalty to his dancers, he steadfastly trusted that they could perform on the same level or better than any other. He would groom his dancers, bringing them up through the ranks to be principals, unlike other companies, which sometimes imported guests that would leapfrog over permanent company members to principal rank, leaving soloists trapped.

ADMINISTRATIVE CHANGES

With Virginia Johnson's artistic leadership in place, changes were also made in administration. In June of 2014, Sharon Gersten Luckman, former executive director of The Ailey Foundation, and Anna Glass, director of 651ARTS, worked as consultants with Johnson and the board, with Luckman staying on for a short time. Anna Glass was then made executive director in April of 2016.

Glass, a Michigander and lawyer who had studied

Left to right: Alexandra Jacob, Gabrielle Salvatto, Fredrick Davis, Emiko Flanagan, and Nayara Lopes in Garland's *New Bach*, 2013 (Photo: Rachel Neville)

dance and history, knew the value of embracing heritage. In a program interview she said, "We want people to see themselves on stage and see their stories on stage." She also said that DTH prioritizes making the arts inclusive, accessible, and reflective of a diverse population. She recognized the importance of preserving DTH history, insisting that nothing ever be jettisoned or deaccessioned without approval of the archivist. Glass and Johnson carried on the DTH legacy by balancing the past with the future. There would be revivals of *Dougla*, *Tones*, *Pas de Dix*, and *New Bach*, and new repertoire in which to feature the Company.

In 2015, for the first time in the history of DTH, another dance company was invited to share its space on a full-time basis. The José Limón Dance Company and administrative staff had rented multiple studio and office spaces scattered throughout Manhattan for over 10 years. Their new space at DTH brought everyone at Limón under one roof. Artistic director Virginia Johnson posited, "The idea that there is another organization here making art . . . aspiring to a communication higher than anything else, is precious. We are rubbing shoulders, sharing air, ideas are percolating . . . it is a sacred space in that sense." Dance Theatre of Harlem was in its 46th year, and the Limón Company in its 70th. This idea to share real estate was beneficial not only for DTH and Limón but for dance in the Harlem community.

However, a real estate issue surfaced. A nearby parking lot owned by DTH, out of financial need, was sold. The sale became a quagmire of local politics concerning the lifting of a deed restriction. Thirty-eight affordable housing units were eventually built on the land located on the corner of 157th Street and St. Nicholas Avenue. The development also included a DTH studio on the project's ground floor.

THE SCHOOL

Endalyn Taylor, followed by Kenya Massey Rodriguez, helmed the School, assisted by Karen Farnum Williams. Isolated engagements continued for both School and Company. A group of young dancers and other artists had the honor and privilege of performing for First Lady Michelle Obama at the Studio Museum in Harlem. While President Obama addressed the United Nations General Assembly, the First Lady hosted a museum event for the spouses of UN diplomats. With her elegance and magnetism, she spoke of the salient arts of Harlem and the accomplishments of its revered artists. She said, "There's a reason why I wanted

First Lady Michelle Obama, Ashley Murphy, and youngsters from the Dance Theatre of Harlem School at the Studio Museum in Harlem, 2013 (Photo: Chuck Kennedy)

to bring you all to Harlem today and that is because this community is infused with the kind of energy and passion that is quintessentially American but that has also touched so many people around the world."

The School's Professional Training Program presented a diaspora project called *Vumbua*, which translates as "to explore" in Swahili. Researched, written, produced, and performed by students, it explored the agonizing journey from Mother Africa to hip-hop, from slavery in the sixteenth century to the founding of DTH. The School presented its annual spring recitals, *Alphabet Soup* in 2014 and *Seasons of Rhythm* in 2015, at the Apollo Theatre.

In December of 2013, the School and Ensemble dancers were on the bill with the Abyssinian Baptist Church Choir for *Ellington at Christmas* at the Apollo, choreographed by Robert Garland. It included Ellington's swingin' jazzy *Nutcracker Suite* and a re-creation of Ellington's *Sacred Music Concerts*.

During the 2013 summer intensive program, with parts of the archive organized and accessible, a class titled Media in Motion: History and Legacy in the Archive was conceived by Nicole Arvin and Judy Tyrus. Students generated experiential models of dance documentation in photography, video, and audio. They developed an appreciation for the past through exposure to the materials. An exhibition of their work was staged for the street festival at the end of the summer intensive program.

The atmosphere becomes electric in the studios during summer intensives. Young dancers from around the world converge for a grueling boot camp in ballet training. Hundreds of dancers flood the halls and studios, lifelong friendships are made, and for the dancers, it becomes a time to scope out the competition and self-evaluate. Extracurricular activities and field trips have included a visit to a Broadway musical and Lemonade on the Terrace, a discussion and Q&A held on DTH's terrace wherein renowned guest teachers share insights.

LEFT: Azama Bashir and Kimberley Ho-Tsai in *Vumbua*, 2013 (Photo: Judy Tyrus)

RIGHT: *Left to right:* staffer Sharon Duncan, Ballet Russe de Monte Carlo prima ballerina Raven Wilkinson, and staffer JoAnn Wong before a Lemonade on the Terrace, 2012 (Photo: Judy Tyrus)

ADVANCING DIVERSITY

In 2015, ABC Television's data reporter Abby Abrams published the costs of training a ballerina over the span of 15 years; the total was conservatively estimated at $120K. She interviewed DTH School administrator Kenya Rodriguez, who said that the School works with students to help them afford all aspects of training, whether that's tuition or an extra pair of shoes. When other schools asked how they can diversify their programs, Rodriguez responded, "You have to practice diversity . . . It's not something we suddenly embark on and it's a one-or two-year project. In particular you have to diversify your faculty. If a child sees themselves reflected in the studio, they're going to be more comfortable, and they're probably going to continue their training more."

It is not unsurprising that DTH has modeled diversity programs for other countries. The US Embassy in Tegucigalpa (Teguz), through the Bureau of Educational and Cultural Affairs, offered Hondurans an experience of diversity through ballet. This was the Company's first visit ever to Central America, with programing whose aim was to highlight the importance of cross-cultural engagement. Master classes, workshops, and performances were presented. Local youths were chosen to dance in a collaborative performance that brought together dancers from divergent cultural backgrounds. As American Ambassador Lisa Kubiske stated, "Dance Theatre of Harlem . . . illustrates the importance of social inclusion and collaboration between individuals of different backgrounds."

Virginia Johnson as artistic director continued to carry forth the idea of diversity when she expressed her opinion about African American choreographers in the *Courier-Journal* (10/23/2014). In speaking of Harlem's own Darrell Grand Moultrie, a choreographer and dancer who created more than 40 works on pointe, she recalled, "Every time I

Left to right, Dylan Santos, Samuel Wilson, Anthony Javier Savoy, Da' Von Doane, and Nayara Lopes in Darrell Grand Moultrie's *Vessels*, 2014 (Photo: Renata Pavam)

saw his work, I thought this is a choreographer with such a vision of ballet as a dynamic and contemporary art form . . . Moultrie's work [*Vessels*] not only fits with the company's mission of presenting the breadth and depth of classical ballet along with contemporary works . . . but it also was a work by a young African-American choreographer in a field that is largely white . . . we are about diversity and presenting the finest work we can." Moultrie, who danced in *Billy Elliot* and *Hairspray* explained, "I thought about what it *infused* in me," having discovered the title for his ballet, *Vessels*. He made the connection between the words *infuse* and *vessel*. "I wanted to make sure this piece infused my artistic expression in the dancers and gave them different ways to express themselves on stage."

EVENTS AND TOURING

New York City Center celebrated the tenth anniversary of their Fall for Dance Festival in 2013, an annual two-week mélange of dance by established legends and new artists of all styles. Sunday Matinées continued and included a special tribute to Geoffrey Holder, a dear DTH family member. The New York Dance and Performance Awards, keeper of the Bessie, celebrated their 30th anniversary in October of 2014. Virginia Johnson presented a Bessie Award for Lifetime Achievement in Dance to Arthur Mitchell. That same year DTH was represented in a new exhibition called *Dance and Fashion* at the Fashion Institute of Technology (FIT). A dress from *Giselle* was on display, and over 30,000 visitors took the opportunity to see the costume from Act II of the original production, designed by Carl Michel.

In 2013 a tour stop included the Israeli Opera in Tel Aviv, supported by the US Embassy in Israel and other organizations. The 2014 tour featured the new ballet, *Vessels*, that premiered in Washington, DC, at the Sidney Harman Hall, hosted by Washington Performing Arts. A partnership between DTH and Washington, DC's City Dance offered residencies for dance artists to train with professionals. The summer of 2014 took the Company to Quebec, Canada, and Innsbruck, Austria, for the Tanzsommer Festival. Touring with a smaller Company became quite manageable. Gone were the semitrucks that carted elaborate sets, props, lighting rigs, theatre cases, and sprung floors. Costumes, shoes, and other supplies were carried by hand in suitcases.

GALAS

THE BALLET GALA SEASON IN NYC, USUALLY IN FEBRUARY, IS ALWAYS ABUZZ WITH MAJOR arts institutions staging spectacular red-carpet fundraising events. These events are carefully calibrated to seek maximum support for the organization's financial future. Vision Gala is the moniker given to DTH's annual fund-raiser, suggesting the organization's mission and prescience in providing youth and adults with the life-changing world of ballet through education and entertainment.

Even though an event planner is hired to stage the festivities, it is the director of individual giving that is the unsung hero, or, in this case, the heroine. Wearing many hats and working behind the scenes since 2002, former director of development and since 2010 the Director of Individual Giving, Sharon Duncan has managed donors, hot celebrities, and unimaginably complex gala logistics. She was once also Mitchell's assistant. When Mitchell hired her, he said, "This will not make you rich, but will give you history." In an interview, Duncan revealed insights into Mitchell's expectations. "He was very good at explaining everything, he had a clear vision. You always had to be on your toes, do your research, and be able to explain yourself. He hated people who chewed gum. He was extremely driven, wanting only excellence. I always made sure that teaching Company class was included in his daily schedule to energize him for the remainder of the day." Duncan remembers him saying that ballet was the art form that saved his life and he believed that it was the answer to everything.

In April of 2011, the Inaugural Vision Gala was held, with the Vision Award bestowed to Arthur Mitchell along with the title of Artistic Director Emeritus. Before invitations were sent out, teasers in the advertising material beckoned, "Be a part of the Return," alluding to Garland's popular ballet *Return*. The 2012 Vision Gala honored Harry Belafonte, and the 2013 Vision Gala's honor-ary chairperson was Chelsea Clinton. She appeared on the red carpet with her husband, Marc Mezvinsky. The couple celebrated Vanessa Williams and her contribu-tion to the arts.

Vision Gala 2014 was held at Cipriani with Billy Joel as honorary chair. The Carl & Lily Pforzheimer Foundation Medal was awarded to 92Y dance educator Jody Arnhold, and the Virtuoso Award feted Valen-tino D. Carlotti of Goldman, Sachs & Company. Patti LaBelle was guest of honor, and students of the school danced to Paul Novosel's piano arrangement of "Over the Rainbow," LaBelle's favorite song.

Ingrid Silva, Dylan Santos, and Choong Hoon Lee in Robert Garland's *Return* (Photo: Rachel Neville)

HITTING THE HIGH C

Arthur Mitchell, the gambler, always bet the highest on his dancers. In the first 1983 version of *Pas de Dix*, all four men would conquer their nail-biting step—*sus-sous*, plié, double *tour*, perfect landing—and Mitchell would rejoice with the dancers in that champion moment. Sometimes, if a dancer was having trouble with a vulnerable step or lift, Mitchell would try to fix it, and it would get worse. Such is the luck of a gambler. Johnson revived *Pas de Dix*.

Pas de Dix, originally staged for DTH by Frederic Franklin, is what DTH teacher Michelle Lucci called "one of the most unforgiving pieces to dance, ever." The men are asked to complete a series of *tours en l'air* and land on a dime—exposed and vulnerable.

Why would an artistic director program a piece that couldn't be picture perfect for every performance? The answer is not a simple one. Like a dancer who masters a series of difficult steps onstage, a company challenged to perform the classical oeuvre, with its technical fireworks, builds artistic muscle. For the DTH staging of *Pas de Dix*, Frederic Franklin said the Company was ready and the challenges could be mastered, and they were. Ballet tradition dictates that these steps in the classics are not changed, removed, or simplified. These are usually breathtaking moments. In *Le Corsaire* and *Swan Lake* the challenge is executing fouettés without becoming too dizzy, losing balance, falling off pointe, or failing to complete—audiences may not even detect a flaw, while balletomanes will leave slightly disappointed. For a dancer, these high-stakes moments can be a nightmare or a triumph.

Michaela DePrince as the Black Swan in the pas de deux from Swan Lake Act III, 2013 (Photo: Rachel Neville)

DIVERGENCE

Johnson's revival of *Pas de Dix* is an affirmation of the Mitchellism that "the real challenge is to never fear a challenge." And the challenges would be many, for both Company and its new director. It would not be easy for Johnson to work within the limitations that reality would impose: the new touring style, a new, scaled-down repertoire, a tighter budget, a new vision, and fewer dancers. These restrictions came with stress and pressure, plus safety issues. Audiences may not realize that the health and safety of dancers depends largely on casting, programming, rest, and recovery. There is only so much workload a dancer's body can withstand before breaking. Even with utmost attention given to preventive care and safety, a dancer's health is precarious. Casting is chancy business—a very good dancer may be prone to injury, and finding a replacement to cover a role can be an administrative nightmare. But the show must go on.

The beginning years of the new company were no doubt challenging, but a safe haven would soon be found. The Coming years would see the fine-tuning of operations, a new direction, a new route. DTH began a period of *divergence*.

Chyrstyn Fentroy and Francis Lawrence in the revival of Marius Petipa's *Pas de Dix* (Photo: Renata Pavam)

The Seasons' Ballets

Donald Byrd's first ballet for DTH, *Contested Space*, is an exploration of contemporary couplings and relationships, examined through the lens of a twenty-first-century post-neoclassical sensibility. On her website, dance critic Wendy Perron said, "The most radical new work that DTH has commissioned since its rebirth is Donald Byrd's *Contested Space*. There's a hard, gotta-have-it edge to it that plunges these young innocents into a darker, more obsessive side of themselves. They rise to the challenge beautifully."

When Love is described by its creator Helen Pickett as "insistent time marks our days. But when we are in love we surrender to unbridled time." The piece was scored by Philip Glass. Laura Di Orio of *Dance Informa* (4/8/2016) said, "With *When Love*, Pickett displays intelligent structure and intent . . . the movement allows the dancers to exude passion and freedom."

Brian Seibert, in his *New York Times* review (4/14/13)

LEFT: Emiko Flanagan and Dustin James performing Helen Pickett's *When Love*, 2012 (Photo: Matthew Murphy)

RIGHT: Robert Garland and young dancers from the DTH School in a rehearsal of *Gloria*, 2012 (Photo: Judy Tyrus)

of the premiere of *Gloria*, declared, "Let every other contemporary ballet company go to the dark side. The future of Dance Theater of Harlem can be brighter. Mr. Garland seems to know the way." *Gloria* uses Francois Poulenc's setting of the Catholic Mass part for choir and small orchestra. Garland dedicated the piece to Calvin O. Butts III, the pastor of the Abyssinian Baptist Church in the City of New York. The original choreography includes the appearance of several young children drawn from the community in which the ballet is performed. Of the New York home season, Siobhan Burke in *The New York Times* (4/25/2014) noted, "The presence of children from the Dance Theater of Harlem School (who were entirely on their game) drives home the message delivered earlier by

Fredrick Davis and Alexandra Jacob in Christopher Huggins's *In the Mirror of Her Mind*, 2012 (Photo: Judy Tyrus)

TOP: The Company *in orans in Garland's Gloria,* 2012 (Photo: Matthew Murphy)

BOTTOM: The Company in Ulysses Dove's *Dancing on the Front Porch of Heaven,* 2013 (Photo: Rachel Neville)

FOLLOWING SPREAD: The Company, 2011 (Photo: Judy Tyrus)

Ms. Johnson, in her curtain speech, that this company is here to inspire a new generation. It seems able to do that best when not beholden to ballet's past."

In Christopher Huggins's *In the Mirror of Her Mind*, "a woman sleeps fitfully reliving past relationships with three men." The lush, sleepy score by Arvo Pärt was the perfect contrast to the emotionally charged dance.

Dancing on the Front Porch of Heaven: Odes to Love and Loss was choreographed by Ulysses Dove for the Royal Swedish Ballet in 1993 during a challenging period in his life. Set to Estonian composer Arvo Pärt's *Cantus in Memory of Benjamin Britten*, Dove's spare but demanding choreography invited dancer and viewer alike to live in each moment as if it were the last. Having lost 13 close friends and relatives, among them his father, Dove explained, "I want to tell an experience in movement, a story without words, and create a poetic monument over people I loved." Dove died of an AIDS-related illness in 1996, at age 49.

Marius Petipa and Nicholas Sergeyev's *Swan Lake Act III*, danced by Samuel Wilson and Michaela DePrince, was a "gala-style excerpt" according to Brian Seibert of *The New York Times* (4/11/2013). He also stated that DePrince "nailed her balances and she can turn—her fouettés nearly carried her offstage." The ballet was staged by Anna-Marie Holmes who learned the role in Saint Petersburg from the great Kirov ballerina, Natalia Dudinskaya.

Beginning in 2013, select ballets from DTH's former repertoire were performed by the new company; these included *New Bach*, *Tchaikovsky Pas de Deux*, *Return*, and *Dougla*.

CHAPTER 11

EVOLUTION

The Seasons 2016–2020

Absorb, become, take something and make it yours.

—*Virginia Johnson*

THE TIMES

- 2016: Donald Trump became President of the United States in a contentious election, later to be impeached and acquitted.

- The #MeToo movement against sexual harassment gained momentum, and the four major Lincoln Center performing arts organizations did not escape scandal for sexual misconduct.

- 2017: Women in Saudi Arabia gained the right to drive a car.

- Gaynor Minden and Freed of London began to make pointe shoes in shades of brown.

- 2019: The opera world lost the legendary performer Jessye Norman, a longtime DTH board member and fervent supporter.

- 2020: The Coronavirus Disease (Covid-19) was declared a pandemic by the World Health Organization.

- Tremendous wildfires burned 3.2 million acres throughout California and the northwest states, the worst fire season ever, attributed to climate change—heralding a new epoch, the Anthropocene.

- The dance world bid farewell to Paul Taylor, Tobi Tobias, Raven Wilkinson, Trisha Brown, Donald McKayle, and, sadly, Arthur Mitchell.

EQUALITY, GENDER, AND SEXUALITY IN 21ST CENTURY BALLET

In 2000, the film *Billy Elliot* told the story of a North Irish boy from a blue-collar family who becomes a danseur with the Royal Ballet. It was made into a musical in 2005. Telling the story from boxing ring to ballet, *Billy Elliot* uncovers decades of dance history when it was claimed that ballet was not for boys. Though the character Billy may be gay, bisexual, or pansexual, the script is silent on the subject. What the script did lay bare was that male dancers in ballet are from the entire spectrum of sexuality.

In the early 2000s, bullying and body shaming were rightly called out, but change comes slowly. Historically ballet carried the painful stigma of being solely a feminine occupation, and if at all, the male danseur on stage was simply a banister for support. A young boy or man kept his dance lessons a secret lest he be bullied and ridiculed. The myth that *all* men who trained in ballet were gay has been dispelled. The male danseur, once used simply as a support railing, is now celebrated as exhibiting virtuosity and strength on stage.

At the 22nd Annual Fire Island Dance Festival in 2016, DTH premiered Darrell Grand Moultrie's *Equilibrium (Brotherhood)*, danced by three DTH male dancers: Jorge Andrés Villarini, Dylan Santos, and Anthony Javier Savoy. It drew on physicality, athleticism, and grace, exploring the importance of male bonding and how it can bring stability to one's life.

Anthony Javier Savoy, Dylan Santos, and Jorge Andrés Villarini performing Darrell Grand Moultrie's *Equilibrium (Brotherhood)* at the Fire Island Dance Festival, sponsored by Dancers Responding to AIDS, a program of Broadway Cares/Equity Fights AIDS, 2016 (Photo: Fire Island Dance Festival)

The portrayal of the sex and sensuality in the DTH canon surfaced in *Bugaku*, where, through Japanese imperial court dance, a heterosexual couple briefly consummate their marriage; Kisselgoff in the *Times* (3/6/1976) said, "*Bugaku* has always been one of the sexiest ballets in the international repertory, and the Harlem Dance Theater's revue like presentation is not alien to its real point of view."

Homoeroticism rarely surfaced onstage at DTH, sexual overtones in *Les Biches*, *Design for Strings*, and *Equus* notwithstanding. *Troy Game*, a DTH all-male ballet, expressed a certain machismo sensuality. Jennifer Dunning in *The New York Times* (6/20/1985) called it "A sexy romp . . . a parade of 13 good-looking male dancers' bodies adorned

by the barest of costumes." *Equilibrium (Brotherhood)* attended to the male mystique, though not as explicitly as dances performed by other companies, such as Matthew Bourne's rendering of *Swan Lake*, popular for casting men in the traditional female parts of the swans.

It is inevitable that in the future, ballet will include more men dancing on pointe. Loosening the constraints of classical ballet will allow choreographers the freedom to express ethereal possibilities, welcoming all genders and identities of those who participate in the art form. The comic vaudeville of Les Ballets Trockadero de Monte Carlo hinted at nonbinary ballet, proving that men can do serious traditional pointe work, and very well at that. The choreographer or company that picks up this mantle will wear the crown. Space and room for transgender and androgynous ballerinas and ballerinos may not yet be a reality; however, this progressive thinking is an eon away from the beginnings of ballet and an age away from the world in which Arthur Mitchell reigned.

While a dancer's sexual preference offstage was of no concern to Mitchell, onstage was a different story. As part of the "silent generation," Mitchell and Balanchine grew up in the conformity of postwar Donna Reed and Disney happiness. Homosexuality was closeted. Mitchell's 1950s values prevailed onstage. He insisted that the man should present the woman, be two steps behind her, and never be effeminate.

Johnson's efforts were to balance worthy tradition with modern sensibility. She celebrated female choreographers and invited them to create new works. Dianne McIntyre, Elena Kunikova, Francesca Harper, and Claudia Schreier provided Johnson with new ideas and choreography. She organized seminars and discussions where choreographers and audiences interacted. These programs showcased the creative process through a woman's eye, as well as the fight for women's equality in education and the workplace.

Johnson recognized that ballet is expensive and creates

Christina Johnson and Donald Williams in George Balanchine's *Bugaku*, c. 1987 (Photo: Martha Swope, ©NYPL)

competition among choreographers, no matter their skin tone, gender, or culture. Gia Kourlas in her *New York Times* article (3/23/2016) "Steps Arranged by Women, with History, at Dance Theater of Harlem" opens with these words:

"Lately, the world of ballet has been scrutinized and criticized for two things: its lack of diversity and the paucity of female choreographers. Dance Theater of Harlem has the first one covered. This season, it will do something

about the second." That something was Johnson's Women Who Move Us initiative, which generated new repertoire for the Company's tours and showcasing women choreographers.

Johnson programming *Agon*, *Dialogues*, *Return*, and *Le Corsaire* grounded the Company and audiences in the familiar—but not without an eye to the future. The Women Who Move Us opened the repertoire to the new and unique. Johnson intensified ballet's relevance for a wider audience. She even echoed Mitchell, the gambler, taking chances: What if a

TOP: Dylan Santos, Da' Von Doane, and Francis Lawrence in Elena Kunikova's *Divertimento*, 2016 (Photo: Rachel Neville)

BOTTOM: The Company in Francesca Harper's *System* (Photo: Rachel Neville)

successful African American *modern dance* choreographer was given the opportunity to stage her first major work on pointe? Dianne McIntyre's premiere of *Change* provided a new source and idiom for the dancers to experience. It also dealt with cultural issues—slavery, civil rights, and African American historical female figures. It gave birth to a ballet that proved prophetic in light of the Black Lives Matter movement. Johnson: "[McIntyre's] whole idiom and way of being is completely different." Johnson wanted her dancers to "understand a different way of moving and a different source for their work."

Beyond her immediate work within the Company, Johnson continued to promote equality in the field of ballet. The Equity Project (TEP), a partnership between DTH and the International Association of Blacks in Dance (IABD) and Dance/USA, was designed to engage participants and move toward full and conscious engagement among ballet companies. Initiated in 2018 to support the advancement of racial equality in professional ballet, this project gave 21 ballet companies across the country the chance to continue what Arthur Mitchell began. Other organizations with DTH dancers at the helm include Ingrid Silva's EmpowerHer New York and Theresa Ruth Howard's Memoirs of Blacks in Ballet. Away from DTH, Takiyah Wallace's Brown Girls Do Ballet® and Jeremy McQueen's The Black Iris Project have championed support for more diversity in ballet and shows the expansion in this area. New-millennium dancers with a cause became vocal, fearless, and expressive, especially through social media and online presence.

The future of ballet will most likely concern itself with the same cultural and social issues taken up in

Alison Stroming, Lindsey Donnell, and Ingrid Silva in McIntyre's *Change*, 2016 (Photo: Kent G. Becker)

contemporary opera, theatre, and literature, as it has always done in history. Ballet will tell of life and how humans live it. Dancers and choreographers will continue to diverge from conventional approaches. This kind of *divergence* was characterized at DTH's 50th anniversary, beginning with its transition from an all-male directorship to an all-female directorship. By 2019, the positions of DTH executive director, artistic director, ballet master, company manager, development director, and marketing and outreach manager had all been filled by women.

THE SCHOOL THRIVES

The School continued to be the cornerstone of the DTH legacy, and 2016 and 2017 were exciting years for the School. With a Company back and touring, the School's attendance spiked. *Take the A-Train* was the 2016 spring School performance at Aaron Davis Hall, which included *A Train Ride of Fun*, written by Paul Novosel and actor/singer/dancer William B. Wesley. Also in 2017, DTH students danced on ABC's *The View*. DTH executive director Anna Glass appeared with Carmen de Lavallade and spoke about the power of dance and the impact of DTH on young lives.

Students in the School as well as Company members were treated to the expertise, cachet, and excitement of being taught by ballet stars of the day: Sascha Radetsky of TV's *Flesh and Bone*, Ethan Stiefel of *Center Stage*, and Gillian Murphy, who appeared in *Center Stage* and married Stiefel in 2015—all American Ballet Theatre principal dancers.

The intersection of education and community has always been a high priority for DTH. Another rare experience for students in 2016 was the opportunity to dance with a live orchestra. The Orchestra of St. Luke's, based in New York City, offered Handel's Water Music as accompaniment. A second program accompanied DTH dancers in Stravinsky's *Pulcinella Suite*, conducted by Damon Gupton.

In 2017, Robert Garland was made director of the School, and master teachers Rachel Sekyi and Augustus van Heerden were named associate directors. In a DTH brochure, for the first time ever, it was stated that the School believes that "art is a platform for social justice." This shift in rhetoric was huge. It spoke volumes of the changing currents in America. The final frontier in the ballet world yet to be conquered was cultural equality among the major ballet companies. When will more dance schools be models of cultural parity and cross-cultural interaction? When would the skin tones of the dancers onstage truly resemble the skin tones of the people of the world?

The *Train Ride of Fun* segment in the 2016 spring school performance in City College's Aaron Davis Hall (Photo: Courtesy of the Dance Theatre of Harlem Archive)

April of 2016 marked the second full Company season since the hiatus. "Power on Point" was the tagline, illustrating the social and aesthetic strength of the art form, as well as the potential of the dancers and Company. It was a season filled with hope, a hope realized with an onstage exaltation called A Black Ballerina Tribute. DTH gathered dancers from across the country to take a bow onstage at City Center. The number was surprising. The stage was flooded with over 40 ballerinas who gave witness to the roots of "Black ballerina power," with luminaries that included Raven Wilkinson, Carmen de Lavallade, and many others. Along with a tribute to Arthur Mitchell, the Vision Award went to singer Gladys Knight, and Joyce Dinkins (wife of New York mayor David Dinkins) received the Carl & Lily Pforzheimer Foundation Medal. The law firm of Latham & Watkins was also honored.

DTH was selected to be included among the premier exhibitions at the new Smithsonian Institution's National Museum of African American History and Culture. Talks began in 2012 between Judy Tyrus and guest curator Kathleen M. Kendrick. By 2016, the "Taking the Stage" section of the inaugural exhibition displayed important DTH artifacts such as sets of flesh-toned pointe shoes, tights from Company members in three shades, two *Giselle* costumes, and a pair of Mitchell's bronzed shoes. By the end of 2020, over seven million people had visited the museum. The artifacts would remain on view until 2026.

In November 2016, the Northwest African American Museum in Seattle presented the exhibition *Dance Theatre of Harlem: 40 Years of Firsts*. A conversation in collaboration with the Frye Art Museum was presented, titled *Dance Theatre of Harlem, A Look Back*, with Vivian Phillips and two former DTH dancers, Kabby Mitchell III and Judy Tyrus. Both artists started their careers with Oakland Ballet, then moved to New York to dance with DTH. Later, Kabby Mitchell became the first African American ballet dancer with Pacific Northwest Ballet. The lively trip down memory lane gave the audience an understanding of their beginnings as artists of color in the ballet world, along with highlights and firsts from their careers. Sadly, just months later, on May 4, 2017, Kabby Mitchell III died suddenly at age 60.

November 2017 marked the first time DTH left a footprint in Poland, Lithuania, and Hungary as American cultural ambassadors and performers. In April of that

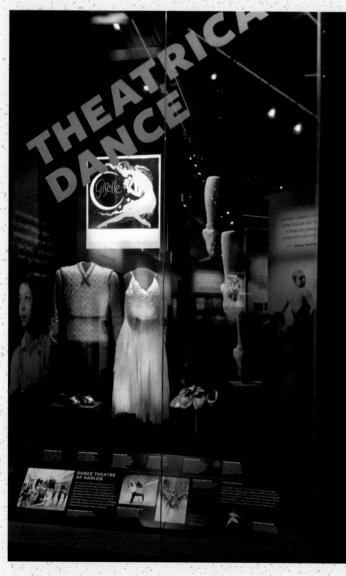

The DTH exhibit at Smithsonian's National Museum of African American History and Culture, 2016 (Photo: Judy Tyrus)

same year, the Sixth Annual Vision Gala was held with the musical Grammy-winning recording artist India.Arie performing with the students of DTH. Homage was paid to the late dance advocate and AGMA union leader Alex J. Dube, who had supported DTH for many years as a union company. DTH kept steadfast in education programs, and in 2018 participated in the Seattle Theatre Group's outreach program Opening Doors to the Arts, with Leslie Odom Jr. from the original cast of the Broadway hit *Hamilton*.

The 2018 season also marked City Center's 75th year and Fall for Dance's 15th anniversary. FFD's commissions included a new ballet by Annabelle Lopez Ochoa for DTH. Jerry Hochman from criticaldance.org stated, "Simply put, Annabelle Lopez Ochoa's *Balamouk* is the finest new work, as choreographed and executed, that I've seen from DTH in a very long time."

In March of 2019 Dance Theatre of Harlem and Alvin Ailey American Dance Theatre celebrated Joan

Myers Brown, founder and artistic director of Philadanco, Philadelphia School of Dance Arts. Brown was Robert Garland's teacher and Garland was Philadanco's youngest member, joining at age 15.

Dance Theatre of Harlem: From Black and White to Living Color, an exhibition, ran concurrently with the Company's performances at the Virginia Arts Festival, held in Norfolk. Written and curated by Judy Tyrus and Paul Novosel, with over 100 photographs and artifacts, it told the DTH story and highlighted the career of ballerina Lorraine Graves. The documentary *Dancing on the Shoulders of Giants* was commissioned by the festival to honor the ballerina. It was produced by Kenny Hopkins with WHRO, aired on PBS, and received an Emmy Award.

The 2018/2019 anniversary season was filled with special celebration. The tradition of Sunday Open House performances continued with a special 50th anniversary

The Company in Annabelle Lopez Ochoa's *Balamouk*, 2018
(Photo: Paula Lobo)

DANCE THEATRE OF HARLEM
From Black And White To Living Color

Photography, Costumes, and Artifacts from The DTH Archive | Curated by Judy Tyrus | Written by Judy Tyrus and Paul Novosel
Layout by Clark Williamson | Graphic Design by Jane G. Cleary | Photo by Rachel Neville
Presented by The Virginia Arts Festival and Slover Library

DANCE THEATRE *of* HARLEM
50th Anniversary

CHRYSLER
MUSEUM *of* ART

VIRGINIA
ARTS FESTIVAL

SLOVER
LIBRARY FOUNDATION

The Andrew W. Mellon Foundation offered a matching grant agreement of $4M if the board raised $1M, totaling a $5M infusion. *The New York Times* (1/14/2020): "Virginia Johnson . . . said the gift would go toward increasing the size of the Company from 18 to 20 dancers, supplementing the organization's lean staff and further encouraging the development of works by women and people of color."

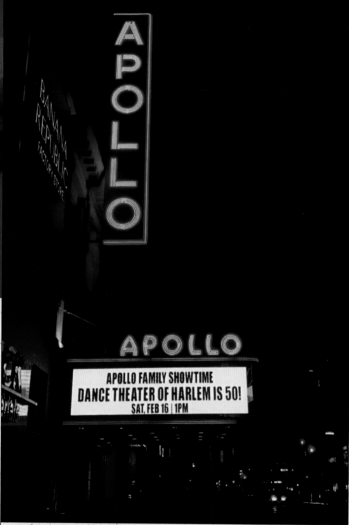

Founders Day Sunday Matinée on February 10, 2019. It included performances by the DTH School, National Black Theatre, the Ailey School, Andromeda Turre/Akua Dixon, Batoto Yetu, Paunika Jones, and pianists Ruoting Li and Adam Kent. Robert Garland led a lecture demonstration at the Apollo Theatre called *Classically Harlem* that harkened back to the early Mitchell years, when the lecture demonstration was the DTH driver of ballet education for audiences.

LEFT: Stephanie Rae Williams on the opening panel of the exhibit *From Black and White to Living Color*, created for the Virginia Arts Festival 2019 (Photo: Rachel Neville)

RIGHT: The Apollo Theater, where Mitchell used to introduce schoolchildren to the magic of dance, 2019 (Photo: Courtesy of the Dance Theatre of Harlem Archive)

ARTHUR MITCHELL

From 2010, when he was named artistic director emeritus, Arthur Mitchell continued to work in the field of dance. Personal appearances included a discussion panel at the 92nd Street Y's Fridays at Noon Series with Darren Walker, Anna Kisselgoff, Tania León, Lydia Abarca-Mitchell, and others. Paunika Jones danced *Balm in Gilead*, and *Agon* was performed by Maria Kowroski and Amar Ramasar.

Mitchell had been driven by the belief that dance can affect social change. He worked with School of American Ballet as a consultant in their Diversity Initiative program launched in 2012. In 2013, American Ballet Theatre created Project Plié to "further expand its diversity and inclusion efforts."

Even though he was on dialysis, in April of that same year he took his third trip to Moscow and St. Petersburg. He was invited to be a featured speaker in the American Seasons Program of the US/Russia Bilateral Presidential Commission, taught master classes, and was the sole American juror at the prestigious XI International Ballet Festival Dance Open in St. Petersburg.

Mitchell placed his personal archive at Columbia University, and his career was celebrated in *Arthur Mitchell: Harlem's Ballet Trailblazer* at the university's Wallach Gallery. The exhibition opened on January 13, 2018, and was a collaboration between the gallery and Columbia's Rare Book & Manuscript division.

A Sunday Matinée was presented in March of 2019 dedicated to the life and legacy of Arthur Mitchell. It was hosted by Alicia Graf Mack and featured singer Patrice Eaton and the Martha Graham II Dance Company.

Mitchell attended DTH's performance at Lincoln Center's 2018 Out of Doors summer concert series. This performance served as the inauguration of the Company's 50th anniversary season. This would be the only opportunity for him to see the dancers performing before casting and restaging his ballet *Tones*, at the invitation of Johnson.

LEFT: Virginia Johnson and Homer Bryant in Mitchell's Tones, 1971 (Photo: Marbeth, Courtesy of the Dance Theatre of Harlem Archive)
RIGHT: Company dancers Dustin James, Amanda Smith, Derek Brockington, and Lindsey Donnell in Tones II (Photo: Kent G. Becker)

Tones was one of the first ballets he choreographed for the Company, in 1970. He was seated in the VIP section. From there he saw his DTH perform his *magnum opus vitae*, live onstage, for the last time.

The new staging of the Mitchell ballet would be known as *Tones II*. Lorraine Graves and Caroline Rocher were asked by Mitchell to assist with the restaging. His ill health prevented him from continuing after two rehearsals. August 17, 2018, was the last time he set foot in studio three. It marked the last time, and for some the first time, that Company members of the fourth generation of dancers would work with the celebrated and venerable "Mr. Mitchell."

Arthur Mitchell died on September 19, 2018, from complications of renal failure. He was 84. He would be remembered in dance history as "the first permanent African American principal male dancer with New York City Ballet," as a founder of Dance Theatre of Harlem, and as the man who gave thousands of people the gift of himself in dance. He had preserved, protected, and renewed the art of dance for all.

A private funeral service was held at the Abyssinian Baptist Church in Harlem. A public memorial service was held on December 3, 2018, at the Riverside Church, with nearly 2,000 people in attendance. Countless more grieved

Arthur Mitchell backstage with a group of children at a lecture demonstration, 1970 (Photo: Marbeth, Courtesy of the Dance Theatre of Harlem Archive)

his passing. The Company performed *Gloria*, Alicia Graf Mack performed *Balm in Gilead*, and *The Greatest* was performed by Paunika Jones and Christopher McDaniel. Cicely Tyson spoke, as well as Jacques d'Amboise, Edward Villella, Kay Mazzo, Carmen de Lavallade, Virginia Johnson, Lorraine Graves, Darren Walker, and Reginald Van Lee. Baba Donald Eaton led the entrance procession with his djembe drummers, Valerie Simpson (of Ashford & Simpson) sang "Reach Out and Touch," and the *Agon* pas de deux was danced by Unity Phelan of NYCB and Calvin Royal III of ABT. The memorial event served as a reunion as well as a turning point in the DTH history, marking the passing of the paternal leader by his thousands of children and family. The new era and future of DTH would now fall to Virginia Johnson and the fourth generation of dancers.

Years before his epiphany on that flight to Brazil, before the official incorporation papers were signed, Dance Theatre of Harlem was created deep inside Arthur Mitchell. Deep inside the young survivor, inheritor of African slavery, a man who struggled, a man who danced. He, the one who felt the aloneness of being different—the only African American dancer in a predominantly Euro-American ballet company, the outlier. He created a home for dancers so that they need not experience the pain and isolation. And so many went on to create their own realities in dance.

Arthur Mitchell once said, "We must ensure that the legacy and flame of DTH remain a beacon to the Harlem's of the world. Using the art of dance and the tools of education, discipline and focus, DTH will continue to encourage everyone, regardless of race, class, creed, ethnicity or color, to strive to become the best they can be." In the words of James Baldwin, "Not everything that is faced can be changed, but nothing can be changed until it is faced." That these words and deeds would be remembered, years after Dance Theatre of Harlem's 50th anniversary.

"50 FORWARD"

The problems of equality in American society are deeply embedded and systemic. They are in ballet as well. Much has been proven at DTH: that ballet is not selective, does not discriminate, and serves all—it offers a space for discipline, and it is played out creatively. Ballet includes other necessary proficiencies from music and theatre to anatomy to geometry. The DTH family model, with dynamics of guiding, nurturing, and supporting, can serve any company very well. Ballet becomes much more than pliés and triple pirouettes. When one is totally invested in the art, one is equipped for success.

It will take time in America for multicultural equality in the arts to fully blossom. In the words of Virginia Johnson: "Dance is a constantly renewing surge of growth, maturity and understanding—it proves itself over and over again."

Looking back through the huge swath of DTH history, and considering the future, the commonality between Mitchell and Johnson that emerges is the *work* of ballet. The *work*, the day-to-day struggle for perfection, connects the past with the future. Again, Virginia Johnson: "The Dance Theatre of Harlem Company returned to its work of bringing people together through art . . . While the world has changed in many ways there is still a distance to go. Ballet is a complex and beautiful human endeavor, the experience of which can change lives. Yes, ballet does have a color. It is the rich color of humanity—in all of its shades. That's what Dance Theatre of Harlem is about—opening minds to what is possible."

The Seasons' Ballets

The 2016 season premiered Garland's *Brahms Variations*, which Brian Seibert of *The New York Times* (4/23/17) described as "exceedingly polite, but such decorum and taste are rare enough to astonish. Moreover, what Mr. Garland has characterized as 'Harlem Swag' comes across in his subtle musicality."

At other times it was danced by Dylan Santos or Stephanie Rae Williams. When performed by Williams, Kathy Ellis of WFPL Radio, Louisville (10/10/2018) said that it "provided the spiritual heart of the evening. [Williams] filled the Whitney stage with the beautifully-linear attitudes of Limón, both informing and being informed by the sublime clarity of Bach's music."

Intended to celebrate jazz in Harlem, Darrell Grand Moultrie's *Harlem on My Mind* included a mash-up of music from Count Basie to Chris Botti. Aside from *The New York Times* criticism of the piece, reviewers were happy with the individual performances.

Christopher Wheeldon's pas de deux, *This Bitter Earth*, was restaged for DTH in 2018. It is set to another mash-up—Max Richter's much overused drone "On the Nature of Daylight" and Dinah Washington's soulful rendition of the 1960s rhythm and blues hit "This Bitter Earth." The program notes read: "The resulting brief encounter between a man and a woman leads one to believe that '. . . this bitter earth may not be so bitter after all.'"

Balanchine's *Valse Fantaisie* received a new production.

DTH performed José Limón's Bachian *Chaconne* (a Baroque dance), a piece Limón choreographed for himself in 1942. Usually a solo piece, for the opening night of the 2017 New York City Center Season, DTH reconfigured it for five dancers, three from DTH and two from the Limón Dance Company.

LEFT: Chyrstyn Fentroy in Robert Garland's *Brahms Variations*, 2016 (Photo: Kent G. Becker)

RIGHT: Stephanie Rae Williams in a rehearsal of José Limón's *Chaconne* (Photo: Andrea Mohin/*The New York Times*/Redux)

In 2017, and again in 2019 due to popular demand, the Pittsburgh Ballet Theatre (PBT) and DTH collaborated at the August Wilson African American Cultural Center. Of the collaboration, Terrance Orr, artistic director of PBT, said, "It's an honor to have this opportunity to collaborate with Virginia . . . This is the first time we've joined forces with another company, and it's an honor to do it with one of the very best . . . I think this performance makes a strong statement about the diversity of talent that we have in ballet and how much richer that makes our art." The programs included a ballet choreographed by Stanton Welch titled *Orange*, a contemporary piece set to music by Baroque master imperator Antonio Vivaldi, in which both companies appeared, along with signature works from DTH and PBT.

For five women and one man, it employed his signature musicality, fleetness, and brilliance. As a new addition to the DTH repertoire, it served as a lively curtain raiser.

The first evening and gala performance of the 2019 season at City Center featured a walk down memory lane with excerpts from *Agon*, *Firebird*, and *Giselle*. Also featured was the stylish film *In Loving Memory*, a tribute to Arthur Mitchell, directed by Daniel Schloss.

LEFT, TOP: The Company in Darrell Grand Moultrie's *Harlem on My Mind*, 2019 (Photo: Rachel Neville)

LEFT, BOTTOM: The Company in George Balanchine's *Valse Fantaisie* (Photo: Dave Andrews, Courtesy of the Dance Theatre of Harlem Archive)

RIGHT: Dance Theatre of Harlem dancers Anthony Santos and Amanda Smith in Stanton Welch's *Orange*, 2019 (Photo: Courtesy of The Pittsburgh Ballet Theatre)

Claudia Schreier's *Passage* was commissioned by the Virginia Arts Festival to remember the 400th anniversary of the 1619 arrival of the first enslaved Africans to reach colonial North America. The piece deals with themes of struggle, hope, and the endurance and perseverance of the human spirit. This piece was piloted exclusively by women, with a new score by Jessie Montgomery conducted by Tania León, costume design by Martha Chamberlain, and lighting by Nicole Pearce. Glass and Johnson presented the piece at the Kennedy Center's Ballet Across America series, sharing the bill with Miami City Ballet and celebrating female creativity and leadership. Johnson was delighted that both the composer and the choreographer of *Passage* were young African American women. She said, "It's time to hear voices that haven't been heard before."

Another collaboration between Miami City Ballet and Dance Theatre of Harlem flowered in Pam Tanowitz's piece *Gustave Le Gray No. 1*. For four dancers and one onstage pianist, the ballet included two dancers from MCB and dancers Anthony Santos and Stephanie Rae Williams from DTH. Sarah L. Kaufman of *The Washington Post* (6/1/2019) said, ". . . formal [choreographic] elements lead to freer expression: thigh-slapping, full-body jiggling, exhausted-on-purpose forward-slumping. Throughout, there's a play of textures: The energy grows soft, then a crisp formation snaps into place."

Another full-circle moment during the 50th anniversary was a DTH appearance at the Solomon R. Guggenheim Museum of Art, where DTH made its official New York City debut in 1971. The Guggenheim's Works &

The Company performing Arthur Mitchell's *Tones II* at the Guggenheim Museum, 2019 (Photo: Robert Altman, Works and Process)

Process presented the Company again dancing Mitchell's *Tones II* in the museum's rotunda. The Company also performed excerpts from George Balanchine's masterpiece *The Four Temperaments*, honoring Balanchine's long-standing patrimony.

The tagline from DTH's 50th anniversary season was "Celebrating Access, Opportunity, and Excellence." The season was a celebration of diversity and equality, the legacy of Dance Theatre of Harlem that will echo for generations.

In the cold, bleak winter of 2020, Company member Dylan Santos staged *Odalisques Variation* from *Le Corsaire*. Though he kept the Petipa choreography, he stripped away the story's "toxic 19th-century social conventions," revealing the sheer beauty of classical dancing. This was the last new touring ballet of the 2019–2020 season.

Robert Garland's *Nyman String Quartet No. 2* was commissioned for the 2019 50th anniversary season. To quote from Brian Seibert's *New York Times* review (4/14/2019), "And at the end . . . the cast turns away, as at the end of *Agon*, but they raise fingers skyward. They might be pointing to Mitchell, somewhere in the stars: People need someone to look up to. Or maybe they're just being aspirational, finding strength in love. Either way, onward and upward is the right idea."

THIS PAGE: Dylan Santos in Robert Garland's *Nyman String Quartet #2*, 2019 (Photo: Kent G. Becker)

FOLLOWING SPREAD: The DTH 50th Anniversary Company, 2019 (*Top Row, Left to Right*) Choong Hoon Lee, Crystal Serrano, Christopher Charles McDaniel, Anthony Santos, Derek Brockington, Alexandra Hutchinson, Alicia Mae Holloway, and Dustin James(*Middle Row, Left to Right*) Yinet Fernandez, Da' Von Doane, Lindsey Donnell, Stephanie Rae Williams, and Ingrid Silva(*Bottom Row, Left to Right*) Amanda Smith, Dylan Santos, Daphne Lee, and Anthony Spaulding (Photo: Cherylynn Tsushima)

THE HISTORY OF DTH HAS NOW BEEN WRITTEN.
MORE QUESTIONS SHOULD BE ASKED.
FUTURE GENERATIONS WILL HAVE GUIDANCE AND
ASPIRATIONS. THE STORY AND LEGACY WILL BE HANDED ON.
"WE HAVE TO MAINTAIN OUR TRADITION
AND WALK INTO THE FUTURE," JOHNSON SAID.
50 FORWARD.

POSTSCRIPT

On Monday, March 16, 2020, a special headline banner on Dance Theatre of Harlem's website announced that all school classes would be suspended, and that the School would remain closed until further notice from both New York city and state governments. It also stated that DTH staff would work remotely. For DTH, thus began the age of COVID.

The World Health Organization announced that the deadly, contagious SARS-COV-2 coronavirus would be characterized as a global pandemic. As of June 2021, more than 3.7 million lives had been lost worldwide. Preventive self-quarantining, mask-wearing, and social distancing became a way of life, and the COVID generation was schooled online from home. Telecommuting changed the way the labor force functioned and reduced pollution levels. Thousands of businesses were shuttered. Broadway went dark and all ballet companies abruptly ceased performing. The 2020 DTH season at City Center was canceled.

Like so many other artists and arts organizations stopped in their tracks by the pandemic, the staff, school, and dancers of DTH pivoted to an online presence to continue its mission. Social media remained active. Videotelephony was used for online classes, meetings, and even dance parties. Bloomberg Philanthropies sponsored DTH on Demand, online classes and presentations that included DTH classics *Giselle* and *Dougla*. The program was billed as a new digital platform to bring "our artistry directly into the homes of our beloved audiences!"

The new reality of quarantine transformed the dancer's living room into a private studio. Virginia Johnson was quick to supply her dancers with a square of Marley flooring. This small island space, to be used for class and rehearsals, would provide a swatch of normalcy. Furniture was cleared; chairs from dining room tables were used as dance barres. Pet cats and dogs joined in. Johnson wanted her dancers to be ready for live performance. Smartphones, computers, and Wi-Fi became crucial for artistic survival.

Company members and alums answered the call to arms. Dance enthusiasts the world over could take class with master DTH teachers in ballet, African dance, and many other styles with a click of the mouse. Rehearsals for ballets were done remotely. In June 2020, the Company began an online collaboration with Dartmouth College to develop *The Hazel Scott Project*, a new work by Tiffany Rea-Fisher about the piano virtuoso who was also an outspoken civil rights activist.

The DTH School held virtual auditions for its online summer intensive in July and August. What's the Step? offered Facebook followers an opportunity to learn a dance combination from *Dougla*. Virtual Sunday Matinées were also presented. The public was invited to panel discussions. One of note, Celebrating Arthur Mitchell, included DTH former principal dancers in conversation with New York City Ballet's Damian Woetzel and Wendy Whelan, she being the first woman appointed associate artistic director of NYCB.

Not until October 2020 would the Company physically dance together, utilizing the "bubble model," a method of on-set quarantining and check-in testing also used on TV and movie sets. The Company took a three-week residency at Kaatsbaan Cultural Park's "bubble" in Tivoli, New York. To assist in recovery from the pandemic, DTH received funds from America's Cultural Treasures Initiative, a grant program conceived by Darren Walker and led by the Ford Foundation, Bloomberg Philanthropies, and others.

On October 19, 2020, the annual Vision Gala was presented on DTH's Facebook and YouTube channels, honoring Jeanine Liburd of the BET Network and Verdun Perry of Blackstone Investments. The 45-minute broadcast, hosted by Emmy Award-winning news correspondent Deborah Roberts, included video premieres of *Breathe* and *Higher Ground*, choreographed by Robert Garland; *Reflections*, by Amy Hall Garner; and *Valor*, choreographed by Christopher Charles McDaniel. Alicia Keys paid tribute with a video montage of DTH dances underscored with her song "Underdog." Also included was "Dancing through Harlem," a video coproduced by Company members Derek Brockington and Alexandra Hutchinson using eight Company dancers. The six-minute video went viral on YouTube.

COVID-19 was not the only significant event of 2020. Black Lives Matter (BLM), a global movement used to combat cultural bias and to promote freedom, liberation, and justice, mobilized people of all cultural heritage to protest. BLM affirmed "the lives of Black queer and trans folks, disabled folks, undocumented folks, folks with records, women, and all Black lives along the gender spectrum . . . working for a world where Black lives are no longer systematically targeted for demise." The killing of George Floyd supercharged the movement with mass protests in cities across America. Confederate statues were toppled and monuments to oppressors removed. The incendiary hate speech of Donald Trump referring to the coronavirus as "Kung Flu" and a "China virus" caused a spike in hate crimes toward Asian Americans.

Lamentably, the same issues of cultural bias that began this book, the same issues of discrimination that led Martin Luther King Jr. to advance civil rights, and those same issues that inspired Karel Shook and Arthur Mitchell to found Dance Theatre of Harlem persisted in 2020, an annus horribilis. But like dancers, humans are resilient.

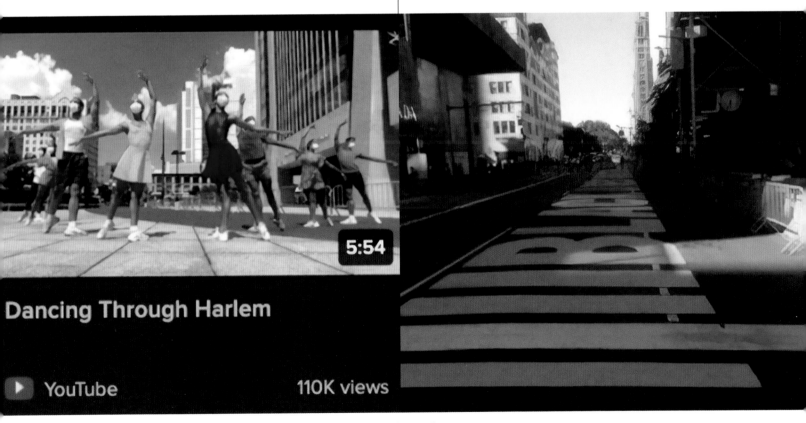

Dancing Through Harlem

5:54

YouTube   110K views

LEFT: A screenshot of the video *Dancing Through Harlem*, 2020 (Photo: Paul Novosel)
RIGHT: "Black Lives Matter" painted by the city with permission of Mayor DeBlasio in front of Trump Tower in New York City (Photo: Paul Novosel)

Progress has been made in cultural acceptance, but not nearly enough. Through periods of survival, Dance Theatre of Harlem called on the strength of its people, and their belief in its mission, to rise and rise again. DTH's determination to offer representation and opportunity to new generations will carry it into the future. It is our hope that the world will follow its lead.

Judy Tyrus and Paul Novosel, December 2020

A FLOURISH

How much can a society change in 50 years? What can one person do in 50 years?
1969 marked the beginning of so many new horizons,
a new dream, another dream
a dream where hope danced its way along a path of mud and marble
with bloody feet
sweat and tears to the war against gravity and balance on a black floor
with child after child man after man and woman after woman
passing through blue crash-barred doors
to learn stance and movement
and thousands and millions of muscles move in concord,
time after time and with note after note of drummed up piano music
of something that sings something of songs of numerous things
that cannot be named but exist---that always existed for eons and eons
that are in the blood and bone
that sculpts the body mind and spirit
leaving nothing but raw human muscle that rests
then awakens afresh and strong and hungry for more road
for more black floor more pliés more tendus more lifts
and more gravity to conquer under pink blue and yellow stage lights
under eyes seeing and feeling
and listening and applauding and loving and wondering
about the dancer who gives more and more and more and more
the mind speeding with thoughts of measurement, trust, grabbing, swirling
jumping and landing in constant hope of landing and landing with grace
the grace obtained from other hearts that surround with love they too
clothed in tights matching skin and skin matching look and look matching culture
and culture matching hair and hair matching headpiece and headpiece matching costume
and costume matching lights and lights matching sets and sets matching story
and story matching characters who dance the dream that dances them.

—Hic liber scriptus est nobis,
Judy Tyrus and Paul Novosel, 2021

AFTERWORD

If one accepts that DTH is the miracle it has so often been called, one must also accept that miracles are really very simple phenomena. They are the result of a highly motivated urge to achieve a state of grace that is healing. Miracles are provoked by necessity, hunger, aspirations, or the need to correct a deranged condition. Miracle workers do not practice sleight-of-hand; they activate atoms in a positive way. Marian Anderson stated it very succinctly when she said of DTH, "God meant this to be!"

Joseph Liebman wrote of DTH, "Emergence! Out of darkness comes illumination. And radiant communication. And it is a cause for joy."

The Dance Theatre of Harlem has come home. Not only from the triumphs of tours across the world but home to the roots of recognition. Home to the new tasks of teaching and learning. Home to the truth of what they are.

For the Dance Theatre of Harlem is more than the dance. More, even, than the nurturing community school it has become—it is intensely dedicated to enriching the young and the old in music, dance, and theatre; the arts which the brain and the hand of man have emblazoned upon the conscience of all humanity.

The Dance Theatre of Harlem is classical ballet that speaks with eloquence to all who have witnessed it, leaping across the artificial barriers of race and ethnicity, of politics and place, of ways and words. The Dance Theatre has transcended all of these. Because this vivid, vital company speaks a special language, a language that our hearts understand well. And it has emerged into a world where achievement is a passport, where talent is nobility, where meritocracy is the only structure acknowledged.

Emergence. Because our Dance Theatre of Harlem has entered the boundaries of our souls. Has uncovered the sense of oneness that abides deep in us all. To experience them is to celebrate their beauty and their truth. And ours, as well.

And it is time.

Karel Shook
New York City
November 18, 1978

Karel Shook watching his students in class (Photo: Marbeth, Courtesy of the Dance Theatre of Harlem Archive)

ACKNOWLEDGMENTS

A book is made by many. We are forever grateful to all those who have brought this work to publication. We treasure the support and efforts of those who believed that it was time to capture the legacy of Dance Theatre of Harlem and granted us the blessing and privilege to do so, especially DTH executive director Anna Glass and artistic director Virginia Johnson, along with their support staff, Sharon Duncan, Jordan Oldham, Keyana Patterson, Melinda Bloom, and Robert Garland.

As with any historic archive, our praise is given to those who have rescued and saved materials for posterity. We are thankful for those with the preternatural insight and energy to recognize the value of the history of Dance Theatre of Harlem. Without these guardians, all is at risk. We acknowledge and salute the work of the past and present gatekeepers of the DTH archive: Michael Scherker, David Lockley, Jorge Arevelo, Ed Schoelwer, Robert Garland, and Theara Ward. We would also like to thank the archive advisors, consultants, and specialists for their expertise and advice: Imogen Smith, Kat Kim Bell, Patsy Gay, Nichole Arvin, Linda Tadic, Libby Smigel, Nancy Watrous, and Rodney Trapp.

Great appreciation is given to funders who have helped begin the preservation of the DTH Archive: Save America's Treasures, the National Park Service, Andrew W. Mellon Foundation, the Dance Heritage Coalition, Bay Area Video Coalition, the Ford Foundation, the National Endowment for the Arts, and generous donors, public and private.

We thank the archive interns and volunteers who helped make our work manageable: Rebecca Hatcher, Jeff Katz, Ashley Swinnerton, Shaqueem Clarke, Aminah Karim, and Nyesha Davis Williams, as well as DTH's quintessential volunteer coordinator, Jackie Thomas, and all of the archive volunteers, especially Kevin Kanesaka. We appreciate those who steadfastly worked to make our physical archive spaces safe and comfortable: Kenneth Thomas, Alberto Recinos, Henry Recinos, and Lillian Recinos.

We have sincere gratitude for those who helped clarify DTH facts, answered our questions of dance pedagogy, or influenced our thinking: Rachel Sekyi, Ronald Perry, Kellye Saunders, Augustus van Heerden, Keith Saunders, Sharon Duncan, Adelheid B. Strelick, Alexis Anderson, Lorraine Graves, Johnny Warrior, Tyrone Brooks, Edward Schoelwer, Michelle Lucci, and Darryl Quinton. Linda Murray and Tanisha Jones of the New York Public Library for the Performing Arts were indispensable.

We are indebted to the press reviewers, critics, journalists, and entertainment writers of public record who, throughout the years, told the DTH story, as well as the photographers who let us see it.

Our admiration goes to our indefatigable editors, Serena and Alana Solin, our publisher, Dafina an Imprint of Kensington Publishing, our acquisitions editor, Esi Sogah, and copy editor Megan Gendell whose support and patient understanding brought this book to life. We acknowledge our counsel, Jeffrey Brandstetter, and accountant, Harmon Burstyn, whose vigilance kept us safe and sound on our writing journey.

And lastly, our devoted friends and loved ones. Without their support, none of this would have been possible: Eileen Novosel, Eric Waldman, Satoko Tyrus, Gilda Waldman, Nurya Adane, Victor Haseman, Roger Koopman, Jeffrey Hannan, David and Jamie Noven, Patrick Loy, Richard Lapka, Robert Kelleher, Janeen Weiss, Fritz Clay,

Anna Marinaccio, Joanne Haase, and Jannette Hawkins. We especially thank Jerry and Helene Dreskin, Judith Nichols, Doris Fiotakis, and ChromaDiverse, Inc.

Our indebtedness reaches to the hundreds of dancers and artists that were not mentioned. It was editorially impossible to mention every person and all instances where praise and gratitude is unequivocally due. These individuals made huge contributions during their time at DTH. It is with utmost respect that we laud and honor the DTH family and all those who have passed through the doors of 466 West 152nd Street.

Staff and Performers of Dance Theatre of Harlem on the historic Pillow Rock at Jacob's Pillow, 2019 (Photo: Grace Kathryn Landefeld)

NOTES AND SUMMARY OF SOURCES

DTH:HMC ONLINE RESOURCES

This book comes with a host of free online ancillary materials at www.DTHbook.org hosted by ChromaDiverse, Inc., a nonprofit organization founded by the authors to promote diversity in the arts. Readers and researchers can access additional resources that include:

- A List of DTH Ballets
- A List of Company Members

- Materials on Multiculturality
- Research Materials, and much more . . .

Sources are not repeated for inclusion in subsequent chapters since a narrative-continuum approach has been taken for the text. Some sources listed were not directly used in the narrative but were used as reference for context or thinking, or used as substantiation for memes and trends. A good amount of sourcing has been used from the Dance Theatre of Harlem Archive; unprocessed materials and some with anonymous authorship have been used. Some Archive press clippings were found without date, author, or publication data. Printed performance programs from 1968 to 2020 have been used as a primary source for dates, repertoire, biographies, ballet notes, billing, and venue information; they are not individually listed in the source summary below but are inventoried at the item level in the DTH Archive as "DTH Inventory of Printed Materials" (by year). Press reviews have been cited within the main chapter text with author/reviewer, name of publication, and date.

KEY: A—DTH Archive; B—Book; BL—Blog; D—Document; E—Email; I—Interviews/Oral Histories; J—Journal; M—Magazine; N—Newspaper Articles; T—Thesis; V—Video; W—World Wide Web; N W may denote that newspaper material was accessed online.

INTRODUCTION

Allen, Theodore W. "Summary of the Argument of *The Invention of the White Race*." J.B. Burnett. W

———. *The Invention of the White Race: Volume 1: Racial Oppression and Social Control*. London: Verso, 1994. B

Dass, Angelica. "Portrait Project Seeks to Document Every Human Skin Tone." PetaPixel, July 7, 2012. W

Melendez, Wilfredo R. "One Race, but Many Cultures." *The Gainesville Sun*, October 11, 2003. N

"The Best: 72 African Wise Proverbs and Inspiring Quotes." Afritorial. BL

CHAPTER 1 ARTHUR MITCHELL

"Alva Gimbel Is Dead; Active Philanthropist." *New York Times*, May 1, 1983, Obituaries. N

Balanchine, George, and Francis Mason. *101 Stories of the Great Ballets*. Garden City, NY: Dolphin Books, Doubleday, 1975. B

"Ballet: 'Clarinade' by Balanchine First New Work to Be at State Theater." *New York Times*, April 30, 1964. N

"Ballet: 'Piege de Lumiere' Has American Premiere; Taras Work Is Danced at State Theater." *New York Times*, October 2, 1964. N

Barnes, Clive. "Dance: 'La Guirlande de Campra' by John Taras; A Good Performance of a Weak Ballet." *New York Times*, December 2, 1966. N

Bourlin, Olga. "Dorothy Leigh Maynor (1910–1996)." *BlackPast*, August 18, 2012, BL

Bowie, Stephen. "Dorothy and Noël." New York Public Library, August 15, 2012. www.nypl.org/blog/2012/08/15/dorothy-and-noel. BL

Columbia University. "Columbia University Libraries Online Exhibitions – Arthur Mitchell: Harlem's Ballet Trailblazer." exhibitions.library.columbia.edu/exhibits/show/mitchell/dance-theatre-of-harlem--compa/press-room. W

Como, William. "Dance Theatre of Harlem," *Dance Magazine*. May 1975. M

Duberman, Martin. *The Worlds of Lincoln Kirstein*. Evanston, IL: Northwestern University Press, 2008. B

Gratz, Roberta Grandes. "A Talk with Arthur Mitchell." *New York Post*, January 2, 1971. N A

Grimes, William. "Dorothy Maynor, 85, Soprano and Arts School Founder, Dies." *New York Times*, February 24, 1996, Arts. N

Gruen, John. *People Who Dance: 22 Dancers Tell Their Own Stories*. 1st ed. Pennington, NJ: Princeton Book Co., 1989. B

———. *The Private World of Ballet*. New York: Viking, 1975. B

Hutter, Victoria. "Arthur Mitchell, Giving Back to the Community." NEA, March 16, 2016. W

Kisselgoff, Anna. "Review/Dance; New Leads, New Look in Balanchine 'Apollo.'" *New York Times*, January 15, 1989. N

Latham, Jacqueline Quinn Moore. "A Biographical Study of the Lives and Contributions of Two Selected Contemporary Black Male Dance Artists – Arthur Mitchell and Alvin Ailey – in the Idiom of Ballet and Modern Dance, Respectively," also known as "The Latham PhD Thesis." 1973. T A

Marcy, Rachel. "Dancers and Diplomats: New York City Ballet in Moscow, October 1962." The Appendix, September 9, 2014. W

Mistretta, Sara. "Arthur Mitchell's Dance Theatre of Harlem." March 30, 2003. T

Mitchell, Arthur. "Agon, An Essay". Publication and date unknown. A

———. "Black Visions '89, Movements of Ten Dance Masters" Excerpt, Arthur Mitchell interviewed James Briggs Murray, n.d. I

Shook, Karel. "Ballet Teachers Talk of Technique." Karel Shook interviewed by Lili F. Rosen. *Dance Scope*, Fall 1979. M

Sparks, Cator. "Arthur Mitchell Interview for Acne Paper 2011." Cator Sparks, September 20, 2018. W

Taylor, Burton. "How the Creole 'Giselle' Took Form," *New York Times*, October 14, 1984. N

Vashti, Lorelei. "How the Four Temperaments Used to Dress." The Australian Ballet, May 28, 2013. W

Notes:

Located at Lincoln Center, the New York State Theater was designed by Phillip Johnson under consultation with George Balanchine. After the New York World's Fair, the state of New York granted ownership to the city, and in turn, the city leased it to City Center of Music and Drama, unassociated with New York City Center on West 55th Street.

Burton Taylor in *The New York Times* (10/14/1984) referred to DTH's *Giselle* as Creole "*Giselle.*" The 1987 film of the ballet titled it *Creole Giselle*, and that title became commonly used. However, the original DTH title of the ballet was simply *Giselle*.

CHAPTER 2 KAREL SHOOK

Annonces, Vieilles. "Duke Ellington's Granddaughter, Mercedes Ellington, Picked to Be Dancer on the Jackie Gleason Show." *Jet Magazine*, September 26, 1963. M

Beckford, Ruth. *Katherine Dunham: A Biography*. New York: M. Dekker, 1979. B

"Billy Wilson and Sonia Van Beers from the Afro-American Dance Company." Jacob's Pillow Dance, 1971. W

Cornish College. "Mission, History, and Values." *Cornish College of the Arts*. www.cornish.edu/cornish-at-a-glance. BL

DeFrantz, Tommy. "Great Performances: Free to Dance – Biographies – William Adolphus Wilson." *Thirteen*, 2001 .W

Fuhrer, Margaret. "Raven Wilkinson's Extraordinary Life: An Exclusive Interview." *Pointe*, June 2, 2014. M

Garafola, Lynn. *Diaghilev's Ballets Russes*. New York: Da Capo, 1998. B

Grant, Dell Omega. "Karel Shook, Dancer, Is Dead; Co-founder Harlem Troupe." *New York Times*, July 27, 1985, Arts. N

Gregory, James. "The Great Depression in Washington State." *Civil Rights and Labor History Consortium/University of Washington*. Depts.washington.edu/depress. W

Holley, Eugene, Jr. "[Unsung Heroes] The Drum Is a Woman: Katherine Dunham." *Ebony*, July 22, 2016. M

Joods Historisch Museum. *Joods Cultureel Kwartier*, July 5, 2019. W

"Katherine Dunham," Dunham Center. June 25, 2019. W

"NYCB – New York City Ballet – Discover." New York City Ballet. www.nycballet.com/Explore/Our-History/NYCB-Chronology/1948-1959.aspx W

"Obituary: Lincoln Kirstein," *The Independent,* January 6, 1996. N

Oxford Reference. "Sonia Gaskell." www.oxfordreference.com/view/10.1093/oi/authority.20110803095844879. W

Rather, Dan. "Dan Rather: America Is Stuck in the Purgatory of Tolerance." *Time*, November 7, 2017. W

Rocha, Gene. "Cornish Connects with Dance Theatre of Harlem." *Cornish College of the Arts.* W

"Serge Diaghilev – Founder." *Russian Ballet History.* W

Shook, Karel. *Beyond the Mist: Selected Poems*. Den Haag: Arta, 1968. B

———. "The First Ten Years," November 18, 1978. A

———. "Karel Shook Letter," December 12, 1964. A

———. "Karel Shook Letters 1964–1966," n.d. A

Sisario, Ben. "June Taylor, 86, Dies; Created 'Gleason' Dances." *New York Times*, May 18, 2004, Arts. N

Tobias, Tobi. "Talking with Karel Shook – Partner in the Dance Theatre of Harlem." *Dance Magazine*, January 1973. M

CHAPTER 3 BIRTH OF A SCHOOL

Burton, Humphrey. *Leonard Bernstein*. London: Faber & Faber, 2017. B

De Mille, Agnes. *America Dances*. New York: Limelight Editions, 1984. B

Dodson, Howard, Christopher Paul Moore, Roberta Yancy, and the Schomburg Center for Research in Black Culture. *The Black New Yorkers: The Schomburg Illustrated Chronology*. New York: John Wiley, 2000. B

Getz, Leslie. *Dancers and Choreographers: A Selected Bibliography*. London: Moyer Bell, 1995. B

Gruen, John. "Dance: Dance Theater of Harlem Keeps its Eye on Change." *New York Times*, June 18, 1989, Arts. N

Haskins, James. *Black Dance in America: A History through its People*. New York: Welcome Rain Publishers, 1999. B

Hodgson, Moira, and Thomas Victor. *Quintet — Five American Dance Companies*. New York: W. Morrow, 1976. B

Kourlas, Gia. "Students Who Hint at What May Lie Ahead for a Venerable Troupe." *New York Times*, February 9, 2012. N

Long, Richard A., and Joe Nash. *The Black Tradition in American Dance*. London: Prion, 1995. B

Marbeth, Karel Shook, and Revlon Foundation. "The Aboutness of Dance Theatre of Harlem." Revlon 1990. A

NYPL. *DTH Oral History*. VHS, 1/2", n.d. V A

O'Reilly, Barb, and William O'Reilly. *Manhattan Dance School Directory*. New York: M. Dekker, 1978. B

Reynolds, Nancy. *The Dance Catalog*. New York: Harmony Books, 1979. B

Shook, Karel. *Elements of Classical Ballet Technique as Practiced in the School of Dance Theatre of Harlem*. New York: Dance Horizons, 1977. B

Sorell, Walter. *Dance in Its Time*. New York: Columbia University Press, 1986. B

Walker-Kuhne, Donna. "Oral Histories 1968–1988." Dance Theatre of Harlem, 1988. I A

CHAPTER 4 BEGINNINGS: THE SEASONS 1968–1971

"'African Goddess' from Philly." *New York Times*. November 19, 1972. N

Allen, Zita. "Dance Theatre of Harlem, Company on a Mission." *Columbia University Libraries*, c. 2017. exhibitions.library.columbia.edu/texhibits/show/mitchell. W

Bailey, Peter. "A Look at Black Classicism." *Routes: A Guide to Black Entertainment*, November 1977. M

Balanchine, George. *Balanchine's New Complete Stories of the Great Ballets*. New York: Doubleday, 1954. B

Barnes, Clive. "Ballet: Mitchell's Troupe." *New York Times*, March 9, 1971. N

———. "Dance Theatre of Harlem at Home on Broadway." *New York Post*, April 18, 1974. N A

———. "Dance: A Black Insight." *New York Times*, April 20, 1974. N

———. "Dance: City Ballet Gala." *New York Times*, May 8, 1971, sec. A. N

———. "Harlem Dance Theater Comes of Age." *New York Times*, December 14, 1971. N

———. "Shaping a Black Classic Ballet," *New York Times*, October 12, 1969. N

Emery, Lynne Fauley. *Black Dance from 1619 to Today, second revised edition*, Princeton Book Company imprint of Dance Horizons Book. Trenton, NJ: 1989. B

Kisselgoff, Anna. "Dance: Harlem at Its Vibrant Best." *New York Times*, May 3, 1975. N

———. "Harlem Dancers Excel at Guggenheim." *New York Times*, January 10, 1971. N

Lyle, Cynthia. *Dancers on Dancing*. New York: Drake Publishers, 1977. B

Maynard, Olga. "Arthur Mitchell & the Dance Theatre of Harlem." *Dance Magazine*, March 1970. M

McDonagh, Don. "Dance Theatre of Harlem Offers Mitchell Excerpts." *New York Times*, December 6, 1969. N

_____."'Strings' and 'Tones' Show Dance Style of Harlem Theater." *New York Times*. April 27, 1974. N

Vaughan, David. "Dance Theatre of Harlem." *Dancing Times*, September 1974. M

Zick, William. "Musicians of African Descent." African Heritage in Classical Music. http://chevalierdesaintgeorges.homestead.com/Musicians.html W

Notes:

Arthur Mitchell is confessional in Lyle's book *Dancers on Dancing* concerning personal life.

Descriptive writings and program notes on the Company's early ballets appear in the archive on hand-typed 8½ × 11 documents without author, signature, date, or attribution. In the case of the discussion of *Holberg Suite* in Seasons' Ballets ("When the curtain rises we see . . ."), the writing style is suspiciously and cautiously judged by Tyrus and Novosel to be written by Karel Shook. Ibid. the material on Otis Redding.

Controversial issues surrounding the Balanchine/Mitchell collaboration on *Concerto for Jazz Band and Orchestra* are discussed in *The Private World of Ballet*, Gruen, 1975.

CHAPTER 5 PINK TIGHTS IN BLACK TEA: THE SEASONS 1972–1976

Barnes, Clive. "Dance: Marathon Final." *New York Times*, November 8, 1972. N

———. "The Extraordinary Achievement of Arthur Mitchell." *New York Times*, May 11, 1975. N

———. "Theatre of Harlem Is Vital and Starling." *New York Times*, April 20, 1974. N

Barr, Sabrina. "Ballerina Precious Adams Explains Why She Won't Wear the Traditional Pink Tights: 'I'm Not Colourblind.'" *Independent*, September 20, 2018. W

Biekert, Mary. "Changing the Face of Ballet: Original Dance Theatre of Harlem Member Reflects on the Company's Wide-Ranging Impact." *The Day*, 2018. W

Blatchford, Nicholas. *Star and Daily News*, April 3, 1973. N

Brennan, Christopher. "U.S. Ballerina Faces Discrimination at Bolshoi Academy." *The Moscow Times*, November 19, 2013. N

Byrne, Emma. "Why Ballet Star Precious Adams Never Wants to Wear Pink Tights." *Evening Standard*, September 19, 2018. W

Carpenter, Erin. "Nude Barre – About." Nude Barre. W

Clarke, Adrian. "Tights Connection to the Beginning of Ballet." *Dancetrain Magazine*. W

"Classic Ballet with Soul." *Time*, March 8, 1976. M

Curtis, Charlotte. "In Ermine Pearls and Jeans, They Came to Dance Theater of Harlem's Gala." *New York Times*, November 14, 1971. N

Dachenbach, Laura. "Turning Pointe." *614 Columbus*, November 1, 2018. BL

"Dance Theatre of Harlem a Stunning Performance." Minneapolis, Minnesota, *Twin City Observer*, June 6, 1973. N

Deen TV. *Story of Ballerina Llanchie Stevenson*. www.youtube.com/watch?v=RvHQofpLAzY. V

Dente, Louise. "CCPTV.ORG: Tribute to Dance Master/Icon, Marie Brooks." Cultural Caravan TV, March 21, 2018. V

Dunning, Jennifer. "A Dancer Who Had a Dream." *New York Times*, April 14, 1974. N

———. "Theatre of Harlem in Dance Premiere of Ancient Voices." *New York Times*, April 28, 1974. N

Ferretti, Fred. "Dance Theater of Harlem Marks Its 10th." *New York Times*, June 18, 1985, Style. N

Forbes, Moriah. "Why Do Only Two Major Dance Suppliers Offer Shoes for Ballerinas of Color?" *D Magazine*, December 11, 2018. BL

Ford, Tanisha C. "Zelda Wynn, Fashion Designer to the Stars." *New York Times*, January 31, 2019, Obituaries. N

Iachetta, Michael. "Pioneer Black Dancers on Broadway." *Daily News*, April 18, 1974. N

Jones, Linda. "More About the Kitchen." *Naturally Curly*, July 1, 2018. W

Kisselgoff, Anna. "Dance: Harlem at Its Vibrant Best." *New York Times*, May 3, 1975. N

———. "The Dance: Harlem Troupe at Its Best." *New York Times*. March 6, 1976. N

Kourlas, Gia. "Bringing Back 'Dougla' Is a Family Affair." *New York Times*, March 30, 2018, Arts. N

Lyddiard, Alan. "8. Royston Maldoom, Berlin, Germany." *Community Arts International*, June 16, 2013. BL

Marshall, Francesca. "English National Ballet Star Attacked for Refusing to Wear Pink Tights on Stage." *Telegraph*, September 20, 2018. N

Mootz, William. "The Dance Theatre of Harlem Even More Pleasing a Year Later." *Courier-Journal*, March 3, 1973. N

Page, Ruth. *Carmina Burana (Court of Love Pas De Deux)*, Chicago Film Archives. 1962. V

Percival, John. "Harlem Return." *Dance and Dancers Magazine*, September 1976. M

Porter, Andrew. *New Yorker*, February 24, 1973. M

Rice, Bill. "Harlem Dancers Pack Sage Center." *Times Record*, January 26, 1973. N

Saal, Hubert. "On Their Toes," *Newsweek*, April 29, 1974. N

Schoelwer, Edward, in discussion with the author, Paul Novosel, New York City, September 2020. I

Tomlinson, Mel A. *Beyond My Dreams*. Teaneck, NJ: Turning Point, 2017. B

Warren, Virginia Lee. "Alva Gimbel: Gives Helping Hand to Many." *New York Times*, January 8, 1971. N

"Why Don't They Make Shoes for Black Ballet Dancers?" *BBC News*, March 11, 2016. www.bbc.com/news/magazine-35629323 W

Williams, Pat. "Dance Theatre of Harlem Gave Islander Rare Treat." *The Amsterdam News*. January 27, 1973. N

Winer, Linda. "Ballet Black: Beautiful but Scarce." *Chicago Tribune*, May 18, 1975. N

Notes:

There were four homecomings in four different years: Harlem Homecoming 1972 at Loew's Victoria Theatre; Harlem Homecoming II 1973 at Loew's; Harlem Homecoming 1986 at City College of New York; and Harlem Homecoming II 1987 at City College.

The feature article in The *Star and Daily News of* Washington, DC concerned Mimes and Masques Theatre for Youth and Howard University's Physical Education Department's joint sponsorship of 18 sold-out lecture demonstrations by DTH. The article also describes dancer Ronald Perry as an agile jumper for North Jr. High School's track team in Great Neck, New York. Blatchford tells, ". . . and when the boy was about 13 and underfoot ('I was like hanging around the house a lot') a friend of the family asked if he'd like to take ballet lessons. This led him to Arthur Mitchell." "He liked my long legs and short torso."

In *Ancient Voices of Children*, an inanimate object comes to life as a woman who represents "every woman." It was danced by China White and six men. The work was wrought as a fertility dance derived from near Eastern and Indian myths. According to Jennifer Dunning in *The New York Times*, ". . . *Ancient Voices of Children* is about memory and the creation of myth. It takes much of its atmospheric coloration from George Crumb's collage of vocal and instrumental music and ghostly sound effects." When it was performed at the ANTA theatre, Balanchine and Kirstein were in the audience.

CHAPTER 6 WORLD STATURE: THE SEASONS 1977–1985

ABT. "Fancy Free." *American Ballet Theatre*, February 24, 2019. W

Anawalt, Sasha. "DTH Means Spirit, Aplomb and Gusto." *Los Angeles Herald Examiner*, August 9, 1984. N

Anderson, Jack. "Dance: New Harlem Theater Season." *New York Times*, January 27, 1983, Arts. N

———. "Dance: New Harlem Theater Season." *New York Times*, January 27, 1983, Arts. N

———. "Review/Dance; Fokine Infuses a Program by the Harlem Troupe." *New York Times*. July 2, 1988. N W

Barnes, Clive. "Harlem Dancers Black Magic at the Met." *New York Post*, n.d. N

Bernheimer, Martin. "Tetley, Too: Harlem Dancers Try Robbins' 'Fancy Free.'" *Los Angeles Times*, May 15, 1985. N

Cummings, Judith. "Marian Anderson Is Back for a Benefit for Harlem Dancers." *New York Times*. March 25, 1978. N.

DeFrantz, Tommy. "Dance Theatre of Harlem – More Resources ." *DHC Treasures*. W

Deitch, Mark. "Return of the Dance Theater of Harlem." *New York Times*. February 18, 1979. N

Dunning, Jennifer. "A Fling with Harlem Dancers." *New York Times*, February 17, 1978. N

———. "Ballet Theater: 'Billy,' 'Sylphides' and 'Fancy.'" *New York Times*, April 22, 1982, Arts. N

———. "Billy Wilson, 59, Director and Choreographer." *New York Times*, August 16, 1994, Obituaries.

———. "Dance Theater of Harlem at the Met." *New York Times*, June 17, 1985, Arts. W

———. "Dance: Harlem Troupe Offers 'Wingborne' and 'Banda.'" *New York Times*, February 14, 1983, Arts. N

———. "A Fling with Harlem Dancers." *New York Times*. February 17, 1978. N

———. "Harlem Dancers and Diaghilev Days." *New York Times*. January 28, 1983. W

Fox, Barbara Figge. "Catch Their Act; Harlem Dancers at McCarter." *Trenton Times*, November 16, 1983. N

Gaiser, Carrie. "Caught Dancing: Hybridity, Stability, and Subversion in Dance Theatre of Harlem's Creole Giselle." *Theatre Journal* 58, no. 2 (July 6, 2006): 269–89. J

Gamboa, Glenn. "Music Hall of Fame Inductee Ron Delsener: I'll Never Retire." *Newsday*, October 21, 2014. N

Gruen, John. "Dance Theatre of Harlem, Feeling Accepted Sets Sights on Artistry." *New York Times*, January 10, 1982. N

Jowers, Christine. "Remembering the Maverick Ballerina, Mia Slavenska, in Film." January 29, 2015. W

Kisselgoff, Anna. "Dance: 'Bugaku' by Harlem Company." *New York Times*. March 20, 1987. N

———. "Ballet: Dance Theater of Harlem." *New York Times*, March 11, 1987, Arts. N

———. "Dance Theatre of Harlem Revives Scheherazade." *New York Times*, January 5, 1981. N

———. "Dance View. New Works by Interesting Choreographers." *New York Times*, March 4, 1979. N

———. "Dance View: The Appealing Harlem Troupe." *New York Times*. January 25, 1981. W

———. "Dance View: A Company Finds a Niche for Itself." *New York Times*. February 20, 1983. W

———. "Dance View: Harlem Dance Theatre Steps Out." *New York Times*, January 31, 1982, Theater. N

———. "Dance View: This 'Giselle' Makes Us Think About What We See." *New York Times*, July 23, 2019. W

———. "Dance: Ballet Theater in MacMillan 'Concerto.'" *New York Times*, May 17, 1981, Arts. N

———. "Dance: Harlem Troupe in a 'Paquita' Premiere." *New York Times*, January 13, 1980. N

———. "Dance: Harlem's One-Act 'Swan Lake.' *New York Times*, January 15, 1981, Arts. N

———. "Harlem Troupe Dances de Lavallade." *New York Times*. February 24, 1979. N

———. "Stepping Out: *A Streetcar Named Desire*." *San Francisco Ballet Magazine*, March 1982. M

Leviant, Doris, and Andre Boissier. "Arthur Mitchell and Dance Theatre of Harlem: Street Talkin' Elegance Sigla: DLAB, December 9, 1982." ARC Typed manuscript interview transcription in photocopy. A

Lyle, Cynthia. *Dancers on Dancing*. New York: Sterling, 1977. B

Michel, Carl. "Carl Michel Designs." *The New York Public Library Archives & Manuscripts*. Archives.nypl.org/dan/23228. W

Pulsipher, Deneb. "African American History Timeline." *BlackPast*. W

Rigney, Jane. "Dance Theatre of Harlem Concludes Season at Met with Two Contrasting Original Works." *New York City Tribune*, July 3, 1985. N

Rosenwald, Peter J. "A Handsome Dance Company Hits Its Stride." *Dance Magazine*, 1980. M

———. "Bayou Lady: DTH's Creole Giselle." *Dance Magazine*, September, 1984.

Schergen, Janek. "Our Mission." Choo-San Goh & H. Robert Magee Foundation. W

Segal, Lewis. "Ballet Review: Dance Theatre of Harlem Revives Fokine's 'Prince Igor.'" *Los Angeles Times*, June 1, 1989. N

———. "Queens to Brussels – a Dancer's Odyssey." *Los Angeles Times*, February 12, 1985. N

"Serenade". *The George Balanchine Trust*. balanchine.com/serenade. W

"Serge Grigoriev – Ballets Russes Archive Guides to Special Collections in Music Division of Library of Congress." Library of Congress, 2014. D

Staff. "Harlem Dance Theatre, an International Treasure." *Daily Gleaner*, July 27, 1985. N

Stage17.tv. "Fan Fare Clip: Faith Prince on Jerome Robbins' Tortured Perfectionism."www.youtube.com/watch?v=hfM6YjKVcNg. V

Switzer, Ellen Eichenwald. *Dancers!: Horizons in American Dance*. New York: Atheneum, 1982. B

Welsh, Anne Marie. "Arthur Mitchell's Multiple Energies." *Washington Star*, February 8, 1981. N

Notes:

Material for this chapter has been extensively taken from the DTH unprocessed archive file folder labeled "25th Anniversary Notes."

Gowns for the Choral Ensemble were designed by Constance Saunders of Reggio, Arthur McGee.

CHAPTER 7 RIDING THE WAVE: THE SEASONS 1986–1996

© 2021 Sesame Workshop®, Sesame Street®, and associated characters, trademarks and design elements are owned and licensed by Sesame Workshop. All rights reserved.

Anderson, Jack. "Bessie Schoenberg, 90, a Mentor for Dancers." *New York Times*, May 15, 1997. N

———. "Bessie Schonberg Remembered as Dancers' 'Collective Mother.'" *New York Times*, July 1, 1997. N

———. "The Dance: 'Harlem Homecoming.'" *New York Times*, March 27, 1986, Arts. N

———. "Review/Dance; A Fast-Paced 'Medea' from Michael Smuin." *New York Times*, May 7, 1992, Arts. N

Berman, Janice. "Dialogues at BAM." *New York Newsday*, April 30, 1992. N

———. "A Tight Weave of Varied Styles." *New York Newsday*, 1987 (n.d.). N

Burns, John T. "Dance Theatre of Harlem: South Africa August–September 1992 – United States Information Service, USIS," November 1992. A D

Cassidy, Suzanne. "Blacks Dance with the Royal Ballet." *New York Times*. December 29, 1990. W

Dunning, Jennifer. "Dance in Review." Re: *Fete Noir, Flower Festival, Genzano*, et al. *New York Times*, June 24, 1991. N W

———. "Milton Rosenstock, Music Director, 74, for Stage and Ballet." *New York Times*, April 28, 1992, Arts. N

———. "Reviews/Dance: Harlem Troupe in a Multifaceted Retrospective." *New York Times*, November 8, 1988, Arts. N

Edelman, Susan. "Meet the New Diverse Faces of the Rockettes." *DNyuz*, October 20, 2019. BL

Fein, Esther. "Harlem Troupe Captivates Moscow." *New York Times*. May 14, 1988. N

Goodman, Walter. "Review/Television: The Very Hard Times of Harlem's Dance Theater." *New York Times*, July 25, 1991, Arts. N

Greskovic, Robert. "Dance Theatre of Harlem at 25." New York: Ballet Review 22, no. 3, Fall 1994, pp. 29–38. J

Gruen, John. *People Who Dance*. Chicago: IPG, Princeton Book Co., 1989. B

"Harlem Dance Contract." *New York Times*, February 14, 1997, Arts. N

"Harlem Dance Troupe, United, Goes on Strike." *New York Times*, January 23, 1997, Arts. N

Kendall, Elizabeth. "Home to Russia: Dance Theatre of Harlem on Tour in the Soviet Union." *Ballet Review*, Winter 1989. J

Kisselgoff, Anna. "Review – Dance; Tetley Premiere by Harlem Troupe." *New York Times*, April 6, 1991, Arts. N

———. "Ballet: Nijinska 'Birches,' by the Harlem Dancers." *New York Times*, January 29, 1983, Arts. N

———. "Dance Review: Harlem Troupe Makes Balanchine Its Own." *New York Times*, March 13, 1995, Arts. N

———. "Dance Review: Reveling in a Repertory's Unpredictability." *New York Times*, July 9, 1989, Arts. N

———. "Dance View: Harlem at a Crossroad." *New York Times*, March 19, 1978. N

———. "'John Henry' and 'Billy the Kid,' A Feast of Folk." *New York Times*, June 6, 1988. N

Kriegsman, Allen. "Harlem's Flawed 'Bugaku.'" *Washington Post*, March 18, 1988. N

Lace, Ian. "A Song for Dead Warriors: Original Score for the San Francisco Ballet Production." Film Music on the Web, *CD Review*, June 2003. W

"NYCB and DTH: Anniversary Reflections." *Ballet Review*, Fall 1994. J

Perpener, John. "John Perpener." *Jacob's Pillow Dance Interactive*. BL

Perry, David. "Anthony Turney – Obit." *David Perry & Associates*, July 4, 2014. BL

Peterson, Gregory J. "What's All White, and Dances in New York?" *New York Times*, May 31, 1985, Opinion. N

Rosen, Lillie. "Ballet Teachers Talk of Technique." *Dance Scope*, Fall 1979. M

Segal, Lewis. "Dance Review: Dance Theatre of Harlem Offers 'Othello.'" *Los Angeles Times*, February 3, 1990. N

Simonson, Robert. "Dancers Walk: Strike at Dance Theatre of Harlem." *Backstage*. 1997 n.d. Updated February 21, 2001, and November 4, 2019. M

Smith, Sid. "Harlem Company on Inventive Tack." *Chicago Tribune*. February 17, 1995. W

Straus, Rachel. "Bessie Schönberg." *Dance Teacher*. September 1, 2010. M W

Trescott, Jacqueline. "House Panel Votes to Kill Arts Agency." *Washington Post*, May 11, 1995. N

Vaughan, David. "About Ballet, in Black and White." *New York Times*, January 23, 1988, Opinion. N

Walker-Kuhne, Donna. "Walker International Communications Group," April 13, 2009. WA

Winship, Frederick. "Dance Theater of Harlem Honors the 'Other' Nijinsky." *United Press International*, June 29, 1989. W

World Health Organization. "WHO: HIV/AIDS." *World Health Organization*. Accessed November 1, 2019. W

CHAPTER 8 TOWARD A NEW MILLENNIUM: THE SEASONS 1997–2004

Campbell, Larry. "Dance Theatre of Harlem – Viraa, Passion of the Blood, Return." *CultureVulture*, January 25, 2002. W

Dunning, Jennifer. "Dance Review: Fresh Faces in Role Debuts." *New York Times*, September 15, 1997. W

———. "Dance Review: From Mannerly Ballet to Ethnic Processional." *New York Times*, September 18, 1997, Arts. N

———. "Tragedy Kindles Dance of Hope." *New York Times*, September 13, 2002, Movies. N

———. "Visions of Ballet as a Multiracial Art Have Been Slow to Spread in the U.S." *New York Times*, February 24, 1997, Arts. N

Gatehouse Media. "Joseph E. Fields." *Miami News*, October 16, 2018. W

Gladstone, Valerie. "DANCE: Still a Mover and Shaker with Harlem on His Mind." *New York Times*, March 14, 1999. N W

Greskovic, Robert. "Ballet Blues: Dance Theatre of Harlem Adapts a 1946 Broadway Flop." *The Wall Street Journal*, July 15, 2003. N

"Harlem Troupe Leads Way to China." *New York Times*, November 7, 2000, Arts. N

Kisselgoff, Anna. "Ballet Review: Classical Cachet and Taut Technique in an Ascent to a Heavenly Wingding." *New York Times*, September 11, 1997, Arts. N

———. "Dance Review: Now That's a Riddle: A Dancing Sphinx." *New York Times*, October 4, 2001, Arts. N

Kourlas, Gia. "Dance Theater of Harlem: Arthur Mitchell's Dream at 50." *New York Times*, April 3, 2019. N

Lazere, Arthur. "Dance Theatre of Harlem." *CultureVulture*, March 9, 2019. W

"Mayor Michael R. Bloomberg and Dance Theatre of Harlem Founder and Artistic Director Arthur Mitchell Announce Reopening of Dance Theatre of Harlem School." *Official Website of the City of New York*, November 30, 2004. W

Parry, Jann. "Dance Review: Jann Parry on Dance Theatre of Harlem, London." *Observer*, April 4, 2004, Stage. N

Robertson, Tatsha. "Famed Harlem Troupe Plans to End Season." *Boston Globe*, September 18, 2004. N

Sekyi, Rachel. "School to China." Email, September 14, 2020. E

Ulrich, Allen. "Dance Theatre of Harlem Satisfies Dream." *SFGate*, February 7, 1998. W

CHAPTER 9 EMERGENCE: THE SEASONS 2005–2010

"About the Museum." *The National Museum of African American History and Culture*, January 4, 2016. W

Adams, Michael Henry. "Opinion – The End of Black Harlem." *New York Times*, May 27, 2016, Opinion. N

"Dance in the Professions: American Ballet Theatre Pedagogy – Dance Education – NYU Steinhardt." *New York University*. W

Dawson, Alene. "What Does the Color 'Nude' Mean Now in an Increasingly Diverse World?" *Los Angeles Times*, July 14, 2016. N

Dunning, Jennifer. "Dance Theater of Harlem Reunion – Dance." *New York Times*, June 26, 2007, Dance. N

———. "Showcase for the World's Young Dancers." *New York Times*, January 28, 2006, Arts. N

Gold, Sylviane. "A Dance Diaspora." *New York Times*, July 3, 2005. N

Grimes, William. "Clive Barnes, Who Gave Dance Criticism a Major Professional Lift, Dies at 81." *New York Times*, November 19, 2008, Dance. N

Harper, Marcellus. "Kevin Thomas and Marcellus Harper Interview." YouTube, n.d. V

Howard, Theresa Ruth. "The Lack of Ballet Technique." *Dance Magazine*, April 28, 2017. W

Humanity in Action. Marie Gørrild et al. "Gentrification and Displacement in Harlem: How the Harlem Community Lost Its Voice En Route to Progress." W

Kaufman, Sarah. "Fabian Barnes, Founder/Director of Dance Institute of Washington, Dies at 56." *Washington Post*, April 12, 2016. N

Kourlas, Gia. "Virginia Johnson to Become Artistic Director at Dance Theater of Harlem." *New York Times*, April 12, 2009, Dance. N

———. "Harlem Troupe Prepares for Act II." *New York Times*, October 29, 2010, Dance. N

———. "Push for Diversity in Ballet Turns to Training the Next Generation." *New York Times*, December 21, 2017, Arts. NW

———. "Virginia Johnson and the Fortunes of Dance Theater of Harlem." *New York Times*, October 29, 2010, Dance. N

———. "Where Are All the Black Swans?" *New York Times*, May 6, 2007. N

Kozinn, Allan. "Dance Theater of Harlem's Executive Director to Step Down." *ArtsBeat*, December 8, 2014. BL

Lucci, Michelle, in discussion with author, Paul Novosel, New York City, September 2018. I

Phillips, Craig. "Breaking Barriers on Stage: African American Ballet Dancers Who Made History." *Independent Lens*, October 5, 2018. BL

Snowdon, Lord. *Interview with Arthur Mitchell*, circa 1970. Typed transcription in manuscript form. Three parts. 39 pp. Two versions, 8½" copy and what appears to be an edited 11" × 14" copy. A I D

Sommers, Charlotte. "'The Nutcracker': Year after Year, It's Always Loved." *Baltimore Sun*, November 27, 1994. N

"Ted T. Kivitt." *Purchase College State University of New York*. www.purchase.edu/live/profiles/148-ted-t-kivitt. W

Timelines of History. "Timeline Black History." timelines.ws/subjects/Black_History.HTML. W

"Tomlinson, Mel". *Ballethnic Dance Company*. W

Notes:

"The Nutcracker: Year after Year, It's Always Loved," by Charlotte Sommers, published in the *Baltimore Sun* references Nicholas Litrenta as a producer.

CHAPTER 10 A NEW COMPANY: THE SEASONS 2011–2015

"A Partnering Lift for 2 Cultural Icons." The Spirit (Upper West Side), October 13, 2015. W

Abrams, Abby. "Raising a Ballerina Will Cost You $100,000." *FiveThirtyEight*, August 20, 2015. BL

Burke, Siobhan. "Flip Sides of a Troupe as It Returns for a 45th-Anniversary Season." *New York Times*, April 25, 2014, Arts. N

"Chelsea Clinton & Husband MA Mezvinsky Attend Charity Event." *People*, October 22, 2018. W M

"Controversial Affordable Housing Project Faces LPC Design Review." City Realty, June 26, 2017. W

Duncan, Sharon; in discussion with authors, Paul Novosel and Judy Tyrus, New York City, October 2018. I

Goodman, J. David. "Builder Acquires Valuable Harlem Plot after Deed Change." *New York Times*, May 13, 2016, New York. N

Halzack, Sarah. "Darrell Grand Moultrie Brings 'Vessels' to Harman Center for the Arts." *Washington Post*, October 19, 2014. N

Jowers, Christine. "DTH & Limón Dance Company Invites You." *The Dance Enthusiast*. W

Kelly, Jack. "The 1% Owns Almost as Much Wealth as the Middle Class: Will the Rich Keep Getting Richer?" *Forbes*, November 12, 2019. M

Kourlas, Gia. "A Phoenix Is Rising on Point." *New York Times*, April 5, 2013, Arts. N

Kozinn, Allan. "Dance Theater of Harlem's Executive Director to Step Down." *ArtsBeat*. *New York Times*, December 8, 2014. BL N

Lee, Felicia R. "Catherine Reynolds to Lead Dance Theater of Harlem." *New York Times*, April 7, 2005, Arts. N

———. "Michelle Obama Visits Studio Museum in Harlem." *New York Times*, September 24, 2013. N

Perron, Wendy. "Dance Theatre of Harlem." *Wendy Perron*, April 23, 2014. BL

Ritzel, Rebecca. "Dance Theatre of Harlem: Some Soar, but Others Are Grounded." *Washington Post*, April 8, 2012. W

Santana, Tamia. "Award Archive." *The Bessies*. BL

Schanfein, Leigh. "Limón Dance Company and Foundation Moves to Harlem." *Dance Informa Magazine*, October 5, 2015. W

Stiglitz, Joseph. "Of the 1%, by the 1%, for the 1%." *Vanity Fair*, March 31, 2011. W

Warerkar, Tanay. "Deed Restriction at Another Valuable Manhattan Site Mysteriously Lifted." *Curbed NY*, May 13, 2016. W

CHAPTER 11 EVOLUTION: THE SEASONS 2016–2020

ABT. "Diversity, Equity, and Inclusion at ABT." *American Ballet Theatre*. W

Bacon-Smith, Camille. "Annenberg Center Live and NextMove Dance Present Dance Theater of Harlem." *Broad Street Review*, March 4, 2019. W

Battle, Allegra. "New Initiative Seeks to Create More Equitable Ballet Companies." *90.5 WESA*, November 13, 2018. W

Bauknecht, Sara. "After Sold-Out Shows in 2017, Dance Theatre of Harlem, Pittsburgh Ballet Theatre Are Partners Again." *Pittsburgh Post-Gazette*, March 11, 2019. W

Becker, Kent G. "Dougla Revival Highlights Dance Theatre of Harlem at City Center." *Ballet Focus*, April 9, 2018. BL

Benedikt, Allison. "Women in Charge: Virginia Johnson." *Slate*, April 8, 2019. W I

"BNY Mellon Presents Pittsburgh Ballet Theatre – Dance Theatre of Harlem." *Pittsburgh Ballet Theatre*. W

Boland, Kathryn. "Arthur Mitchell: Trailblazer." *Dance Informa Magazine*, October 6, 2018. W

Bomboy, Erin. "Dance News: Dance Theatre of Harlem Makes First Eastern European Tour in 48-Year History." *The Dance Enthusiast*, November 8, 2017. W

Brandt, Amy. "The Standouts of 2017: Chyrstyn Mariah Fentroy and Da'Von Doane in 'Brahms Variations' for Dance Theatre of Harlem." *Pointe*, January 11, 2018. W

"Dance Theatre of Harlem – New York City Center." *New York City Center*. W

Di Orio, Laura. "Dance Review: Dance Theatre of Harlem at City Center." *Dance Informa Magazine*, April 15, 2016. W

Duberman, Martin. *The Worlds of Lincoln Kirstein*. Evanston, IL: Northwestern University Press, 2008. B

Dunning, Jennifer. "Arthur Mitchell Is Dead at 84; Showed the Way for Black Dancers." *New York Times*, September 21, 2018, Obituaries. N

Ebershoff, David. "How a Group of Gay Male Ballet Dancers Is Rethinking Masculinity." *New York Times*, November 5, 2018. W

Ellis, Kathi E. B. "Dance Theatre of Harlem Brings Passion and Precision to Ky. Center." *89.3 WFPL News Louisville*, November 10, 2018. W

Finley, Taryn. "This Digital Platform Is Highlighting the Forgotten History of Black Ballet." *Huffington Post*, February 27, 2017, Black Voices. W

Forsyth, Sondra. "BWW Review: Dance Theatre of Harlem Revives Dougla, Holder's Incandescent Masterpiece." *BroadwayWorld*, April 9, 2018. W

Garcia, Sophia. "The New York City Ballet's Blinding Diversity Problem." *The New School Free Press*, October 26, 2017. BL

Giuliano, Charles. "Dance Theatre of Harlem." *Berkshire Fine Arts*, July 12, 2019. W

Greene, Leonard. "Virginia Johnson." *Brownstone NYU*, March 1985. M

"Harlem Dance Legend to Go to Russia." *Caribbean Life*, April 4, 2012. W

Hochman, Jerry. "Dance Theatre of Harlem: Mutual Admiration." *CriticalDance*, April 10, 2018. BL

———. "Fall for Dance 2018: First Two (and a Half) Programs." *CriticalDance*, October 8, 2018. BL

Howard, Theresa Ruth. "Dance Theatre of Harlem Kicks Off Ballet Across America with a New Ballet by Claudia Schreier." *Pointe*, May 28, 2019. W

———. "Op-Ed: A Radical Reimagining of Ballet for 2018." *Dance Magazine*, January 11, 2018. W

Jennings, Luke. "Why Are There So Few Black Ballet Dancers?" *Huffington Post*, September 11, 2012, Culture & Arts. W

Kenyon, Sandy. "'Dance Theatre of Harlem' Honors Late Founder at The Apollo." *ABC7 New York*, February 13, 2019. W

Kisselgoff, Anna. "The Dance: Harlem Troupe at Its Best." *New York Times*, March 6, 1976. N

Kourlas, Gia. "Arthur Mitchell, Ballet's 'Grandfather of Diversity.'" *New York Times*, January 20, 2018, Arts. N

———. "Steps Arranged by Women, with History, at Dance Theater of Harlem." *New York Times*, March 23, 2016, Arts. N

———. "When Two Men Fall in Love on the Ballet Stage, and Why It Matters." *New York Times*, January 20, 2018, Arts. N

Latus, Janine. "The Dance Theatre of Harlem Defies Expectations – and Genres – as the Country's First Primarily African-American Dance Company." *Virginian-Pilot*, December 9, 2018. M

Libbey, Peter. "Dance Theater of Harlem Awarded Its Biggest Gift Yet." *New York Times*, January 14, 2020. N

Macaulay, Alastair. "Fall for Dance Festival at City Center – Review." *New York Times*, October 28, 2011, Dance. N

Macdonald, Moira. "Kabby Mitchell III, First Black Dancer with Pacific Northwest Ballet, Dies." *Seattle Times*, May 11, 2017. W

Marshall, Alex. "Brown Point Shoes Arrive, 200 Years after White Ones." *New York Times*, November 4, 2018. W

Mattingly, Kate. "Dance Theatre of Harlem Lively, Magisterial in Ogden Debut." *Utah Arts Review*, November 2019. J

McDonald, Jo. "Ballet Brothers: Bringing Male Dancers Together." *Dance Informa Magazine*, March 4, 2019. BL

Molzahn, Laura. "Review: Dance Theatre of Harlem Honors Past as Well as Political Present." *Chicago Tribune*, November 19, 2016. W

Nedzhvetskaya, Nataliya. "Iconic American Ballet Dancer Comes to Russia Again." *The Moscow Times*, April 11, 2012. W

Novak, Jill. "The Six Living Generations in America." *Marketing Teacher*, May 8, 2014. W

Osenland, Kurt. "Gay in Ballet: Two Men Defying Traditions in the Dance World," *Out Magazine*, March 28, 2017. W

Perez, Guillermo. "Famed Dance Companies Team to Present Geoffrey Holder Classic." *Miami Herald*, January 22, 2019. W

Priscilla, Frank. "Why Are There So Few Black Ballet Dancers?" *Huffington Post*, September 11, 2012. W

"Race, Equity, and Otherness in Ballet and Society." *Albertine Books*. www.albertine.com/events/race-equity-and-otherness-in-ballet-and-society. W

"Review: After 50 Years, Dance Theater of Harlem Looks Back and Up." *New York Times*, April 4, 2019. N

Seibert, Brian. "Review: Dance Theater of Harlem Regains Its Footing." *New York Times*, December 22, 2017, Arts. N

———. "Review: With 'Dougla,' Dance Theater of Harlem Recalls Past Glory." *New York Times*, June 8, 2018, Arts. N

Siegel, Adam Rei. "Fire Island Dance Festival Features Five Premieres, Shatters Fundraising Record." *Dancers Responding to AIDS*. W

Sjostrom, Jan. "Dance Theatre of Harlem Celebrates Its 50th with a Neoclassical-to-Funky Show." *Daily Commercial*, May 3, 2019. W

Stieg, Cory. "Finally, a Company Made Pointe Shoes Specifically for Women of Color." *Refinery29.com,* January 30, 2017. W

Strum, Lora. "BWW Review: Dance Theatre of Harlem Sets Tone for the Future of Ballet." *Broadway World,* June 3, 2019. W

Sucato, Steve. "A Pittsburgh Ballet Theatre Collaboration with Dance Theatre of Harlem Yields Generally Positive Results." *Pittsburgh City Paper,* March 22, 2017. N W

Sulcas, Roslyn. "Matthew Bourne's 'Swan Lake' Is All Male." *New York Times,* October 8, 2010, Dance. N

Tonguette, Peter. "Theater Review – Dance Theatre of Harlem: Gloriously Performed Ballet Is Effervescent." *Columbus Dispatch,* November 17, 2018. W

Tschebull, Johanna. "The Equity Project: Increasing the Presence of Blacks in Ballet." *International Association of Blacks in Dance,* September 20, 2018. W

Watson, Denise. "'Dance Theatre of Harlem from Black and White to Living Color Exhibit." *Virginian-Pilot,* May 9, 2019. W

———. "Dance Theatre of Harlem Premieres a Piece That Evokes the Fight and Fortitude of Virginia's, and America's, Beginnings." *Virginian-Pilot,* May 10, 2019. W

Wingenroth, Lauren. "Jonathan Stafford and Wendy Whelan Will Lead New York City Ballet." *Dance Magazine,* February 28, 2019. W

Zuchowski, David. "Pittsburgh Owl Scribe: Pittsburgh Ballet Collaborates with Dance Theatre of Harlem." *Pittsburgh Owl Scribe,* March 7, 2017. BL

AFTERWORD

Shook, Karel. "Social Aspects" from "The First Ten Years." November 18, 1978. A

POSTSCRIPT

Black Lives Matter. blacklivesmatter.com. W

Blumberg, Perri Ormont. "NYC Ballet Dancers Stay Flexible with Creative Dance-from-Home Setups." *New York Post,* August 27, 2020. BL

"Broadway Update on Performance Cancellations." *The Broadway League,* October 9, 2020. W

DeParle, Jason. "The Coronavirus Generation." *New York Times,* August 22, 2020, Sunday Review. N

DiAngelo, Robin J. *White Fragility: Why It's So Hard for White People to Talk about Racism.* New York: Penguin Random House, 2019. B

Homan, Timothy R. "A List of the Statues across the US Toppled, Vandalized or Officially Removed amid Protests." *The Hill,* June 12, 2020. W

Knight, David. "What's 'Colorism'?" *Teaching Tolerance,* Fall 2015. W

Li, Eric P. H., Hyun Jeong Min, and Russell W. Belk. "Skin Lightening and Beauty in Four Asian Cultures." *ACR North American Advances,* NA-35, 2008. J D

Moynihan, Colin. "New Initiative Will Grant $156 Million to Arts Groups Run by People of Color." *New York Times,* September 25, 2020. N

Rankine, Claudia. "I Wanted to Know What White Men Thought about Their Privilege. So I Asked." *New York Times,* July 17, 2019. N W

Rather, Dan. "Dan Rather: America Is Stuck in the Purgatory of Tolerance." *Time,* November 7, 2017. W

Rowes, Barbara. "It's No Stretch to Call Lydia Abarca One of Ballet's Most Under-Recognized Stars." *People,* October 18, 1979. W

Shalvey, Kevin. "A New Study Has Linked the Rise in Anti-Asian Online Hate Speech with President Donald Trump's COVID-19 Rhetoric." *MSN,* March 27, 2021. (Originally published in *Insider. com.*) W

Staff. *Dance Theatre of Harlem Online Newsletter.* Email, 2018 through 2020. A

WHO. "Archived: WHO Timeline – COVID-19." *World Health Organization,* April 27, 2020. W

Williams, Stephanie Rae. Interviewed by Paul Novosel, New York City, July 2020. I

LIST OF MUSICIANS

This list includes staff pianists, conductors, members of
the DTH Percussion Ensemble and the Dance Theatre of Harlem Chorus

Lydia Abarca
Freda Afonin
Irina Alabina
Clara Antoine
Wilbur Archie
Carlos Baeza
Therman Bailey
Mark Barksdale
Robert Bass
Lorraine Baucum
Gerasin Bekkerman
Victoria Bell
George Benson
Sylvia Bhourne
Gilbert Bigenho
Barbara Bilach
Rudolph Bird
Esther Blue
Angela Bofill
Dorcas Bravo
Odilia Campbell
Gladys Celeste
James Cherry
Michael Cherry
Coty Cockrell
Anthony Cofield
Debbie Corpier
Muriel Costa-Greenspon
Joe Cross
Charles Darden
Mark di Minno
Debra Dorfmann
Mariette Drummond
Leslie B. Dunner
Donald Eaton
William Engle
Mikhail Ermolov

George Ewell
Melody Fader
Fina Farberg
Jesse Featherstone
Oleg Felzer
Marisa Fleming
Patrick Flynn
Cheryl Freeman
Robert Fuchs
Harry Fuchs
David Gagne
Mallory Gaines
Stacy Gaines
Marcus Galante
Patrick Gallagher
Taana Gardner
Roberta Gilliam
Phillip Gilmore
Bill Gladd
Valerie Glavin
Gregory Gnau
Allan Greene
Felipe Hall
Ivan Hampden
Jamal Hardeman
Ben Harney
Paul Hastil
Rodney Hazen
Luther Henderson III
Adrianne Hill
Clarissa Howell
Kenneth Hull
Derrick Inouye
Mariana Iskhakova
Isaiah Jackson
Cliff Jackson
Adrian Johnson

Leona Johnson
Jacqueline Jones
Donald Joyce
Sedor Kabalin
James Kay
Craig Kitt
David La Marche
Bruce Lazarus
Tania León
Svetlana Litvinoff
Raymond Lowey
John Madden
Bob Marbach
Roman Markowicz
Michele Marks
Jerry McCants
Kim McLeod
Jonathan McPhee
James Mironchik
Michael Mironchik
Mejin Moon
Kevin Moss
Steven Nettles
Deborah Newmark
David Nichols
Michael Nosal
Paul Novosel
Charles Olaker
Renee Ong
Gitiim Oyil-Chakamoi
Lidiya Popelyash
Clifford Priester
Michael Pryor
Greg Reeves
Sally Ricketts
Mary Roarke
Rudolph Romero

Milton Rosenstock
William Rozenwasser
Vadim Rubinskiy
Karl St. Charles
Brenda J. Saunders
Michael Schumacher
Ed Seaman
Lauren Shapiro
Earl Shendell
Bella Shiukashvili
Tatyana Sirota
Noel Smith
Patricia Smith
Gary Sojkowski
Boyd Staplin
Mort Stine
Elena Tchina
Vanessa Theard
Michael Thomas
Curnell Thompson
David Tice
Donna Tiller
Cedric Tolley
Ivan Torzs
Edwina Tyler
Anival Vazquez
Andrew Violette
Diane Volpe
Johnny Warrior
Pamela Watson
Crystal Williams
Arthur Woodley
Elena Zelinskaya
William Zucker

DANCE THEATRE OF HARLEM REPERTOIRE

Title, Choreographer, Premiere Date

Acid Dreams and Nightmare, Robert Garland, May 3, 1996

Adagietto #5, Royston Maldoom, November 6, 1976

Adrian (Angel on Earth), John Alleyne, March 11, 1997

After Corinth, Walter Raines, April 29, 1975

Afternoon of a Faun, Jerome Robbins, March 8, 1971

Agon, George Balanchine, June 27, 1971

Allegro Brillante, George Balanchine, May 1, 1975

Ancient Voices of Children, Milko Šparemblek, May 19, 1973

Apollo, George Balanchine, March 20, 2004

Bach Passacaglia, Arthur Mitchell and Rachel Sekyi, May 25, 1993

Balamouk, Annabelle Lopez Ochoa, October 5, 2018

Balm in Gilead, Arthur Mitchell, n.d.

Banda, Geoffrey Holder, January 19, 1982

Bele, Geoffrey Holder, November 13, 1973

The Beloved, Lester Horton, December 11, 1971

Billy the Kid, Eugene Loring, June 28, 1988

Biosfera, Arthur Mitchell, June 17, 1970

Black Swan Pas de Deux, Marius Petipa, November 9, 2012

Brahms Variations, Robert Garland, May 14, 2016

Breathe, Robert Garland, October 19, 2020

Breezin, Arthur Mitchell, May 8, 1977

Bugaku, George Balanchine, April 25, 1975

The Cape, Gail Kachadurian, March 23, 1989

Caravansarai, Talley Beatty, April 18, 1975

Carmen and Jose, Ruth Page, May 12, 1972

Carmina Burana, Ruth Page, May 13, 1972

Chaconne, José Limón, April 1, 2017

Change, Dianne McIntrye, February 2, 2016

The Combat, William Dollar, November 6, 1975

Coming Together, Nacho Duato, April 8, 2015

Concerto Barocco, George Balanchine, June 17, 1970

Concerto for Jazz Band and Orchestra, Arthur Mitchell and George Balanchine, May 6, 1971

Concerto in F, Billy Wilson, February 4, 1986

Contested Space, Donald Bryd, February 7, 2012

Crossing Over, Robert Garland, April 8, 1997

Dalabar, Vincent Sekwati Mantsoe, May 16, 1997

Dancing on the Front Porch of Heaven, Ulysses Dove, October 4, 2013

Design With Strings, John Taras, April 25, 1974

Dialogues, Glen Tetley, April 2, 1991

Divertimento, Elena Kunikova, February 17, 2016

Doina, Royston Maldoom, February 18, 1978

Doin' It, Arthur Mitchell, August 14, 1978

Don Quixote, Marius Petipa, April 23, 1975

Dougla, Geoffrey Holder, April 16, 1974

Episode, Peter Pucci, July 1, 1905

Equilibrium (Brotherhood), Darrell Grand Moultrie, July 16, 2016

El Mar, Arthur Mitchell, May 8, 1977

Equus, Domy Reiter-Soffer, January 21, 1982

Etosha, Ron Cunningham, March 22, 1994

Every Now and Then, William Scott, April 25, 1975

Fall River Legend, Agnes de Mille, February 3, 1983

Fancy Free, Jerome Robbins, May 13, 1985

Far But Close, John Alleyne, November 16, 2012

Fete Noire, Arthur Mitchell, January 8, 1971

Firebird, John Taras, January 12, 1982

Flower Festival in Genzano, August Bournonville, March 22, 1990

Footprints Dressed in Red, Garth Fagan, June 18, 1986

Forces of Rhythm, Louis Johnson, December 12, 1971

The Four Temperaments, George Balanchine, February 20, 1979

Fragments, Lowell Smith, n.d.

Frankie and Johnny, Ruth Page and Bentley Stone, May 21, 1981

Fun and Games, Arthur Mitchell, March 8, 1971

Ginastera, Billy Wilson, March 26, 1991

Giselle, Jean Coralli and Jules Perot, July 18, 1984

Glinka Pas de Trois, George Balanchine, January 17, 2012

Gloria, Robert Garland, November 9, 2012

Graduation Ball, David Lichine, February 1, 1983

The Greatest, Arthur Mitchell, May 8, 1977

Greening, Glen Tetley, January 9, 1980

Ground, Alonzo King, May 7, 1996

Gustave le Grey No. 1, Pam Tanowitz, n.d.

Haiku, Walter Raines, July 20, 1973

Hallmark, Robert Garland, n.d.

Harlem on my Mind, Darrell Grand Moultrie, September 29, 2017

His Love is Everlasting, Royston Maldoom, March 25, 1978

Holberg Suite, Arthur Mitchell, May 21, 1970

Higher Ground, Robert Garland, October 19, 2020

In the Glow of the Night, Choo San Goh, April 5, 1997

In the Mirror of Her Mind, Christopher Huggins, August 17, 2011

Introducing, Choo San Goh, September 21, 1978

Invasion, Royston Maldoom, February 18, 1978

John Henry, Arthur Mitchell, June 28, 1988

The Joplin Dances, Robert Garland, March 15, 1995

La Mer, Domy Reiter-Soffer, May 16, 1985

The Lark Ascending, Alvin Ailey, October 20, 2012

Las Hermanas, Sir Kenneth MacMillan, April 30, 1996

Laurencia Pas de Six, Vaktang Chabukiani, November 6, 1972

Le Corsaire, Karel Shook, December 22, 1973

Les Biches, Bronislava Nijinska, January 27, 1983

Les Noces, Bronislava, Nijinska, June 27, 1989

Manifestations, Arthur Mitchell, November 6, 1975

Medea, Michael Smuin, March 19, 1992

Memento Mori, Augustus van Heerden, September 6, 2000

Mendelssohn's Concerto, William Dollar, November 4, 1975

Mirage, Billy Wilson, February 27, 1997

The Moor's Pavane, José Limón, April 11, 1997

New Bach, Robert Garland, September 25, 2001

Nyman String Quartet No. 2, Robert Garland, March 1, 2019

Odalisques Variations (from Le Corsaire), Marius Petipa, January 19, 2020

Ode to Otis, Arthur Mitchell, February 2, 1969

One by One Equals Two, Arthur Mitchell, c. 1969

Orange, Stanton Welch, March 14, 2019

Othello, John Butler, July 7, 1982

Paquita, Marius Petipa, January 11, 1980

A Pas de Deux for Phrygia and Spartacus, Lowell Smith, September 25, 2001

Pas de Dix, Marius Petipa, January 25, 1983

Passage, Claudia Schreier, May 3, 2019

Passion of the Blood, Augustus van Heerden, September 25, 2001

past-carry-forward, Thaddeus Davis and Tanya Wideman Davis, October 17, 2013

Phoenix Rising, Arthur Mitchell and Billy Wilson, March 24, 1987

Piano Movers, David Gordon, June 24, 1985

Prince Igor, Michel Fokine, June 30, 1988

The Prodigal Son, George Balanchine, March 10, 1995

Return, Robert Garland, September 21, 1999

Rhythmetron, Arthur Mitchell, May 21, 1970

Ribbon in the Sky, Arthur Mitchell, November 25, 1990

The River, Alvin Ailey, March 26, 1993

Romeo and Juliet, Gabriella Taub-Darvash, March 4, 1976

Rondo Capriccioso, Bronislava Nijinska, June 27, 1989

Saffron Knot, Istvan Rabovsky, March 28, 1986

Sasanka, Vincent Sekwati Mantsoe, April 8, 1997

Scheherazade, Michel Fokine, January 3, 1981

Secret Silence, Carlos Carvajal, February 22, 1979

Sensemaya, Carmen de Lavallade, February 22, 1979

Serenade, George Balanchine, February 27, 1979

Shapes of Evening, Carlos Carvajal, September 19, 1978

Signs and Wonders, Alonzo King, March 11, 1998

Six Piano Pieces (Harlem Style), David Fernandez, February 8, 2012

A Song for Dead Warriors, Michael Smuin, March 16, 1993

Songs of Mahler, Michael Smuin, February 15, 1984

Songs of the Auvergne, Geoffrey Holder, January 19, 1982

Soul on Pointe, Louis Johnson, April 28, 1998

South African Suite (first version), Arthur Mitchell, Augustus van Heerden, Laveen Naidu, May 1, 1998

South African Suite (second version), Arthur Mitchell, Augustus van Heerden, Laveen Naidu, March 30, 1999

Sphinx, Glen Tetley, September 28, 2001

Spiritual Suite (from Dance In Praise of His Name), Arthur Mitchell, August 5, 1976

Square Dance, George Balanchine, February 3, 1983

St Louis Woman: A Blues Ballet, Michael Smuin, July 8, 2003

Stabat Mater, Michael Smuin, September 14, 2002

Stars and Stripes, George Balanchine, August 7, 1984

A Streetcar Named Desire, Valerie Bettis, January 14, 1982

Swan Lake, Act II, Marius Petipa and Frederic Franklin, January 8, 1980

Sweetheart of my Dreams, Keith Saunders, n.d.

Sylvia Pas de Deux, Frederic Franklin, February 8, 1983

System, Francesca Harper, January 1, 2016

Tchaikovsky Pas de Deux, George Balanchine, May 17, 1977

Thaïs, Frederick Ashton, July 9, 2003

This Bitter Earth, Christopher Wheeldon, March 11, 2018

Timperturbably Blue, Arthur Mitchell, February 23, 1970

Toccata E Due Canzoni, John McFall, February 5, 1986

Tones, Arthur Mitchell, June 19, 1970

Tones II, Arthur Mitchell, March 1, 2019

Tributary, Robert La Fosse and Robert Garland, May 25, 2000

Troy Game, Robert North, February 9, 1978

Twist, Dwight Rhoden, September 21, 1999

Untitled (Work in Progress), Arthur Mitchell, August 8, 1977

Valse Fantaisie, George Balanchine, April 8, 2018

Variations Serieuses, Choo San Goh, September 21, 1978

Vessels, Darrell Grand Moultrie, October 17, 2014

Viraa, Laveen Naidu, September 25, 2001

Voluntaries, Glen Tetley, September 26, 1984

Walk in the Light, Arthur Mitchell, August 15, 1978

When Love, Helen Pickett, October 20, 2012

Wingborne, Loyce Houlton, February 10, 1983

Wings, Louis Johnson, April 16, 1974

Please visit www.DTHbook.org for an up-to-date list of ballets performed by the Dance Theatre of Harlem Company.